EDEN
INSIGHTs

&

The Lost Books of Adam and Eve

S.N.Strutt

ISBN 978-1-78222-889-9

CREDITS: The Forgotten Books of Eden, include a translation originally published in 1882 of the "First and Second Books of Adam and Eve", translated **first from ancient Ethiopic to German by Ernest Trumpp and then into English by Solomon Caesar Malan,** and a number of items of Old Testament pseudepigrapha, such as reprinted in the second volume of R.H. Charles's Apocrypha and Pseudepigrapha of the Old Testament (Oxford, 1913).

Artwork: front cover by Susanne Strutt

www.suzannestruttartist/instagram.com

www.suzannestruttartist/facebook.com

Book design, layout and production management by Into Print
www.intoprint.net
+44 (0)1604 832149

DEDICATION

I would like to dedicate this book to a future 'new world' wherein true love and peace reign supreme.

– S.N.Strutt (Author)

PREFACE

'**EDEN INSIGHTS**' is a running commentary on: '**The Lost Books of Adam and Eve.**'

In writing this book, 'Eden Insights', I believe that there is a lot of 'original text' and many 'deep truths' in the Lost Books of Adam and Eve.

'**Eden Insights**' takes us from the Garden of Eden and the subsequent 'Fall of man' all the way to the Great Flood. This book shows in detail, how evil came into the world, and shows many of the temptations put to Adam and Eve, that are not even mentioned in the Bible.

It shows how intensely difficult and painful it was for Adam and Eve to have to leave the beautiful and heavenly Garden of Eden.

It mentions the rebellion of Satan and the fallen angels, of Genesis 6 infamy.

These Lost books of Adam and Eve show Satan up for what he really is: a nasty pesky devil that seeks only to destroy God's Creation and his people. It shows in detail how the world became corrupted and overcome through temptation.

It was in fact so intense just before the Great Flood of Noah, that most of the 'children of Seth' came down from the 'mountain' and joined the evil sons of Cain in rebellion against God. As a result, only three men, and their families remained righteous before the Great Flood: Methuselah, Lamech and Noah. All the others became evil.

This book 'Eden Insights' also contains amazing 'glimpses' from other apocryphal books, such as the Books of Enoch, Jubilees, Jasher and others, which help to fill in the gaps - to give a much fuller picture as to what really happened in Pre-Flood times. For **more** about *this book* see my **website** page: 'EDEN INSIGHTS' - www.outofthebottomlesspit. co.uk/448356559

CONTENTS

PREFACE   3

THE FORMAT OF THIS BOOK   9

INTRODUCTION   10

1 THE CRYSTAL SEA   12

2 ADAM AND EVE LEAVE THE GARDEN OF EDEN   19

3 THE PROMISE OF 5 ½ DAYS   23

4 THE CAVE OF TREASURES   29

5 EVE TAKES THE BLAME   32

6 GOD'S REPRIMAND   35

7 ANIMALS AT PEACE   39

8 'BRIGHT NATURE' GONE!   41

9 THE TREE OF LIFE   43

10 WATER   46

11 PARADISE LOST   48

12 DARKNESS   50

13 NIGHT AND DAY   53

14 PROPHECIES ABOUT CHRIST   58

15 SALVATION   60

16 THE FIRST SUNRISE   61

17 THE SERPENT   63

18 WARS WITH THE SERPENT   64

19 THE ANIMALS AS FRIENDS   67

20 ADAM PROTECTS EVE   69

21 ADAM AND EVE 'AS DEAD'   70

22 ADAM CRIES FOR HELP.   73

23 THE FIRST ALTAR   75

24 LIFE & DEATH OF CHRIST   77

25 GOD THE MERCIFUL   79

26 ETERNAL LIFE   80

27 TEMPTED   83

28 SATAN THE DECEIVER   86

29 THE DEVIL EXPOSED   88

30 SPECIAL PRESENTS   90

31	THREE TOKENS	92
32	PRAYERS	94
33	SATAN'S LIES	96
34	FOOD AND DRINK	98
35	THE WORD OF GOD	103
36	FIGS	104
37	'WORKS' CAN'T REDEEM A SOUL	105
38	THE FULFILMENT OF 5500 YEARS	107
39	FEAR TO EAT	108
40	HUNGER	109
41	THIRST	110
42	THE 3RD PROPHECY ABOUT CHRIST	112
43	ARSON	117
44	FIRE	119
45	HELL	121
46	DELIVERANCE	123
47	THE DEVIL'S TRICKS	125
48	5TH APPARATION OF SATAN	126
49	RESURRECTION	129
50	NAKEDNESS	132
51	SHEEP SKINS	134
52	TO SEW A SHIRT	136
53	THE GREAT FLOOD	138
54	EXPLORING	141
55	GOD VERSUS SATAN	143
56	DIVINE COMFORT	147
57	HIDEOUS FIGURE OF SATAN	149
58	THE 53RD DAY	152
59	THE 8TH APPARITION OF SATAN	153
60	THE DEVIL IN DISGUISE	156
61	LED ASTRAY	160
62	FRUIT TREES	163
63	THE TWO FIG TREES	165
64	EARTHLY FOOD	167

65 THE GARDEN IS LOST! 169

66 TO WORK 171

67 MORE TRICKS 173

68 SATAN THE DESTUCTIVE MASTER 176

69 THE 12TH APPARITION 180

70 THE 13TH APPARITION OF SATAN 182

71 ADAM TO MARRY EVE? 185

72 TEMPTING MAIDENS 187

73 ADAM AND EVE GET MARRIED 190

74 BIRTH OF CAIN AND LULUWA 193

75 BIRTH OF ABEL AND AKLIA 195

76 CAIN IS JEALOUS OF ABEL 198

77 CAIN AND ABEL GROW APART 200

78 THE IST MURDER IS PLANNED 202

79 CAIN IS CURSED 209

LOST BOOKS OF ADAM AND EVE BOOK II

1 (80) CAIN MARRIES LULUWA 216

2 (81) 3RD SON BORN TO ADAM AND EVE 219

3 (82) SATAN AS A TEMPTRESS 221

4 (83) THE HIDEOUS DEVIL 224

5 (84) SETH TEMPTED AT SEVEN YEARS OLD 227

6 (85) CONSCIENCE RESCUES SETH 230

7 (86) SETH MARRIES AKLIA 233

8 (87) ADAM PREDICTS THE GREAT FLOOD 235

9 (88) DEATH OF ADAM 240

10 (89) THE FIRST MAN TO DIE 243

11 (90) SETH BECOMES HEAD OF THE TRIBE 246

12 (91) ENOS 253

13 (92) THE CHILDREN OF CAIN 258

14 (93) TIME PASSES 261

15 (94) CAVE OF TREASURES BECOMES A SHRINE 262

16 (95) CONTENTION 264

17 (96) JARED BECOMES 'MARTINET' 268

18 (97) JARED'S CHILDREN FALL 281

19 (98) BACKSLIDING   284
20 (99) THE REVOLT   287
21 (100) JARED PREDICTS THE FLOOD   295
22 (101) ONLY THREE RIGHTEOUS MEN ARE LEFT   301

APPENDIX

I: ORIGIN OF THE LOST BOOKS OF ADAM AND EVE   308
II: WHAT HAPPENED IN THE GARDEN OF EDEN?   309
III: THE CRYSTAL SEA - DARK NATURE   311
IV: TWINS   312
V: TRIPLE HELIX   314
VI: 5500 YEARS OR 5 ½ DAYS?   315
VII: 7000 YEAR TIME-TABLE   317
VIII: BIBLICAL NUMEROLOGY   318
IX: 4000 OR '5500' YEARS FROM CREATION?   319
X: EXTREME LONGEVITY   320
XI: FALLEN ANGELS OR NEPHILIM   321
XII: THE HEAVENLY CITY   323
XIII: CRITIQUE   328
XIV: ACCOUNTABILITY   330
XV: LONGEVITY CHART ADAM TO JOSEPH LONGEVITY CHART - www.outofthebottomlesspit.co.uk/450264991   334
XVI: MY OTHER BOOKS   335
XVII: USEFUL TOPIC LINKS   336

THE FORMAT OF THIS BOOK

i) The original text from the 'Lost Books of Adam and Eve' will be surrounded by boxes to make it easier to notice the original text.

ii) I have typed a chapter of the 'Lost Books of Adam and Eve' and included in each chapter my commentaries, which are just that: my opinions and speculations and inspiration gleaned from much study of the subject matter. My hope is simply that others by doing further investigations will prove the things that I have written to their own satisfaction.

iii) I have also put cross-references to the Bible, and other Apocryphal books where appropriate.

iv) Details: The first 'comment' in each chapter, will be noted as being 'Comment:1' & then C.2, C.3, etc. I have done this to make it easier as a study book to find the different comments and information. In some chapters I have made a lot of comments, and in others I have made few or no comments. Some of the time the story just speaks for itself.

v) The original text from the Lost Books of Adam and Eve is in slightly larger text than either the 'comments' or 'Bible verses.

vi) Three different types of writing are used. One for the original text, and another type of writing for my comments, and yet another for the Bible verses.

vii) The longest commentaries and conclusions are in the 'Appendices' of this book.

viii) The KJV of the Bible is what is quoted most of the time in this book.

INTRODUCTION

There are a total of 79 chapters for The Lost Book of Adam and Eve Book I and 22 chapters to Book II.

[**Suggestion**]: Please read the following chapters about Adam and Eve from Genesis: 1.26-31, & Chapter 2 & 3 as an introduction to this story. Here is a link to those exact chapters on my website: BIBLE PASSAGES - www.outofthebottomlesspit.co.uk/450264991)

THE 'LOST BOOKS OF ADAM AND EVE'
BOOK 1

CHAPTER 1

The Crystal Sea

God commands Adam expelled from the Garden of Eden to live in the Cave of Treasures.

> 1 On the third day, God planted the Garden of Eden in the East of the earth, on the border of the world eastward, beyond which towards the sun-rising one finds nothing but water that encompasses the whole world and reaches to the borders of heaven.

C.1 What does it say in Genesis about the Garden of Eden and the 'third day'?

Genesis 1.12-13 The land produced vegetation: plants bearing seed according to their kinds and trees bearing fruit with seed in it according to their kinds. And God saw that it was good. [13] And there was evening, and there was morning—the *third day*.

Genesis 2.8-9 And the Lord God planted a garden eastward in Eden; and there he put the man whom he had formed. And out of the ground made the Lord God to grow every tree that is pleasant to the sight, and good for food, the tree of life also in the midst of the garden, and the tree of knowledge of good and evil.

C.2 The title above chapter 1 reads: The Crystal Sea. What is the Crystal Sea? This is a big topic, and this title would seem to connect the beginning of the biblical story of Creation with the very end of the story – The New Heaven and the New Earth.

C.3 Notice the word expression 'border of the world' & 'borders of heaven' What do these expressions mean? It would appear, that on the earth there are portals that connect one realm with another. In the case of a *'border of the world*, and *'borders of heaven'* it would appear that the story is simply making a connection with the physical and spiritual realms.

C.4 Look at the following verses from both the **Book of II Esdras,** and also the **Book of Enoch**, both of which are very interesting apocryphal books.

II Esdras 6 .1 And he said unto me, 'At the beginning of the 'circle of the earth', before the portals of the world were in place, and before the assembled winds blew, and before the rumblings of thunder sounded, and before the flashes of lightning shone, and before the foundations of paradise were laid.

Enoch 18.1 I saw the treasuries of the winds. I saw how he had furnished with them the whole creation and the firm foundation of the earth. I saw the cornerstone of the earth. I saw the four winds which bear the earth and the firmament of heaven.

Rev: 4.6 'Before the throne *there was* a sea of glass, like crystal.'

Rev: 15.2 'I saw as it were a sea of glass mingled with fire.

> 2 And to the north of the Garden of Eden there is a sea of water, clear and pure to the taste, unlike anything else: so that through the clearness thereof, one may look into the depths of the earth.

C.5 How is it possible to '*look into the depths of the earth*' by just looking into a Crystal Sea or lake? Very strange observation. That sounds mysterious and almost like stating that it was like looking into a crystal ball and being able to see things extremely far away, and in this case, they had the ability to investigate the depths of the earth. Could there have been a portal in the waters? Look at the following verse from the Book of Enoch:

Enoch 33.2 'I saw the ends of the earth, whereon the heaven rests and the portals of heaven open.

<RELATED: TOP SECRET SERIES—PART 28: Enoch's Portals Meets Sanderson's Vile Vortices » SkyWatchTV>

C.6 It certainly sounds like a spiritual domain concerning these waters of the Crystal Sea to the north of the Garden of Eden.

C.7 The description of the sea of water is like nothing that I have heard of before. It would appear that this water originated from a river coming out of the Garden of Eden. Is seems that we are seeing an illustration of the far future with the New Heaven and the New Earth when the Crystal City New Jerusalem has finally come down to the surface of the earth. This is what is stated in Revelations chapter 22.

Revelations 22.1-2 And he showed me a pure river of water, clear as crystal, proceeding out of the throne of God and of the Lamb. 2 In the midst of the street of it and on either side of the river was there the tree of life, which bare twelve manner of fruits and yielded her fruit every month, and the leaves of the tree were for the healing of the nations.

C.8 There were rivers of living waters pouring out from the throne of God into the Garden which had the potential of giving eternal life to both Adam and Eve and the vegetation in the Garden of Eden.

C.9 The Bible tells us that a river flowed through the Garden, and it divided into four rivers when leaving the Garden. Adam and Eve in 'going through the gate of the Garden of Eden' in effect passed through a dimensional portal.

C.10 We know as a fact that it was not God's intent for the waters of life to continue feeding the rivers that flowed outside of the Garden of Eden.

C.11 Adam and Eve had lost the blessing of being in the Garden. God specifically had stated that 'less they also take their hand to the tree of life and live forever' in their now sinful and downgraded state, therefore God had them kicked out of the Garden of Eden.

Genesis 3.22-23 And the Lord God said, Behold, the man is become as one of us, to know good and evil: and now, lest he put forth his hand, and take also of the tree of life, and eat, and live for ever: Therefore, the Lord God sent him forth from the garden of Eden, to till the ground from whence he was taken.

C.12 I propose that even if God took away some of the supernatural abilities of the Garden: that perhaps for a little while some immortal powers remained, such as being able to 'see afar off' as if it were 'close by' (a power which is mentioned in this Lost **Book of Adam and Eve Book 1: Ch 8.2**)

C.13 The description in the verse 2 above, which I quote again here as the verse is truly puzzling in its content, as we today certainly don't have the powers of sight to be able to look *deep* into the earth: *'And to the north of the Garden of Eden there is a sea of water, clear and pure to the taste, unlike anything else: so that through the clearness thereof, one may look into the depths of the earth'*.

> 3 And when man washes himself in it, he becomes clean of the cleanness thereof, and white of its whiteness – even if he were dark.

C.14 Here we can see that this water is no ordinary water, as it cleanses whosoever goes into it in, a way that sounds distinctly like spiritual waters.

C.15 These waters are from the River of Life and the Tree of Life. Verse 3 is simply telling us, that if one fell into the waters of the River of life, you would be completely cleansed of all the evil that you had committed.

C.16 For this reason God had the Tree of life and presumably the Rivers of Life protected by His angels, so that no one was allowed to bathe in these waters until it was God's time, which happens once God has created the New Heaven and the New Earth. That will also be when the Heavenly City will come down to dwell on the earth at the end of the Golden Age of the Millennium.

C.17 Mentioning the word 'dark' is probably referring to 'dark spiritually.' Like the fallen angels and the most wicked people imaginable from all of time. Does this mean that evil can be forcibly altered? [See **Appendix III** for more on this topic]

C.18 How long were Adam and Eve in the Garden of Eden before they got kicked out? Well, the Apocryphal book of Jubilees gives us some insight, stating that it was 7 years.

Book of Jubilees 3.15 Adam and his wife were in the Garden of Eden for 7 years tilling and keeping it, and we (angels) gave him work and we instructed him to everything that is suitable for tillage.

> 4 And God created that sea of his own good pleasure, for He knew what would come of the man that He would make: so that after he had left the Garden of Eden on account of his transgression, men should be born in the earth. Among them are righteous ones who will die, whose

14

> souls God would raise at the last day when all of them will return to their flesh, bathe in the water of that sea, and repent of their sins.

Book of Jubilees: 3.17-18

17 And after the completion of 7 years, which he had completed there, 7 years exactly [8A.M] and in the 2nd month, on the 17th day of the month, the serpent came and approached the woman and came and said unto the woman, "Hath God commanded you saying,

18 Ye shall not eat of every tree of the Garden. And she said unto it, 'Of all the fruit of the trees of the Garden God hath said unto us, eat; but of the fruit of the tree which is in the midst of the Garden Ye shall not eat thereof, neither shall Ye touch it lest ye die!

C.19 Verse 4 is full of meaning as it is stating that God knew that mankind would fall and have to leave the paradise of the Garden of Eden which was God's intent in the first place.

C.20 As for bathing in the waters of the River of Life or the Crystal Sea which apparently is formed from the waters of the River of Life as mentioned in the Book Revelation.

Rev.22:1-3 Then the angel showed me the **river of the water of life**, as **clear as crystal**, flowing from the throne of God and of the Lamb down the middle of the great street of the city. On each side of the river stood the tree of life, bearing twelve crops of fruit, yielding its fruit every month. And the leaves of the tree are for the healing of the nations. No longer will there be any curse. The throne of God and of the Lamb will be in the city, and his servants will serve him.

> 5 But when God made Adam go out of the Garden of Eden, He did not place him on the border of it northwards. This was so that he and Eve would not be able to go near to the sea of water where they could wash themselves in it, be cleansed from their sin, erase the transgressions that they had committed and be no longer reminded of it in the thought of their punishment.

C.21 The famous writer Rebecca Springer wrote 'Within Heaven's Gates' in late 19th century. Her book was about her own 'Life after Death experience' in visiting Heaven. She stated that she was led to the 'River of life' to wash away the 'evil memories of her early life and to purify her soul' in order to enter fully into the atmosphere of heaven.

> 6 As to the Southern side of the Garden of Eden, God did not want Adam to live there either because when the wind blew from the north, it would bring him on that Southern side, the delicious smell of the trees of the Garden.

> 7 Wherefore God did not put Adam there. This was so that he would not be able to smell the sweet smell of those trees, forget his transgressions and find consolation for what he had done by taking delight in the smell of the trees and yet not be cleansed from his transgressions.

C.22 We have all heard of aromatic herbs and spices how that they can affect our moods, well apparently even more so the herbs and spices and trees of the Garden of Eden. As mentioned above, some waters or even plants have been known to cause blissful 'forgetfulness' which if one has committed crimes would be a wonderful 'escape'. Just like that scene in the **Matrix I** where the traitor talks to the 'machine agents' and states 'Ah ignorance is bliss!'

C.23 To make sure that they acknowledged their crimes, God was not going to let Adam and Eve live too close to the Southern border of the Garden of Eden where they might fall into a spiritual slumber of 'bliss' and forget all that they had done wrong.

> 8 Again, also, because God is merciful and of great pity, and governs all things in a way that he alone knows – He made our father Adam live in the Western border of the Garden of Eden, because on that side the earth is very broad.
>
> 9 And God commanded him to live there in a cave in a rock – Cave of Treasures below the Garden of Eden.

C.24 The Tree of Life and the River of life were originally in the Garden of Eden but later were moved up to the Heavenly City as mentioned clearly in Revelations 22.

Rev 22.2 "In the midst of the street of it, and on either side of the river, *was there* the tree of life, which bare twelve *manner of* fruits, *and* yielded her fruit every month: and the leaves of the tree *were* for the healing of the nations."

C.25 What happened to the Garden of Eden? Is the Garden of Eden the same place as Paradise as mentioned by Jesus? Where did God eventually move it to? According to the ancient Jewish mystical Book the Zohar, as well as the Torah the Garden of Eden exists inside a 'hollow earth.' eden.pdf (koshertorah.com)

I talked about this in my first book '**Out of the Bottomless Pit.**'

C.26 Here is an interesting verse about Enoch, the 7th from Adam in the ancient Hebrew Book of Jubilees.

Jubilees: 4.23 'And he, Enoch was taken from among the children of men, and we (the angels of God) conducted him into the **Garden of Eden** in majesty and honour and behold there he writes down the condemnation and judgement of the world and all the wickedness of the world.'

C.27 When was Enoch taken to the Garden of Eden by the angels? Enoch was translated when he was 365 years old. He was born in the year 622 After Creation – so that would mean that he was translated to the spirit world and taken to the Garden of Eden in order to write things down about the wickedness of mankind in the year 987 AC (**A**fter **C**reation) **See APPENDIX XV: BIBLICAL LONGEVITY TIMECHART FROM ADAM TO JOSEPH:** LONGEVITY CHART - www.outofthebottomlesspit.co.uk/450264991

C.28 It is stated that Enoch was the first human to write things down by divine guidance. Here is a verse from the Book of Enoch about the fabulous Garden of Eden, described from an aerial view, when Enoch was flying with an angel over the face of the earth:

Book of Enoch 32.3-6:

3 And I came to the **Garden of Righteousness** and saw beyond those trees many large trees growing there and of goodly fragrance, large, incredibly beautiful, and glorious, and the **Tree of Wisdom**, whereof they eat and know great wisdom.

4 That tree is in height like the fir and its leaves are like those of the Carob tree; and its fruit it like clusters of the vine, very beautiful, and the fragrance of the tree penetrates afar.

5 Then I said, "How beautiful is the tree, and how attractive it its look!"

6 Then Rafael, the Holy angel who was with me answered me and said, "This is the 'Tree of Wisdom', of which thy father Adam old in years (now in your time) and thy aged mother Eve who were before thee have eaten and they learnt wisdom, and their 'eyes were opened' and they knew that they were naked, and they were driven out of the Garden."

C.29 Did Eve eat an apple, or was the fruit like the 'clusters of the vine'? According to this above verse 4 from the Book of Enoch, the Tree of Wisdom, or the Tree of the 'Knowledge of Good and Evil', it would appear that Eve did not eat an apple, but the fruit was like unto 'clusters of the vine' or rather large grapes.

C.30 The Garden of Eden was the one place where Adam and Eve, as the first created humans - had an immortal body. Not yet eternal, as they were not allowed to eat of the Tree of Life in the Garden, but nevertheless immortal bodies with tremendous powers of vision hearing and an incredible connection with the realms of the spirit world.

C.31 When the spirits of the saints come back to get their physical bodies then the flesh and spirit will be fully combined into not just an immortal body such as Adam and Eve had whilst in the Garden of Eden, but an eternal body that can never be harmed or destroyed.

1 Cor. 15.40-41 'There are also celestial bodies, and bodies terrestrial: but the glory of the celestial is one, and the glory of the terrestrial is another.' 'There is one glory of the sun, and another glory of the moon, and another glory of the stars: for one star differs from another star in glory'.

Daniel 12.3 They that we wise shall shine as the brightness of the firmament and they that win many to righteousness as the stars for ever and ever.

C.32 One day the righteous will freely be allowed to eat of the Tree of Life.

Revelation 2.7 To him that overcomes will I give to eat of the tree of life, which is in the midst of the paradise of God.

Revelation 22.2 "In the midst of the street of it, and on either side of the river, *was there* the tree of life, which bare twelve *manner of* fruits, *and* yielded her fruit every month: and the leaves of the tree *were* for the healing of the nations."

Revelation 22.14 "Blessed are those who wash their robes, that they may have the right to the tree of life and may go through the gates into the city.

BOOK of ENOCH: 25.4-6 And this beautiful and fragrant Tree (of Life) will be given to the righteous and the humble.
5 From its fruit, life will be given to the chosen by the house of the Lord, the Eternal King.

6 Then they will rejoice with joy and be glad in the Holy place. They will each draw the fragrance of it into their bones, and they will live a long life on earth, as your fathers lived. And in their days sorrow and pain, and toil and punishment, will not touch them."

CHAPTER 2

ADAM AND EVE LEAVE THE GARDEN

> 1 But when our father Adam and Eve went out of the Garden, they walked the ground on their feet, not knowing they were walking.

C.1 According to this story, Adam and Eve were apparently not accustomed to 'walking' in the way that we physically do today. So, how were they accustomed to getting around inside the Garden of Eden?

C.2 It is amazing that apparently, they could not even walk out of the Garden of Eden without 'holding God's hand' - as this beautiful Story of Adam and Eve Book 1 tells us.

C.3 I would propose that the Garden of Eden was created as an 'in between world' or a higher dimension than the earth - part spiritual and part physical to prepare Adam and Eve for the much harsher existence that they would soon have to endure once they left the Garden of Eden.

C.4 Well, if they were not 'walking' in the Garden of Eden, then how did they get around? I propose from the evidence of those who have had spirit trips in one form or another or even 'Life After Death' experiences, that they floated along.

C.5 In many 'out of body' experiences people said that they sort of 'floated along' rather than walked along as we do physically on the earth. Whilst in the Garden of Eden, Adam and Eve had many freedoms and pleasures which were all lost as soon as they left the Garden.

> 2 And when they came to the opening of the gate of the Garden of Eden and saw the broad earth spread before them, covered with stones large and small, and with sand, they feared and trembled, and fell on their faces, from the fear that came over them and they were as dead.

C.6 Clearly the physical life was something vastly different than what they were used to in the Garden of Eden. They were leaving the protection of the paradise of the Garden of Eden, where they had been waited on hand and foot by the angels and spirit helpers, but now they had lost all that or rather almost. Well, at least that is what they thought initially.

> 3 Because – whereas until this time they had been in the Garden of Eden land, beautifully planted with all manner of trees – they now saw themselves in a strange land, which they knew not, and had never seen.

C.7 The world outside the Garden of Eden was harsh terrain, and they needed to be fully alert from the moment they stepped out of the Garden.

> 4 And because when they were in the Garden of Eden they were filled with the grace of bright nature and they had not hearts turned toward earthly things.

C.8 Here is another interesting detail that whilst in the Garden of Eden Adam and Eve had a 'bright nature'. In other words, they were more like the beings of light in heaven and as described in the Book of Daniel chapter 12 .3 'They that be wise shall shine as the stars of the firmament'.

C.9. In my book '**Esdras Insights'** chapter 7, which is based on the apocryphal book of **II Esdras,** we read the following about those who are saved and have been given their resurrected bodies:

7.48 Their faces shine like the sun and how they are to be made like the light of the stars, being incorruptible from then on.

7.62 The faces of those have practiced **self-control** shall shine more than the stars.

C.10 Moses's face was shining when he came down with the 10 Commandments on the tablets of stone from Mt Sinai having spent 40 days and nights in the presence of God.

EXODUS 24. 39 'And it came to pass, when Moses came down from mount Sinai with the two tables of testimony in Moses' hand, when he came down from the mount, that Moses knew not that the skin of **his face shone** while he talked with him.'

C.11 THE TRANFIGURATION OF JESUS: In the New Testament, the Transfiguration of Jesus is an event where Jesus is transfigured and becomes radiant in glory upon a mountain. The Synoptic Gospels (Matthew 17:1-8, Mark 9: 2-8, Luke 9.28-36) all describe it, and the Second Epistle of Peter also refers to it 2 Peter 1:16-18 It has also been hypothesized that the first chapter of the Gospel of John alludes to it John 1:14

On the mountaintop, Jesus begins to shine with bright rays of light. Then the Old Testament figures Moses and Elijah appear next to him, and he speaks with them. Both figures had eschatological roles: they summarize the law and the prophets, respectively. Jesus is then called: Son: by the voice of God the Father, as in the Baptism of Jesus: **SOURCE**: Transfiguration of Jesus - Wikipedia

C.12 This detail about Adam and Eve having a 'bright nature' whilst in the Garden of Eden, proves that the Garden of Eden was in a higher spiritual dimension or higher frequency, as some would put it. There are examples in the Bible when certain people were seen to shine with light: Moses when he came down from the mountain of Sinai having spent 40 days and nights in the presence of God - it is said that his face shone. It is also said of Jesus at his transfiguration that he shone – that was about one week before his crucifixion and resurrection.

C.13 When Adam and Eve were in the Garden they had different bodies of light like the Saints and celestial beings in heaven. Adam and Eve could apparently see through the barriers of the spirit world and see the very throne of God and his angels and ministering spirits. They could even see things that were far off as though they were close up.

C.14 There is also an interesting book by Douglas Hamp about the 3rd Helix. According to the book 'Corrupting the Image' Book 1 there used to be a 3rd DNA strand in the human genome called the triple helix instead of the double helix that we as humans presently have in the nucleus of each of our cells.

C.15 It is a controversial topic, but according to Douglas Hamp: The triple helix has apparently been lost from our physical bodies at some time in history and either when Adam and Eve came out of the Garden of Eden or more likely at the time of the Great Flood when people's lifespan dropped considerably due to changes in conditions in the earth itself as well as in the human body. One of the qualities of the triple helix was 'luminescence' or 'having a bright nature'. How does he know that? Well, I suggest you read his books.

C.16 Due to other qualities and abilities that people still had in the times before the 'Great Flood' God little by little turned off more and more of man's 'special abilities', due to increased disobedience. What were man's special abilities in the far past? Did mankind used to have more gifts of perception? <See the **APPENDIX** for more on this topic>.

---

5 Therefore God had pity on them; and when He saw them fallen before the gate of the Garden of Eden, He sent His Word to our father Adam and Eve and raised them from their fallen state.

C.17 'He sent His Word' … There are many verses like that in the Bible such as:

Psalm 107.20 'He sent his word, and healed them, and delivered *them* from their destructions.

C.18 The big question here is: Could Adam and Eve still see their Creator 'The Word of God', after they had left the Garden of Eden or did the Word of God now only speak to them in their thoughts, as what has happened to most people who enquired of the Lord ever since?

C.19 The Bible tells us that when Adam and Eve were still in the Garden of Eden that the Lord Himself came and talked with them in the 'cool of the day'.

Genesis 3.8 'And they heard the voice of the LORD God walking in the garden in the cool of the day.'

C.20 What or better said *who* is the 'Word of God'? The Bible and the apocryphal books all make it clear that the 'Word of God' is the creator of the universe – Jesus who became the Messiah.

Jn 1.1 In the beginning was the Word and the Word was with God and the Word was God. –

C.21 The Bible also tells us in Revelation 3.14 that Jesus was the beginning of the creation of God and was the 'only begotten Son of God as also brought out so well in the oldest book in the world - the Book of Enoch – See my book 'Enoch Insights' for a lot more details on the 'Son of God'. All through the Old Testament and even further back in time such as the Book of Enoch - it is always made clear that there are two distinct beings in both God the Father and God the Son - Daniel 7

Daniel 7.13-14 'I saw in the night visions, and behold, one like the Son of man came with the clouds of heaven, and came to the Ancient of days, and they brought him near before him. [14] And there was given him dominion, and glory, and a kingdom, that all people, nations, and languages, should serve him: his dominion is an everlasting dominion, which shall not pass away, and his kingdom that which shall not be destroyed.

Enoch chapter 105.1 'For I and My Son will be united with them forever in the paths of uprightness in their lives, and ye shall have peace: rejoice ye children of uprightness. Amen.

CHAPTER 3

The promise of 5 and a half days

---

1 God said to Adam, "I have ordained on this earth days and years, and you and your seed shall live and walk in it, until the days and years are fulfilled; when I shall send the Word that created you, and against which you have transgressed, the Word that made you come out of the Garden of Eden and that raised you when you were fallen.

C.1 What is the Word that created you? The Word of God is Jesus according to the gospel of **John:1.1-3:**

1 In the beginning was the Word and the Word was with God and the Word was God.

2 The same was in the beginning with God.

3 All things were made by Him and without Him was not made any thing that was made.

---

2 Yea, the Word that will again save thee when the five days and a half are fulfilled."

3 But when Adam heard these words from God, and of the great five days and a half, he did not understand the meaning of them.

4 For Adam was thinking that there would be but five days and a half for him, to the end of the world.

5 And Adam wept, and prayed God to explain it to him.

6 Then God in His mercy for Adam who was made after His own image and similitude, explained to him, that these were 5,000 and 500 years; and how One would then come and save him and his seed.

C.2 This book is not the only one which mentions this strange number of 5500. Briefly put - apparently, many people at the time of Christ stated that the world was 5500 years old when Christ was born.

C.3 There has always been a conflict in 'time issues' between the Masoretic text: as used in the KJV of the Bible and the Greek Septuagint (300 BCE) which is a Greek version of the Hebrew Bible (or Old Testament), including the Apocrypha, made for Greek-speaking Jews in Egypt in the 3rd and 2nd centuries BC and adopted by the early Christian Churches.

C.4 I mentioned how that someone had altered the biblical timeline in the

Septuagint by adding 100 years to each of the those from Seth down to the grandfather of Abraham- thus having added an extra 1500 years to the timeline.

C.5 Why would someone do that? See my other book for the answers - **'JASHER INSIGHTS'**]

C.6 Well, thank God for the KJV of the Bible because one can easily count backwards from Christ starting with both Joseph and Mary and trace their ancestry all the way back to Adam at about 4004 BCE.

C.7 Many thought that the world would come to an end at the 6000-year mark which according to the 5500 Timeline from Creation to Christ has already come and gone at around 500 AD.

C.8 Perhaps the 5500 years is to be interpreted in a different way than the traditional way of some of the ancients. How come we have better genealogies as in the KJV of the Bible to go by today, than the church fathers had available almost 2000 years ago? Now that is a good question.

C.9 The point here is that the 5500 years is mentioned in other books apart from the 'Lost Books of Adam and Eve' - but could the number of years have been misinterpreted in the far past?

C.10 Could it be perhaps measuring the time from 500 years after Creation unto the year 6000 A.M (Anno. Mundi) when Christ will return in the 2nd coming?

C.11 God is telling Adam and Eve that no matter what they try to do in penitence and asking for forgiveness, they will not be allowed back into the Garden until 5500 years have passed! Why this strange number of 5500 and not exactly 6000 years? What exactly could this mean? (**See Appendix for more on this topic**)

> 7 But God had before that made this covenant with our father, Adam, in the same terms, ere he came out of the garden, when he was by the tree whereof Eve took the fruit and gave it him to eat.

C.12 The Lord Creator made a 'Covenant of Obedience' with Adam and Eve – as long as they obeyed, they got to stay in the heavenly Garden of Eden; but if they disobeyed and ate of the Tree of the Knowledge of Good and Evil then they would surely die.

C.13 Adam and Eve did die spiritually when they ate the forbidden fruit, and thus were forced to leave the Garden of Eve as they had become both corrupted and mortal.

> 8 Inasmuch as when our father Adam came out of the garden, he passed by that tree, and saw how God had then changed the appearance of it into another form, and how it withered.

C.14 The tree of the 'Knowledge of Good and Evil' had withered! This reminds me of the story of Jesus and His disciples and the fig tree. – **Matthew 21: 18-22; Mark 11:12-14,20-24** Jesus cursed it saying, 'Let no fruit grow on thee henceforward forever 'By the next morning the fig tree was withered'.

C.15 Jesus was talking about Israel as being withered and Israel was destroyed in 70 AD - 40 years after the Pharisees killed Him, their own Saviour. That action did not save Israel - she incurred the full Wrath of God in 70 AD, by the hand of the Romans for killing His only begotten Son.

C.16 In this story of Adam and Eve, perhaps the point of the Tree of the Knowledge of Good and Evil being withered was to show that from that point on in time man's knowledge would be mostly evil and thus withered and cursed by its Creator - as has been the case for the past almost 6000 years. Man's inventions have been mostly for evil and for his ultimate destruction.

---

9 And as Adam went to it, he feared, trembled, and fell down; but God in His mercy lifted him up, and then made this covenant with him.

10 And, again, when Adam was by the gate of the garden, and saw the cherub with a sword of flashing fire in his hand, and the cherub grew angry and frowned at him, both Adam and Eve became afraid of him, and thought he meant to put them to death. So, they fell on their faces, and trembled with fear.

C.17 The Cherub with the flaming sword is not the traditional baby angel with tiny wings. The Cherub was a mighty angel.

Genesis 3.24 After he drove the man out, he placed on the east side of **the Garden of Eden** cherubim and a flaming sword flashing back and forth to guard the way to the tree of life.

C.18 The cherubim are normally seen guarding the Throne of God as in Revelation 4 and Ezekiel chapters 1 & 10. Also known as the 4 Beasts around God's Throne.

---

11 But he had pity on them, and showed them mercy; and turning from them went up to heaven, and prayed unto the Lord, and said:

12 " O Lord Thou didst send me to watch at the gate of the garden, with a sword of fire.

13 "But when Thy servants, Adam and Eve, saw me, they fell on their faces, and were as dead. O my Lord, what shall we do to Thy servants?"

14 Then God had pity on them, and showed them mercy, and sent His Angel to keep the Garden.

> 15 And the Word of the Lord came unto Adam and Eve and raised them up.

James 4.10 'Humble thyself therefore in the sight of God and he shall lift thee up.'

> 16 And the Lord said to Adam, "I told thee that at the end of five days and a half, I will send my Word and save thee.

C.19 Here again, we see the Lord mentions His promise of five and a half days or 5500 years, until He as the Word of God shall save mankind. N.B Repetition in the scriptures is generally to emphasize the importance of what is being announced.

C.20 According to these Books of Adam and Eve 5500 years until Salvation seem to be an important statement.

> 17 "Strengthen thy heart, therefore, and abide in the Cave of Treasures, of which I have before spoken to thee."

C.21 The Cave of Treasures Was called that because God in time gave different treasures for Adam and Eve to put in the cave including gold, myrrh, and frankincense. When people such as the old patriarchs died, they were eventually buried in this 'Cave of Treasures' including Adam and Eve.

C.22 There is already a lot written about the Cave of Treasures both in old Jewish writings and Christian writings. Obviously originally Adam and Eve had to have a physical place to live. The Cave of Treasures however came to mean a lot more than just a cave.

C.23 Later in time we read in the Book of Jasher concerning Abraham buying a cave to bury Sarah his wife. Why is it that there was a direct link between the Cave of Treasures and the place where Abraham bought for burying his wife Sarah in Machpelah?

C.24 Machpelah was a sort of 'double cave' that was reported in ancient Hebrew writings to be linked to the Cave of Treasures. It is reported that when Abraham went into the Cave of Machpelah that he saw the bodies of Adam and Eve? Adam reportedly talked with him! How was that even possible. Was the Cave an actual portal to Inner Earth where the Garden of Eden used to be as recorded in the Zohar and ancient Hebrew writings.

Source: https://godssecret.wordpress.com/category/hebron-machpelah

C.25 The first time Abraham entered the cave, he saw Adam and Eve and a light emanating from the Garden of Eden (Zohar 1:128b). In the painting, a procession of people enters under a vaulted ceiling into hidden chambers within. They proceed towards a light which shines and illuminates the scene. It is here in Hebron that the end of temporal life connects to the next world and eternity. The quintessential image of Hebron is the Cave of Machpelah. *Machpelah* comes from the root Hebrew word *kaful*, double, referring to the double cave and to the four special couples buried there: Adam and Eve, Abraham and Sarah, Isaac and Rebecca, Jacob, and Leah.

SOURCE: The Cave of Machpelah - Chayei Sarah Art - Parshah (chabad.org)

C.26 Why did Adam and Eve live in the Cave of Treasures and not in a proper house or a castle or something more dignified and treated like royalty one might ask – after all they were God's first Creations, and one might expect some sort of glory for them? It was the Lord who commanded them to live there. Why? The answer to that question of course is - humility. So many people on earth have the 'get rich quick' mentality, but they do not want to be taught how they should behave properly, courteously and with all the fruits of God's Spirit.

Galatians 5.22-23 For the fruit of the spirit is love, joy, peace, long-suffering, gentleness, goodness, faith, meekness, temperance against such there is no law.

C.27 Christ Himself is described as coming to earth in humility and not in pride and arrogance like so many of the world's leaders of today who are not here to 'serve the people' but to 'serve up' the people and devour them. - Revelations 18

Rev.18.23-24 And the light of a candle shall shine no more at all in thee; and the voice of the bridegroom and of the bride shall be heard no more at all in thee: for thy merchants were the great men of the earth; for by thy sorceries were all nations deceived.

[24] And in her was found the blood of prophets, and of saints, and of all that were slain upon the earth.

> 18 And when Adam heard this Word from God, he was comforted with that which God had told him. For He had told him how He would save him.

C.28 It is wonderful for this Lost book of Adam and Eve glorifies the Creator as Jesus Himself as the 'Word of God' who would eventually come down to earth as the only Begotten Son of God to save all of mankind from the works of the Devil. Apart from the Bible in John chapter 1.1 and the Book of Enoch and the Book of Daniel chapter 7, there are few books which directly come out and lift up Jesus as being the Creator and also the Son of God who God had hidden away for a long time.

C.29 It is true that Jesus the Creator did die for the sins of all of mankind 4000 years later according to the KJV of the Bible, although some would say that it was exactly 5500 years later especially to those who adhere to the Septuagint teachings of the Biblical time chronology. Who was right about it? What do you think?

C.30 I would state as I did above, that yes, Jesus saved us sinners, but mankind as represented by Adam and Eve as the very first man and woman on this planet have not yet re-entered into the Garden of Eden at least not on the earth as it used to be before.

C.31 There is only one example that I have heard about and that is in the book of Jubilees where it mentions that after Enoch was translated that he was taken by the angels to the Garden of Eden, where he wrote about the coming Great Flood and the coming Wrath of God.

Jubilees Ch 4.24 'And he was taken from among the children of men and we conducted into the Garden of Eden in majesty and honour and behold he writes down the condemnation and the judgement of the world and of all the wickedness of the children of men.

C.32 The Garden of Eden is also mentioned as being especially important to God Himself as a specific location on the earth:

Jubilees Ch 4.27 For the Lord has four places on earth, the Garden of Eden, and the Mount of the East, and this mountain on which thou art this day. Mount Sinai and Mt Zion which will be sanctified in the New Creation for a sanctification of the earth; through it will the earth be sanctified from all its guilt and its uncleanness throughout the generations of the world.

C.33 God in the book of Jubilees was talking with Moses on the mountain and revealing that the Garden of Eden would be part of the New Heaven and New Earth in the future in probably the Millennium after Christ has returned for the 2nd time or 1000 years later after the Millennium when God has created a New Heaven and a New Earth.

CHAPTER 4

The Cave of Treasures

1 But Adam and Eve wept for having come out of the garden, their first abode.

2 And, indeed, when Adam looked at his flesh, that was altered, he wept bitterly, he and Eve, over what they had done. And they walked and went gently down into the Cave of Treasures.

II Esdras 3.13 For the first Adam, burdened with an evil heart, transgressed, and was overcome, as were all who were descended from him, thus the disease became permanent. The law was in the people's heart along with the <u>evil root</u>, but what was good departed and the <u>evil remained</u>.

C.1 *'His flesh was altered'* How exactly had their flesh been altered? *'And they went gently down into the Cave of Treasures'.* They went 'gently' because they were unaccustomed to having to walk and were therefore like small children learning to walk. In the Garden of Eden, they had floated along just like the inhabitants in heaven. Adam and Eve having been kicked out of the Garden of Eden, were now totally broken-hearted and they no longer had the will or enthusiasm to face this new and foreboding world of the unknown.

3 And as they came to it Adam wept over himself and said to Eve, "Look at this cave that is to be our prison in this world, and a place of punishment!

C.2 Adam makes it sound in verse 3, as if they are entering Hell itself! It is true that God had to provide a good place for Adam and Eve to live in the physical world, but to Adam and Eve after just having left the bright, beautiful, and celestial Garden of Eden, the earth life looked like a prison of limitations, pains, and sorrows by comparison to what they had just lost, as well as a *'place of punishment'*.

4 "What is it compared with the garden? What is its narrowness compared with the space of the other?

2 Esdras 7.5-6 'The entrances of this world were made narrow and sorrowful and toilsome, they are few and evil, full of dangers, and involved in great hardships. But the 'entrances of the greater world (spirit world) are broad and safe' and really yield the fruit of immortality. Therefore, unless the living pass through the difficult and vain experiences, they can never receive those things that have been reserved for them.

> 5 "What is this rock, by the side of those groves? What is the gloom of this cavern, compared with the light of the garden?

1 Jn 1.5 "This then is the message which we have heard of him, and declare unto you, that God is light, and in him is no darkness at all."

> 6 "What is this overhanging ledge of rock to shelter us, compared with the mercy of the Lord that overshadowed us?

Psalm 91.1 'He that dwelleth in the secret place of the Most High shall abide under the shadow of the Almighty.'

> 7 "What is the soil of this cave compared with the garden-land? This earth, strewed with stones; and that, planted with delicious fruit-trees?"
>
> 8 And Adam said to Eve, "Look at thine eyes, and at mine, which afore beheld angels in heaven, praising; and they, too, without ceasing.
>
> 9 "But now we do not see as we did: our eyes have become of flesh; they cannot see in like manner as they saw before."

C.3 Here is some very important information, as it is stating that Adam and Eve had been more than mortal when they were still in the Garden of Eden and that now they had lost their immortality. Their eyes before leaving the Garden of Eden were full of spiritual light and they had powers of sight unequalled by human beings.

C.4 In the Garden of Eden, Adam and Eve had 'heavenly eyes' that could see long distances, seeing far away objects as though they were close up. The Bible itself does not make much distinction from the time Adam and Eve were in the Garden and then had to live outside the Garden, as to the nature of their bodies.

> 10 Adam said again to Eve, "What is our body to-day, compared to what it was in former days, when we dwelt in the garden?"

C.5 Adam is bemoaning the fact that their whole bodies were glorified whilst they were in the Garden of Eden, and they were much closer to the ways of heaven and the spirit world than the earthly.

C.6 Why was it so much more like heaven than the earth when God had just created the physical earth? Well, God created the Garden of Eden, first of all.

II Esdras: 3.4 And thou did lead him into the Garden (of Eden) which thy right hand had planted <u>before</u> the earth appeared.

C.7 It would seem, that the Lord was making an important point in separating the spiritual world from the physical world.

C.8 Man came from the celestial to the physical realm to be tested and tried and to see if he would turn to God through his many trials and afflictions or would he go the way of the flesh or even worse, the excessive carnality and lusts of both Satan and his fallen angels?

C.9 It was exceedingly difficult for Adam and Eve, having been kicked out of the Garden of Eden and still remembering what the celestial life was like - especially when many of their former powers and abilities were now very much limited and even taken away altogether.

11 After this Adam did not like to enter the cave, under the overhanging rock; nor would he ever have entered it.

12 But he bowed to God's orders; and said to himself, "Unless I enter the cave, I shall again be a transgressor."

C.10 Adam was starting to learn to submit to God and learning to trust Him in a new harsher world where he could no longer readily see God.

C.11 Remember that according to the Bible and this Lost Book of Adam and Eve that whilst in the garden of Eden, the angels had taught Adam how to till the ground and how to sow, plant, cultivate and harvest. Initially when Adam and Eve had been forced from the Garden of Eden they were in great shock, but eventually all that they had been taught in the Garden of Eden for 7 years would have been a big help for them in carving out the wilderness that they now found themselves in and enabling them to make it into a beautiful place - with God's help.

CHAPTER 5

Eve Takes the Blame

> 1 Then Adam and Eve entered the cave, and stood praying, in their own tongue, unknown to us, but which they knew well.

C.1 The original language as spoken by Adam and Eve was in Hebrew according to the Book of Jubilees. (**See my book 'Jubilees Insights'**)

Jubilees 12.26 'And I opened his mouth and his ears and his lips, and I began to speak with him in Hebrew, in the tongue of creation.'

> 2 And as they prayed, Adam raised his eyes, and saw the rock and the roof of the cave that covered him overhead, so that he could see neither heaven, nor God's creatures. So, he wept and smote heavily upon his breast, until he dropped, and was as dead.

C.2 Adam and Eve were accustomed to praying and looking up above them and seeing into heaven and possibly even God's Throne and the 4 Beasts or Seraphim surrounding the throne of God and countless millions of angels.

Revelation 4.6 And before the throne *there was* a sea of glass like unto crystal: and in the midst of the throne, and round about the throne, *were* <u>four beasts</u> full of eyes before and behind.

C.3 Prayer for Adam and Eve was not some deeply pious religious ceremony that they performed, but it was their very life with God. It was the most important part of their existence to be able to be in direct communication with God. To be with God always was rather like a small baby still in the 'womb of the Garden of Eden' totally shielded and totally cared for by his mother.

C.4 It is the longing of millions of people today to regain that original relationship with God, where we can actually 'see Him' as Adam and Eve could in the Garden of Eden.

Jn 3.2 "Beloved, now are we the sons of God, and it doth not yet appear what we shall be: but we know that, when he shall appear, we shall be like him; for we shall see him as he is."

1 Cor 13.12 For now we see through a glass, darkly; but then face to face: now I know in part; but then shall I know even as also I am known.

> 3 And Eve sat weeping; for she believed he was dead.
>
> 4 Then she arose, spread her hands towards God, suing Him for mercy and pity, and said, "O God, forgive me my sin, the sin which I commit-

ted, and remember it not against me.

5 "For I alone caused Thy servant to fall from the garden into this lost estate; from light into this darkness; and from the abode of joy into this prison.

6 "O God, look upon this Thy servant thus fallen, and raise him from his death, that he may weep and repent of his transgression which he committed through me.

7 "Take not away his soul this once; but let him live that he may stand after the measure of his repentance, and do Thy will, as before his death.

8 "But if Thou do not raise him up, then, O God, take away my own soul, that I be like him; and leave me not in this dungeon, one and alone; for I could not stand alone in this world, but with him only.

9 "For Thou, O God, didst cause a slumber to come upon him, and didst take a bone from his side, and didst restore the flesh in the place of it, by Thy divine power.

10 "And Thou didst take me, the bone, and make me a woman, bright like him, with heart, reason, and speech; and in flesh, like unto his own; and Thou didst make me after the likeness of his countenance, by Thy mercy and power.

11 "O Lord, I and he are one and Thou, O God, art our Creator Thou are He who made us both in one day.

C.5 This is a beautiful declaration by Eve. It is wonderful when you feel specially joined to someone in spirit as well as in body and you feel that you are truly one with them in every way. That is an excellent definition of a good marriage.

Genesis 2:24 'Therefore shall a man leave his father and his mother and shall cleave unto his wife: and they shall be one flesh.'

12 "Therefore, O God, give him life, that he may be with me in this strange land, while we dwell in it on account of our transgression.

13 "But if Thou wilt not give him life, then take me, even me, like him;

that we both may die the same day."

14 And Eve wept bitterly and fell upon our father Adam from her great sorrow.

C.6 This chapter is a touching story and how hurt Eve felt in seeing Adam lying apparently *'as dead'* because of their sins that they had committed against their Creator.

C.7 Adam and Eve had not fully appreciated the great blessings that they had in the Garden of Eden to the point of being totally obedient to God and now they had been thrust out into a seeming world of total darkness -the physical world – that at first looked both rough and barren. It filled them with great sorrow to realize exactly 'what' they had just lost.

2 Cor 7:10 "For godly sorrow worketh repentance to salvation not to be repented of: but the sorrow of the world worketh death."

CHAPTER 6

God's Reprimand

> 1 But God looked upon them; for they had killed themselves through great grief.
>
> 2 But He would raise them and comfort them.

C.1 Was it true that Adam and Eve killed themselves as according to the Lost books of Adam and Eve? I think it highly unlikely, as it is certainly not written about in the Bible. I think that what the original story meant was that Adam and Eve were overcome by grief and remorse to the point of wanting to die or feeling 'dead in spirit' - and thus the flesh simply followed as in a very severe depression with suicidal thoughts? Adam and Eve felt like the modern expression 'I felt like killing myself.' I felt like jumping off a cliff! That is Satan's temptation to kill oneself by jumping off a bridge or something.

C.2 Remember that God had warned Adam and Eve that if they ate of the Tree of the 'Knowledge of Good and Evil' then they would die! They did die spiritually, and they clearly noticed that their whole appearance was different.

C.3 Adam and Eve could only be rescued by Salvation by the Creator Himself who in this very book had promised to come to the earth in person to save them from all their sins and reconcile them to God.

C.4 The truth is that although Adam and Eve had been kicked out of the Garden of Eden they were still protected to some degree by God's angels. The Lord did still come and see them when sent by God the Father according to this book.

C.5 In the Garden they could see Jesus the Creator (The Word of God) and all the heavenly beings - but now that they had been thrust out of the Garden of Eden into this seemingly barren wasteland where in general, they could neither see nor perceive the heavenly beings - which caused them to despair of life itself.

C.6 Adam and Eve had not yet learned that God and his angels were still very much with them and would still love and care for them, although once they left the Garden of Eden, God and his angels and ministering spirits were now for the most part invisible. They learned little by little that God was still very much there and still lovingly caring for them personally, as He had also done so when they were still inside the Garden of Eden.

C.7 Because of their sins in the Garden of Eden they had to learn the hard way. Defeat teaches us a lot! We learn from it! All Adam and Eve had to do was 'cry out to God' and He would answer in the form of sending His Son – the Creator of all things to visit Adam and Eve and to instruct them as in the following situation. The question is could Adam still actually see Jesus the Creator in the early days when they had first been booted out of their heavenly home of the wonderful Garden of Eden?

> 3 He, therefore, sent His Word unto them; that they should stand and be raised forthwith.
>
> 4 And the Lord said unto Adam and Eve, "You transgressed of your own free will, until you came out of the garden in which I had placed you.
>
> 5 "Of your own free will have you transgressed through your desire for divinity, greatness, and an exalted state, such as I have; so that I deprived you of the bright nature in which you then were, and I made you come out of the garden to this land, rough and full of trouble.

C.8 When Satan tempted Eve in the Garden, he lied to her in promising her that she could become as a goddess! She already had a 'Bright nature' and was already like a goddess whilst in the Garden of Eden and had been 'waited on' by angels.

C.9 Satan is the Father of all the children of PRIDE. He used the temptation for something that Eve thought that she did not have at the time, to trick and lure her and Adam away from God's highest will. God's highest will, was to obey and trust Him that He knew best and had their best interests at heart.

> 6 "If only you had not transgressed My commandment and had kept My law and had not eaten of the fruit of the tree, near which I told you not to come! And there were fruit trees in the garden better than that one.
>
> 7 "But the wicked Satan who continued not in his first estate, nor kept his faith; in whom was no good intent towards Me, and who though I had created him, yet set Me at naught, and sought the Godhead, so that I hurled him down from heaven, he it is who made the tree appear pleasant in your eyes, until you ate of it, by hearkening to him.

Luke 10.18 'I beheld Satan falling like lightning from heaven.'

Rev. 12:4 "And his tail drew the third part of the stars (angels) of heaven and did cast them to the earth: and the dragon (Satan) stood before the woman, which was ready to be delivered, for to devour her child (Jesus the Creator) as soon as it was born."

> 8 "Thus have you transgressed My commandment, and therefore have I brought upon you all these sorrows.

> 9 "For I am God the Creator, who, when I created My creatures, did not intend to destroy them. But after they had sorely roused My anger, I punished them with grievous plagues, until they repent.

1Peter 3.9 The Lord is not slack concerning his promise, as some men count slackness; but is longsuffering to us-ward, not willing that any should perish, but that all should come to repentance.

10 "But, if on the contrary, they still continue hardened in their transgression, they shall be under a curse for ever.

Jude 1.6 'The angels which kept not their first estate but left their own habitation, he hath reserved in everlasting chains under darkness unto the judgment of the great day.

C.10 Could it be that in the original writings of the 'Lost Books of Adam and Eve' were written in Pre-Flood times?

C.11 Why do I think that the original Lost books of Adam and Eve were probably written in Pre-Flood times? The answer to that is simple: in this very book Adam and Eve instruct their descendants to write about what had happened to them. The first human to write was either Enoch 7th from Adam or Cainan 4th from Adam according to the Apocryphal books of Jubilees and Jasher. **BIBLICAL LONGEVITY TIMECHART FROM ADAM TO JOSEPH:** LONGEVITY CHART - www.outofthebottomlesspit.co.uk/450264991

C.12 There was a big interest in 300-100 BCE in scholars making excellent copies of original manuscripts. Many of those manuscripts had apparently been incredibly old. There was a big interest in making excellent copies of them and selling them to the biggest library in the world in Alexandria in Egypt and which was built in the 3rd century BCE.

C.13 This is why the Septuagint version of the Bible was assembled in Egypt and was translated into Greek. Greek was the language of the then 5th 'world empire' of the Greeks in 300 BCE. Egypt was part of the Grecian empire in 300 BCE and was referred to as the Seleucid quarter, or Southern part of the Grecian empire.

C.14 Notice that many of the original apocryphal books were re-assembled at that same time or from 300-100 BCE, such as the Book of Enoch, Jubilees, Jasher and these Lost Books of Adam and Eve.

C.15 Did that just happen? Was the motive in assembling of all these ancient books to preserve them or was it as a direct result of the great Library in Alexandria, which paid good money for copies of original books? Not that that matters, as 'all things work together for good' – (Romans 8.28), and more copies of original books were made which was a particularly good thing, as books do not last more than 200 years, or they will disintegrate into dust.

C.16 The greatest library in the world at Alexandria was sadly eventually destroyed in a fire apparently. A loss of up to 1,000,000 books. When was the library destroyed well no one seems to be sure about that one? Some suggest the library was destroyed by accident by Julius Caesar in 48 BCE in his conquests of the Grecian empire. Others say that the Great library of Alexandria was destroyed around 390 AD.

C.17 The Library of **Alexandria** flourished under the patronage of the Ptolemaic dynasty and functioned as a major centre of scholarship. It was built in the third century BC. Library of Alexandria - Simple English Wikipedia, the free encyclopaedia

C.18 Assuming that the great Library at Alexandria was indeed deliberately burned down for nefarious reasons:

Why would a conqueror burn down a gigantic ancient library as the one at Alexandria in Egypt?

Well, as is still quoted by the 'elite rulers' of today 'Knowledge is Power' and as the great historian Toynbee stated, 'Power corrupts, and 'Absolute Power' corrupts absolutely'.

World leaders always end up thinking that they are more than human, as they are indeed often inspired by Satan himself.

Rulers of the past including Hitler and the communists ended up 'burning the books' so to speak. To destroy knowledge is often one of their aims, to keep the masses in darkness, ignorance and blissfully controlled. Their motto is 'The truth is whatever 'they say it is' at any given moment.'

The Rise of Alexandria

Alexandria, one of the greatest cities of the ancient world, was founded by Alexander the Great after his conquest of Egypt in 332 BC. After the death of Alexander in Babylon in 323 BC, Egypt fell to the lot of one of his lieutenants, Ptolemy. It was under Ptolemy that the newly founded Alexandria came to replace the ancient city of Memphis as the capital of Egypt. This marked the beginning of the rise of Alexandria: Who Destroyed the Great Library of Alexandria? | Ancient Origins (ancient-origins.net)

CHAPTER 7

Animals At Peace

> 1 When Adam and Eve heard these words from God, they wept and sobbed yet more; but they strengthened their hearts in God, because they now felt that the Lord was to them like a father and a mother; and for this very reason, they wept before Him, and sought mercy from Him.

C.1 I believe that we have God the Father and Jesus the Son (Creator) and the Holy Spirit as the Mother of the Trinity. If this is true and it can be proven using scriptures (See my book: **JASHER INSIGHTS**) then Adam and Eve did not really have anything to worry about when they got kicked out of the Garden of Eden as they had parents and the Creator to take of them - although now the spirit world was invisible for the most part.

C.2 God truly loved Adam and Eve and did take very good care of them which Adam and Eve learned about over the time of their lives.

> 2 Then God had pity on them, and said: "O Adam, I have made My covenant with thee, and I will not turn from it; neither will I let thee return to the garden, until My covenant of the great five days and a half is fulfilled."

C.3 What did God mean by the strange incomplete number of five and a half?

> 3 Then Adam said unto God, "O Lord Thou didst create us, and make us fit to be in the garden; and before I transgressed, 'Thou made all beasts come to me, that I should name them'.

Gen.2:19 And out of the ground the LORD God formed every beast of the field, and every fowl of the air; and brought them to Adam to see what he would call them: and whatsoever Adam called every living creature, that was the name thereof.

> 4 "Thy grace was then on me; and I named everyone according to Thy mind; and Thou made them all subject unto me.

C.4 Adam had prayed and asked God Himself what to call the animals. Adam had been learning to depend on God through prayer in the Garden of Eden. God gave him all the answers because He took the time with God and asked Him.

C.5 Simple enough to hear from God one might say - but how many things simply do not happen in peoples' lives in modern times, because they have not learned this basic lesson: Get quiet before God and ask Him about everything.

C.6 God loves to answer our questions, I can personally assure you. Adam certainly did the right thing in asking God what to do and in this case - what to name the different animals that God had just created whilst Adam and Eve were still in the Garden of Eden.

---

5 "But now, O Lord God, that I have transgressed Thy commandment, all beasts will rise against me and will devour me, and Eve Thy hand-maid; and will cut off our life from the face of the earth.

6 "I therefore beseech Thee, O God, that, since Thou hast made us come out of the garden, and hast made us be in a strange land, Thou wilt not let the beasts hurt us."

7 When the Lord heard these words from Adam, He had pity on him, and felt that he had truly said that the beasts of the field would rise and devour him and Eve, because He, the Lord, was angry with them two on account of their transgression.

8 Then God commanded the beasts, and the birds, and all that moves upon the earth, to come to Adam and to be familiar with him, and not to trouble him and Eve; nor yet any of the good and righteous among their posterity.

9 Then the beasts did obeisance to Adam, according to the command-ment of God; except the serpent, against which God was wroth. It did not come to Adam, with the beasts.

C.7 According to the Book of Jubilees all the animals could talk with Adam and Eve whilst they were in the Garden. They lost this ability of communicat-ing with the animals once they left the Garden of Eden.

Jubilees 3.28 And on that day was closed the mouths of all the beasts, and of cattle and of birds, and whatever walks and whatever moves, so that they could no longer speak; for they had all spoken with one another with one lip and one tongue.

Jubilees 3.30 And to Adam alone did he give the wherewithal to cover his shame, of all the beasts (creatures) and cattle.

CHAPTER 8

"Bright Nature" Gone!

> 1 Then Adam wept and said, "O God, when we dwelt in the garden, and our hearts were lifted up, we saw the angels that sang praises in heaven, but now we do not see as we were used to do; nay, when we entered the cave, all creation became hidden from us."

C.1 'All creation became hidden to us. What does that mean? Adam and Eve obviously had had a direct link to the spiritual realm before getting kicked out of the Garden of Eden and now they felt abandoned, simply because they could no longer see into the spirit world.

C.2 *'We saw all the angels'*: It obviously meant a lot to them, and it also was a great disappointment to Adam and Eve that they could no longer see the angels and experience the delight of their praises to God.

C.3 Why? All who have 'seen these things' and even participated in them described themselves as being in a type of 'ecstasy' and an amazing feeling of euphoria.

C.4 Who in their right mind would want to leave such a beautiful atmosphere of praise and worship of the Living God?

C.5 So, it must have been very tough for Adam and Eve to leave all that. It has been similarly described by many people in their 'Life and Death' experiences. In many cases they simply did not want to return to the painful and trying physical life, because of the Joys that await God's children in heaven.

C.6 This would indicate that we are all supposed to praise God much more for His blessings and protection, His great Love for us and for His light in our lives through His giving us the treasure of His Word - Jesus.

Jn 1.51 And he saith unto him, 'Verily, verily, I say unto you, Hereafter ye shall see heaven open, and the angels of God ascending and descending upon the Son of man.'

Psalm 22.3 But thou art holy, O thou that 'inhabits the praises' of Israel.

> 2 Then God the Lord said unto Adam, "When you were under subjection to Me, thou had a bright nature within thee, and for that reason could thou see things afar off. But after thy transgression thy bright nature was withdrawn from thee; and it was not left to thee to see things afar off, but only near at hand; after the ability of the flesh; for it is brutish."

C.7 The 'bright nature' of angels and resurrected saints that Adam and Eve had in the Garden of Eden is mentioned - where they had eyes that could see things far away and conceivably many other abilities which they lost due to their transgressions in the Garden of Eden. Whilst in the Garden of Eden, Adam and Eve could clearly see 'deep into the realms behind this physical realm'.

C.8 'After the ability of the flesh for it is brutish' -This is certainly telling us a lot about mankind and the carnal mind.

Gal. 5:17 For the flesh lusts against the Spirit, and the Spirit against the flesh: and these are contrary the one to the other: so that ye cannot do the things that ye would.

Romans 8:7 Because the carnal mind is enmity against God: for it is not subject to the law of God, neither indeed can be.

---

3 When Adam and Eve had heard these words from God, they went their way, praising and worshipping Him with a sorrowful heart.

C.9 Praising God is the highest form of worship. See the psalms for so many prayers of praise and worship of God as written about by King David in 1000 BCE

Psalm.9:1 I will praise thee, O LORD, with my whole heart; I will shew forth all thy marvellous works.

Psalm: 86.12 I will praise thee, O Lord my God, with all my heart: and I will glorify thy name for evermore.

---

4 And God ceased to commune with them.

CHAPTER 9

Water from the Tree of Life

> 1 Then Adam and Eve came out of the Cave of Treasures, and drew near to the garden gate, and there they stood to look at it, and wept for having come away from it.

C.1 There is a warning in the scriptures of 'not looking back' when God wants you to go in a different direction. Otherwise, if you disobey it will lead to sadness and tears of regret.

Luke 17:32 'Remember Lot's wife' [She turned back to look at Sodom and Gomorrah being destroyed with fire and brimstone by God and immediately turned into a pillar of salt]

> 2 And Adam and Eve went from before the gate of the garden to the southern side of it, and found there the water that watered the garden, from the root of the Tree of Life, and that parted itself from thence into four rivers over the earth.
>
> 3 Then they came and drew near to that water and looked at it; and saw that it was the water that came forth from under the root of the Tree of Life in the garden.

C.2 God had commanded in the Book of Genesis:

Genesis 3:22 And the LORD God said, Behold, the man is become as one of us, to know good and evil: and now, lest he put forth his hand, and take also of the tree of life, and eat, and live for ever:

C.3 God did not want Adam and Eve to go anywhere near the Tree of Life and therefore live forever in their 'Fallen state'.

II Esdras 3.13 For the first Adam, burdened with and evil heart, transgressed and was overcome, as were also all who were descended from him, thus the disease became permanent. The law was in people's hearts along with the evil root, but what was good departed, and evil remained.

II Esdras 4.17 For a grain of evil seed was sown in Adam's heart from the beginning, and how much ungodliness it has produced until now, and will produce until the time of the threshing comes. Consider for yourself how much fruit of ungodliness a grain of evil seed has produced. When heads of grain without number are sown, how great a threshing floor they will fill.

Genesis 3.23 Therefore the LORD GOD SENT HIM FORTH FROM THE GARDEN OF EDEN, TO TILL THE GROUND FROM WHENCE HE WAS TAKEN.

Genesis 3.24 So he drove out the man; and he placed at the east of the garden of Eden Cherubims, and a flaming sword which turned every way, to keep the way of the tree of life.

---

4 And Adam wept and wailed, and smote upon his breast, for being severed from the garden; and said to Eve:

5 "Why hast thou brought upon me, upon thyself, and upon our seed, so many of these plagues and punishments?"

6 And Eve said unto him, "What is it thou hast seen, to weep and to speak to me in this wise?"

7 And he said to Eve, "See thou not this water that was with us in the garden, that watered the trees of the garden, and flowed out thence?

8 "And we, when we were in the garden, did not care about it; but since we came to this strange land, we love it, and turn it to use for our body."

C.4 Adam and Eve realise that what they had taken for granted as when they were inside the Garden of Eden has now been lost. In the idyllic Garden of Eden, they did not even need to use water to drink or wash themselves. Now in the physical domain they desperately needed water to both drink and bathe. This clearly shows that the Garden of Eden was in a higher dimension than the physical earth as there they did not even need to drink water.

C.5 Whilst in the Garden of Eve, Adam and Eve must have been drinking in spiritual waters to sustain their bodies.

Jn.7.38 'He that believes on Me as the scriptures have said out of his belly shall flow rivers of living waters.

C.6 It is stated that a river ran through the Garden of Eden and then parted into four rivers as it left the Garden.

Genesis 2:10 'And a river went out of Eden to water the garden; from hence it was parted and became into four heads.'

C.7 Were the waters coming out of the Garden of Eden mixed with the 'waters of the Tree of life' as mentioned in Revelations 22 where the Garden of Eden is restored?

Rev.22.1-2 Then the angel showed me the river of the water of life, as clear as crystal, flowing from the throne of God and of the Lamb. Down the middle of the great street of the city. On each side of the river stood the tree of life, bearing twelve crops of fruit, yielding its fruit every month. And the leaves of the tree are for the healing of the nations.

C.8 That will be the Eternal age that will be ushered in by God Himself after the Great White throne Judgement and the Heavenly City comes down to the surface of the earth.

C.9 Adam and Eve did not live forever in their physical state. However, they did live an exceptionally long time or over 900 years. How was that even possible? (See the **Appendix**)

> 9 But when Eve heard these words from him, she wept; and from the soreness of their weeping, they fell into that water; and would have put an end to themselves in it, so as never again to return and behold the creation; for when they looked upon the work of creation, they felt they must put an end to themselves.

C.10 If it is true that the waters coming out of the Garden of Eden contained the 'waters of life' then God must have cut them off sometime after Adam and Eve had been sent out of the Garden of Eden.

CHAPTER 10

Water

> 1 Then God, merciful and gracious, looked upon them thus lying in the water, and nigh unto death, and sent an angel, who brought them out of the water, and laid them on the seashore as dead.

C.1 Did this happen - that they were dead? Or was it simply an expression of their exasperation of their own folly for having lost their world of Paradise and their 'bright nature' In this new world they were like small children who hardly knew how to do anything, and they kept fumbling and stumbling – until they were taught how to do things in this new physical world by God Himself as well as his angels.

> 2 Then the angel went up to God, was welcome, and said, "O God, thy creatures have breathed their last."

C.2 The angel is announcing to God that Adam and Eve have collapsed and 'given up' on themselves. They were in a bad state.

> 3 Then God sent His Word unto Adam and Eve, who raised them from their death.
>
> 4 And Adam said, after he was raised, "O God, while we were in the garden we did not require, or care for this water; but since we came to this land, we cannot do without it."
>
> 5 Then God said to Adam, "While thou was under My command and was a bright angel, thou knew not this water.

C.3 Why is it written 'whilst thou was a bright *angel*'? Now that is a mystery? Was Adam ever an angel? No, not as far as we know, so why does the text call him an angel. If the text is to be believed, then it must simply mean that Adam and Eve had a 'bright nature' like unto an angel, and not that they themselves were angels.

Hebrews 2.7 'Thou made him a little lower than the angels; thou crowned him with glory and honour, and didst set him over the works of thy hands:

> 6 "But after that thou hast transgressed My commandment, thou canst not do without water, wherein to wash thy body and make it grow; for it is now like that of beasts and is in want of water."

7 When Adam and Eve heard these words from God, they wept a bitter cry; and Adam entreated God to let him return into the garden and look at it a second time.

C.4 It appears that the real problem here is that Adam and Eve do not accept that they have been kicked out of the Garden of Eden for their sins and that now is the time to adapt to the new situation and to move on and forget about trying to get back into the Garden.

8 But God said unto Adam, "I have made thee a promise; when that promise is fulfilled, I will bring thee back into the garden, thee and thy righteous seed."

C.5 At least God had promised them that eventually their righteous children along with them would find both salvation from their sins and an eternal home in Heaven.

9 And God ceased to commune with Adam.

CHAPTER 11

Paradise Lost

1 Then Adam and Eve felt themselves burning with thirst, and heat, and sorrow.

2 And Adam said to Eve, "We shall not drink of this water, even if we were to die. O Eve, when this water comes into our inner parts, it will increase our punishments and that of our children, that shall come after us."

3 Both Adam and Eve then withdrew from the water and drank none of it at all; but came and entered the Cave of Treasures.

4 But when in it, Adam could not see Eve; he only heard the noise she made. Neither could she see Adam but heard the noise he made.

5 Then Adam wept, in deep affliction, and smote upon his breast; and he arose and said to Eve, "Where art thou?"

6 And she said unto him, "Lo, I am standing in this darkness."

7 He then said to her, "Remember the bright nature in which we lived, while we abode in the garden!

8 "O Eve! remember the glory that rested on us in the garden. O Eve! remember the trees that overshadowed us in the garden while we moved among them.

9 "O Eve! remember that while we were in the garden, we knew neither night nor day. Think of the Tree of Life, from below which flowed the water, and that shed lustre over us! Remember, O Eve, the garden-land, and the brightness thereof!

10 "Think, oh think of that garden in which was no darkness, while we dwelt therein.

11 "Whereas no sooner did we come into this Cave of Treasures than

darkness compassed us round about; until we can no longer see each other; and all the pleasure of this life has come to an end."

C.1 'No one would condemn a child for being afraid of the dark – the condemnation today is when grown men are afraid of the light'.

John 3:19-20"And this is the condemnation, that light has come into the world, and men loved darkness rather than light, because their deeds were evil. For everyone who does evil hates the light and does not come to the light, lest his deeds should be exposed."

C.2 There are indeed great lessons here for Adam and Eve of learning 'to be broken' and humble and to learn to accept God's will that for the foreseeable future they would not be allowed back into the 'Garden of Eden', as they now lived in the physical domain.

C.3 The sample of the 'righteous' would eventually be helpful once they had returned to the spirit world after they died. Their lives were a lesson to the whole spirit world as to how to behave and what was right and what was wrong and how to learn to submit to God's will under duress with both new and difficult circumstances in a situation when you no longer had the privilege of seeing God or 'straight into heaven'. One had to live by faith in order to be righteous. The following is a verse which shows the contrast between those that walk in pride and those who are humble.

Habakkuk 2.4 [4] Behold, his soul which is lifted up is not upright in him: but the just shall live by his faith.

CHAPTER 12

Darkness

> 1 Then Adam smote upon his breast, he, and Eve, and they mourned the whole night until dawn drew near, and they sighed over the length of the night in Miyazia.

C.1 Where is Miyazia? The dictionary does not seem to know exactly where it is except to quote this book of the 'Lost Books of Adam and Eve'.

C.2 Well, we do not know where it originally was before the Great Flood. Why do I say that? According to biblical experts on Creationism - the truth be known; the topography of the entire planet was completely different before the Great Flood. The land masses were different in shape and the seas were lower down, so names given of places before the Flood can not necessarily be recognized as the same places that they are called today in modern times.

C.3 However, I think what happened was that starting with Noah and his sons, they remembered the names of key land masses, seas, mountains, and rivers from before the Great Flood.

C.4 After the Great Flood with the whole world totally changed in topography, they started giving the Pre-Flood names to the new lands and seas around them including the rivers which after the Great Flood must have been totally different from before the Great Flood.

C.5 There is a big mystery concerning the topography of the earth which I will talk about later. What if the earth is actually hollow and Noah had travelled from the inner earth to the outer earth, so that in general mankind came to live where we do now – on the outer surface of the earth for the very first time?

C.6 There are so many Bible and Apocryphal Book verses to support this idea.

C.7 If true, then why is this basic information deliberately kept hidden? You tell me!

C.8 Like I said, there are great mysteries as to where did Atlantis fit into the picture and other super empires like it in Pre-Flood times? Let us talk about that later.

C.9 Just to whet your appetite, the ancient books from India describe a super-race which had flying machines and lasers or crystal technology some 5000 years ago. If it was true, then according to the biblical time-charts, that would put those super empires around 500 years before the Great Flood in the so-called 'Golden Age' of the Fallen angels, the Giants, and the demi-gods.

C.10 I recently saw the movie the 'Gods of Egypt', which had some similar concepts. What I would add is, that what is portrayed in 'Gods of Egypt' happened earlier and in Pre-Flood times.

C.11 The largest pyramids were certainly not built by the Egyptians, although traditionally, they have taken the credit for them.

C.12 The Egyptians simply did not have the advanced technology to the build the pyramids. That is a major topic in itself, which I will talk much more about in my next book '**OUT OF THE BOTTOMLESS PIT II',** which will be about the paranormal.

---

2 And Adam beat himself, and threw himself on the ground in the cave, from bitter grief, and because of the darkness, and lay there as dead.

3 But Eve heard the noise he made in falling upon the earth. And she felt about for him with her hands and found him like a corpse.

4 Then she was afraid, speechless, and remained by him.

C.13 Adam and Eve needed to face up to the new life on the physical earth & all its difficult challenges which in turn would teach them a lot of needed lessons and teach them godly wisdom, which comes only through 'trial and error' experiences such as they are going through in this story.

---

5 But the merciful Lord looked on the death of Adam, and on Eve's silence from fear of the darkness.

6 And the Word of God came unto Adam and raised him from his death and opened Eve's mouth that she might speak.

7 Then Adam arose in the cave and said, "O God, wherefore has light departed from us, and darkness come over us? Wherefore dost Thou leave us in this long darkness? Why wilt Thou plague us thus?

8 "And this darkness, O Lord, where was it ere it came upon us? It is such, that we cannot see each other.

9 "For, so long as we were in the garden, we neither saw nor even knew what darkness is. I was not hidden from Eve, neither was she hidden from me, until now that she cannot see me; and no darkness came upon us, to separate us from each other.

10 "But she and I were both in one bright light. I saw her and she saw me. Yet now since we came into this cave, darkness has come upon us, and parted us asunder, so that I do not see her, and she does not see me.

C.14 Had God indeed plagued Adam and Eve with darkness? No, of course not! They just did not yet know what night and day were - as they had never experienced it before, having come from the 'land of light' where they had had a 'bright' nature.

C.15 They would fail to gain important wisdom by only staying in the Garden of Eden. God knew Adam and Eve would literally 'fall from grace'.

C.16 The physical life was designed to teach Adam and Eve, and of course by inference - all of us - many important lessons and give us wisdom. A wisdom which you simply could not learn in the spirit world where everything was perfect.

CHAPTER 13

Night and Day

1 Then when God, who is merciful and full of pity, heard Adam's voice, He said unto him:

2 "O Adam, so long as the good angel was obedient to Me, a bright light rested on him and on his hosts.

C.1 Here God is clearly talking about Satan and His fall due to his rebellion against God along with the Fallen Angels like unto him.

3 "But when he transgressed My commandment, I deprived him of that bright nature, and he became dark.

C.2 This verse is showing us that Satan and his angels fell long before the physical creation. For Satan to have shown up in the Garden of Eden at the very beginning of Creation, he had obviously already fallen. Something dark in terms of rebellion went on in the spirit world long before the physical world was created. We can expand on that later.

4 "And when he was in the heavens, in the realms of light, he knew naught of darkness.

5 "But he transgressed, and I made him fall from heaven upon the earth; and it was this darkness that came upon him.

Ezekiel 28.13-18 Thou hast been in Eden the Garden of God .14 Thou art the anointed cherub that covers... Thou was upon the holy mountain of God; thou walked up and down in the midst of the stones of fire... Thou was perfect in thy ways until iniquity was found in thee... Thy heart was lifted up because of thy beauty... Thou has corrupted thy wisdom by reason of thy brightness... Therefore, I will cast thee as profane out of the mountain of God... and I will destroy thee, O covering cherub, from the midst of the stones of fire.

Isaiah 14.12-15 How art thou fallen from heaven, O Lucifer, son of the morning! how art thou cut down to the ground, which didst weaken the nations! For thou hast said in thine heart, I will ascend into heaven, I will exalt my throne above the stars of God: I will sit also upon the mount of the congregation, in the sides of the north: I will ascend above the heights of the clouds; I will be like the Most High. Yet thou shalt be brought down to hell, to the sides of the pit.

6 "And on thee, O Adam, while in My garden and obedient to Me, did

> that bright light rest also.

Dan.12.3 'They that be wise shall shine as the brightness of the firmament' (stars)

> 7 "But when I heard of thy transgression, I deprived thee of that bright light. Yet, of My mercy, I did not turn thee into darkness, but I made thee thy body of flesh, over which I spread this skin, in order that it may bear cold and heat. 'I made thee thy body of flesh, over which I spread this skin, in order that it may bear cold and heat'.

C.3 This last verse if we can believe it is telling us perhaps something very new to our way of thinking:

Genesis 2.7 'And the LORD God formed man *of* the dust of the ground and breathed into his nostrils the breath of life; and man became a living being'.

C.4 This above verse is telling us that first Adam and Eve had a spiritual body that was 'bright' along with some sort of an immortal physical body whilst they were still in the Garden of Eden, but that when they came out of the Garden of Eden they became 'fully physical' including God putting skin and other physical organs into their bodies.

C.5 Traditionally, we as Bible students or even biblical experts, have the impression that Adam and Eve were basically just the same body-wise when they were in the Garden of Eden, as when they came out of the Garden of Eden.

C.6 It does indeed seem logical that Adam and Eve had a 'bright' nature whilst in the Garden of Eden and that they did indeed lose many of their spiritual powers once they left the Garden.

> 8 "If I had let My wrath fall heavily upon thee, I should have destroyed thee; and had I turned thee into darkness, it would have been as if I killed thee.

C.7 God is telling Adam that he could had destroyed him and turned him into darkness and destroyed him but instead he 'down-graded' him.

> 9 "But in My mercy, I have made thee as thou art; when thou didst transgress My commandment, O Adam, I drove thee from the garden, and made thee come forth into this land; and commanded thee to dwell in this cave; and darkness came upon thee, as it did upon him (Satan) who transgressed My commandment.

C.8 Adam and Eve in a real sense had to be downgraded to the mortal life of sin and temptations. Satan and mankind were both 'downgraded' because of disobedience to the Lord God.

10 "Thus, O Adam, has this night deceived thee. It is not to last for ever; but is only of twelve hours; when it is over, daylight will return.

C.9 Did the Lord God Creator make the physical realm in a very different way than the spiritual realm? If so, why did He do it that way? Our physical dimension is 'The land of orbs' or 'spheres' as described by another writer. The physical realm depends on night and day as afforded by the gradual turning or spinning of the moon on its axis each day and around the earth every 28 days which has a profound affect upon our lives in so many ways. What about the make-up of the whole physical universe? It depends upon time itself. The spirit world in contrast is not limited by time, which makes it sound very interesting in possibilities, and something to look forward to.

C.10 Notice the 'wording' 'has this night deceived you?' Adam through lack of experience was afraid of the dark. Satan is always willing to try and make us afraid of the unknown.

11 "Sigh not, therefore, neither be moved; and say not in thy heart that this darkness is long and drags on wearily; and say not in thy heart that I plague thee with it.

12 "Strengthen thy heart and be not afraid. This darkness is not a punishment. But, O Adam, I have made the day, and have placed the sun in it to give light; in order that thou and thy children should do your work.

13 "For I knew thou shouldest sin and transgress and come out into this land. Yet would I not force thee, nor be heard upon thee, nor shut up; nor doom thee through thy fall; nor through thy coming out from light into darkness; nor yet through thy coming from the garden into this land.

C.11 God knew in advance that Adam and Eve would eventually sin and fall from Grace. The whole point of the Garden of Eden was to show us that we cannot be genuinely good and righteous without God's grace and without faith and total trust in Him. It is probably incorrect to state that Adam and Eve were closer to God in the Garden of Eden. In a real sense they got much closer to God after they had been kicked out of the Garden, as they realised that they were totally helpless and had to totally depend on God for everything and so they got very desperate in prayer with Him and of course he solved all their problems. That is what good parents would do for their small children whilst they are still helpless and know little.

14 "For I made thee of the light; and I willed to bring out children of

> light from thee and like unto thee.

1 Thess. 5.4 -5 But ye, brethren, are not in darkness, that that day should overtake you as a thief. Ye are all the children of light, and the children of the day: we are not of the night, nor of darkness.

> 15 "But thou didst not keep one day My commandment; until I had finished the creation and blessed everything in it.

C.12 What does God mean here by one day? According to the Book of Jubilees Adam lived 7 years in the Garden of Eden until Satan was allowed to tempt them at the Tree of the Knowledge of Good and Evil:

JUBILEES 3.17 And after the completion of seven years, which he had completed there, even years exactly, [8 A.M] and in the 2nd month on the 17th day of the month the Serpent came and approached the woman, and the serpent said unto the woman, 'Hath God said that ye shall not eat of the fruit of the Garden… [A.M = Anno Mundi = total years of the existence of the world.]

C.13 Perhaps when God says Adam and Eve did not last 1 day – He meant that from the time Satan was allowed into the Garden of Eden that on the very same day he tempted Eve, that sadly Adam and Eve immediately fell from grace.

> 16 "Then I commanded thee concerning the tree, that thou eat not thereof. Yet I knew that Satan, who deceived himself, would also deceive thee.
>
> 17 "So I made known to thee by means of the tree, not to come near him. And I told thee not to eat of the fruit thereof, nor to taste of it, nor yet to sit under it, nor to yield to it.

C.14 God knew exactly what would happen, and that if Adam and Eve went anywhere near the Tree of the Knowledge of Good and Evil that the temptation would be too great and that they would fall from grace. He also knew that Satan was very much 'tied up' with the Tree of the Knowledge of Good and Evil. This is why God had very strongly admonished Adam and Eve to never go near that tree. We will talk about this more later.

> 18 "Had I not been and spoken to thee, O Adam, concerning the tree, and had I left thee without a commandment, and thou had sinned it would have been an offence on My part, for not having given thee any order; thou wouldst turn round and blame Me for it.

C.15 We cannot blame God for our mistakes and problems as God Himself does not tempt any man or woman.

James 1.3 "Let no man say when he is tempted, I am tempted of God: for God cannot be tempted with evil, neither tempts he any man:"

19 "But I commanded thee, and warned thee, and thou didst fall. So that My creatures cannot blame me; but the blame rests on them alone.

20 "And, O Adam, I have made the day for thee and for thy children after thee, for them to work, and toil therein. And I have made the night for them to rest in it from their work; and for the beasts of the field to go forth by night and seek their food.

21 "But little of darkness now remains, O Adam; and daylight will soon appear."

CHAPTER 14

Prophecy about Christ

1 THEN Adam said unto God: "O Lord, take Thou my soul, and let me not see this gloom anymore; or remove me to some place where there is no darkness."

2 But God the Lord said to Adam, "Verily I say unto thee, this darkness will pass from thee, every day I have determined for thee, until the fulfilment of My covenant; when I will save thee and bring thee back again into the garden, into the abode of light thou longest for, wherein is no darkness. I will bring thee, to it in the kingdom of heaven."

C.1 The Lord God has promised that He will come to the earth and save all mankind and that one-day Adam and Eve will return to the Garden of Eden, in the Kingdom of Heaven.

3 Again said God unto Adam, "All this misery that thou hast been made to take upon thee because of thy transgression, will not free thee from the hand of Satan, and will not save thee.

Genesis 3:15 [15]And I will put enmity between thee and the woman, and between thy seed and her seed; it shall bruise thy head, and thou shalt bruise his heel.

C.2 This above verse in Genesis is especially important, as God is saying that he will make a difference between the 'seed of Satan' and the Woman's seed. From the woman and mankind would be born the Messiah who would crush the head of Satan and bring Salvation to all who came to the Saviour.

4 "But I will. When I shall come down from heaven, and shall become flesh of thy seed, and take upon Me the infirmity from which thou suffer, then the darkness that came upon thee in this cave shall come upon Me in the grave, when I am in the flesh of thy seed.

C.3 Jesus who is the Lord Creator promises that he himself will don the robes of flesh to save or redeem mankind including Adam and Eve.

5 "And I, who am without years, shall be subject to the reckoning of years, of times, of months, and of days, and I shall be reckoned as one of the sons of men, in order to save thee."

Revelation 1.8 "I am the Alpha and the Omega, *the* Beginning and *the* End," says the Lord, "who is and who was and who is to come, the Almighty."

Hebrews 2.9 But we see Jesus, who was made a little lower than the angels for the suffering of death, crowned with glory and honour; that he by the grace of God should taste death for every man.

Hebrews 2.10 For it became him, for whom are all things, and by whom are all things, in bringing many sons unto glory, to make the captain of their salvation perfect through sufferings.

Isaiah 53.4 Surely, he hath borne our griefs, and carried our sorrows: yet we did esteem him stricken, smitten of God, and afflicted.

Isaiah 53.5 But he was wounded for our transgressions, he was bruised for our iniquities: the chastisement of our peace was upon him; and with his stripes we are healed.

Acts 4.12 'Neither is there salvation in any other: for there is no other name under heaven given among men whereby we must be saved.'

6 And God ceased to commune with Adam.

CHAPTER 15

Salvation

1 Then Adam and Eve wept and sorrowed by reason of God's word to them, that they should not return to the garden until the fulfilment of the days decreed upon them; but mostly because God had told them that He should suffer for their salvation.

1Pe 3.18 For Christ also hath once suffered for sins, the just for the unjust, that he might bring us to God, being put to death in the flesh, but quickened by the Spirit:

CHAPTER 16

The first sunrise

1 After this Adam and Eve ceased not to stand in the cave, praying and weeping, until the morning dawned upon them.

2 And when they saw the light returned to them, they restrained from fear, and strengthened their hearts.

3 Then Adam began to come out of the cave. And when he came to the mouth of it, and stood and turned his face towards the east, and saw the sun rise in glowing rays, and felt the heat thereof on his body, he was afraid of it, and thought in his heart that this flame came forth to plague him.

4 He wept then, and smote upon his breast, and fell upon the earth on his face, and made his request, saying:

5 "O Lord, plague me not, neither consume me, nor yet take away my life from the earth."

6 For he thought the sun was God.

C.1 It is interesting how many cultures did come to worship the sun in one way or the other, and we hear of the sun-god Ra.

C.2 In the Book of Jubilees when Abraham was young, he was asking God questions about the sun and moon the stars and wondering if they were gods. After prayer and observation, he concluded that they were not gods and certainly not the Creator.

Jubilees 12.16 'Abram sat up throughout the night on the new moon of the 7th month to observe the stars from the evening to the morning, in order to see what would be the character of the year 17 And a word came into his heart, and he said: All the signs of the stars and the signs of the moon and of the sun are all in the hand of the Lord. Why do I search them out?

C.3 Abraham went on to pray that God would deliver him from evil spirits which trick the mind and had become common after the Great Flood.

Jubilees 12.20 Deliver me from the hands of evil spirits who have dominion over the thoughts of men's hearts. And let the me not lead me astray from thee My God and stablish thou me and my seed forever that we go not astray from henceforth for evermore.

C.4 The book of Jubilees reveals how that after the Great Flood the origin of evil spirits was from the disembodied spirits of the giants, the sons of the fallen angels and women who had been wiped from the face of the earth at the time of the Great Flood.

Jubilees 10.1 And in the third week of this Jubilee the unclean demons began to lead astray the children of the sons of Noah, and to make err, and to destroy them.

C.5 Here was Noah's pray for this sons' protection after the Great Flood:

Jubilees 10.5 And thou know how Thy Watchers (Fallen angels), the fathers of these (bad) spirits (the Giants) acted in my day: and as for these spirits which are living, imprison them and hold them fast in the place of condemnation, and let them not bring destruction on the sons of thy servant, My God; for they are malignant and created in order to destroy.

C.6 For much more on this above topic see my book '**Jubilees Insights'**.

---

7 Inasmuch as while he was in the garden and heard the voice of God and the sound He made in the garden, and feared Him, Adam never saw the brilliant light of the sun, neither did the flaming heat thereof touch his body.

8 Therefore was he afraid of the sun when flaming rays of it reached him. He thought God meant to plague him there with all the days He had decreed for him.

9 For Adam also said in his thoughts, as God did not plague us with darkness, behold, He has caused this sun to rise and to plague us with burning heat.

10 But while he was thus thinking in his heart, the Word of God came unto him and said:

11 "O Adam, arise and stand up. This sun is not God; but it has been created to give light by day, of which I spake unto thee in the cave saying, 'that the dawn would break forth, and there would be light by day.'

12 "But I am God who comforted thee in the night."

13 And God ceased to commune with Adam.

CHAPTER 17

The Serpent

1 Then Adam and Eve came out at the mouth of the cave and went towards the garden.

2 But as they drew near to it, before the western gate, from which Satan came when he deceived Adam and Eve, they found the serpent that became Satan coming at the gate, and sorrowfully licking the dust, and wriggling on its breast on the ground, by reason of the curse that fell upon it from God.

3 And whereas aforetime the serpent was the most exalted of all beasts, now it was changed and become slippery, and the meanest of them all, and it crept on its breast and went on its belly.

4 And whereas it was the fairest of all beasts, it had been changed, and was become the ugliest of them all. Instead of feeding on the best food, now it turned to eat the dust. Instead of dwelling, as before, in the best places, now it lived in the dust.

5 And, whereas it had been the most beautiful of all beasts, all of which stood dumb at its beauty, it was now abhorred of them.

Ezekiel 28.13-18 Thou hast been in Eden the Garden of God .14 Thou art the anointed cherub that covers… Thou was upon the holy mountain of God; thou walked up and down in the midst of the stones of fire… Thou was perfect in thy ways until iniquity was found in thee… Thy heart was lifted up because of thy beauty… Thou has corrupted thy wisdom by reason of thy brightness… Therefore, I will cast thee as profane out of the mountain of God… and I will destroy thee, O covering cherub, from the midst of the stones of fire.

6 And, again, whereas it dwelt in one beautiful abode, to which all other animals came from elsewhere; and where it drank, they drank also of the same; now, after it had become venomous, by reason of God's curse, all beasts fled from its abode, and would not drink of the water it drank; but fled from it.

CHAPTER 18

War with the serpent

WHEN the accursed serpent saw Adam and Eve, it swelled its head, stood on its tail, and with eyes blood-red, did as if it would kill them.

2 It made straight for Eve, and ran after her; while Adam standing by, wept because he had no stick in his hand wherewith to smite the serpent, and knew not how to put it to death.

3 But with a heart burning for Eve, Adam approached the serpent, and held it by the tail; when it turned towards him and said unto him:

4 "O Adam, because of thee and of Eve, I am slippery, and go upon my belly." Then by reason of its great strength, it threw down Adam and Eve and pressed upon them, as if it would kill them.

5 But God sent an angel who threw the serpent away from them and raised them up.

6 Then the Word of God came to the serpent, and said unto it, "In the first instance I made thee glib, and made thee to go upon thy belly; but I did not deprive thee of speech.

7 "Now, however, be thou dumb; and speak no more, thou and thy race; because in the first place, has the ruin of my creatures happened through thee, and now thou wish to kill them."

8 Then the serpent was struck dumb, and spake no more.

C.1 'The serpent was struck dumb'. It is interesting that it is mentioned that the serpent could speak with Adam and Eve, and this is mentioned in the Bible and in the Apocryphal books. It is also mentioned that Adam and Eve could talk with the other animals when they lived in the Garden and I think especially in the beginning when God brought all the animals to Adam, so that he could name them.

Genesis: 2.19 So the LORD God formed out of the ground every animal of the field and every bird of the air and brought them to Adam to see what he would call them; and whatever the man called a living creature, that was its name.

C.2 Look at the following unique verse mentioning the day the animals and birds ceased talking with mankind. This happened when Adam and Eve left the Garden of Eden.

Jubilees 3.28 And on that day was closed the mouth of the beasts, and of all cattle and of the birds and of whatever walks, and of whatever moves, so that they could no longer speak: for they had all spoken one with another with one lip and one tongue.

C.3 There are, however, a few examples where even after the Great Flood God 'opened' the mouth of a particular animal and it was allowed to talk to mankind as in the beginning of the Creation. There is the story of Balaam's donkey in the Bible in Numbers 22.

Numbers 22.28 And the Lord opened the mouth of the ass, and she said unto Balaam, 'What have I done unto thee that has hast smitten me these three times?

C.4 There is also the story of a wolf talking with Jacob in the Apocryphal Book of Jasher:

JASHER 43.43 'And the Lord opened the mouth of the beast to comfort Jacob with his words.' [See my book **Jasher Insights**]

> 9 And a wind came to blow from heaven by command of God that carried away the serpent from Adam and Eve, threw it on the seashore and it landed in India.

C.5 That is an interesting detail that the serpent was thrown far away to the 'land of India'. Is India a land where there are many serpents or snakes and other reptiles?

Apparently, India has 300 different types of dangerous snakes with over 60 of them poisonous and deadly including the cobra:

C.6 N.B. Until recently, the no.1 cause of death in India was by snakebite. Is it just a coincidence that this story from the Lost Books of Adam and Eve Book 1 mentions the serpent being originally cursed by God at the time of Adam and Eve, and cast into the land of India where to this day the serpent is both feared and worshipped by the Hindu religion and where they believe in many snake-gods and other reptilian forms which can be even half human and half snake?

C.7 Many of the 'snake gods' can actually be traced back to before the great Flood or around 5000 years ago.

C.8 5000 years ago according to the KJV of the Bible was around 500 years before the Great Flood. This was the exact time of the Fallen angels and giants having established their empires on the earth known today as the golden Age of the demi-gods. Empires such as Atlantis and Lemuria and the Land of Mu. All on the outer surface of the earth at a time when mankind probably lived on the inner surface of the earth. [**See my book 'Out of the Bottomless Pit'** about the 'Hollow Earth' & for more on the snake gods of

India]

C.9 For more on the 'snakes' in India: https://english.alarabiya.net/
perspective/features/2017/09/07/Once

CHAPTER 19

Animals as friends

1 But Adam and Eve wept before God. And Adam said unto Him:

2 "O Lord, when I was in the cave, I said this to Thee, my Lord, that the beasts of the field would rise and devour me and cut off my life from the earth."

C.1 There were no devouring beasts or *'the beasts of the field that would rise and devour me' at the beginning of Creation. God had commanded that both mankind and the animals were to be herbivores and not carnivores.*

Genesis .1.29-30 Then God said, "I give you every seed-bearing plant on the face of the whole earth and every tree that has fruit with seed in it. They will be yours for food. [30] And to all the beasts of the earth and all the birds in the sky and all the creatures that move along the ground—everything that has the breath of life in it—I give every green **plant** for food." And it was so.

C.2 In general the carnivorous nature was introduced to both man and animals after the Great Flood.

C.3 There was an exception to what I have just mentioned, in the creation of nasty dangerous hybrid carnivorous creatures created by the Fallen angels by altering the DNA of other creatures - which we can talk about later.

Genesis 9.2-3 And the fear of you and the dread of you shall be upon every beast of the earth, and upon every fowl of the air, upon all that moves upon the earth, and upon all the fishes of the sea; into your hand are they delivered. [3] Every moving thing that lives shall be meat for you; even as the green herb, have I given you all things.

3 Then Adam, by reason of what had befallen him, smote upon his breast, and fell upon the earth like a corpse; then came to him the Word of God, who raised him, and said unto him,

4 "O Adam, not one of these beasts will be able to hurt thee; because when I made the beasts and other moving things come to thee in the cave, I did not let the serpent come with them, lest it should rise against you, make you tremble; and the fear of it should fall into your hearts.

5 "For I knew that that accursed one is wicked; therefore, would I not let it come near you with the other beasts.

6 "But now strengthen thy heart and fear not. I am with thee unto the

end of the days I have determined on thee."

CHAPTER 20

Adam protects Eve

THEN Adam wept and said, "O God, remove us to some other place, that the serpent may not come again near us, and rise against us. Lest it find Thy handmaid Eve alone and kill her; for its eyes are hideous and evil."

C.1 We all wish that the Devil did not exist along with all the evils, and sometimes it is indeed a very tough trial for us humans in many ways. For Adam and Eve, it was the shock treatment as they were not accustomed to having to face the Evil.

C.2 The key is to always see life as a challenge and see the evil as but a large wave over which one can surf, especially when you do have a great surfboard made by God Himself - Salvation in His Son Jesus the Messiah. In a way, it is a great surfboard to face all the challenges of life itself. Just hold onto God's promises in His word.

C.3 Once Adam and Eve got accustomed to the big spiritual and physical struggle, they began to get both wiser and stronger.

2 But God said to Adam and Eve, "Henceforth fear not, I will not let it come near you; I have driven it away from you, from this mountain; neither will I leave in it aught to hurt you."

C.4 More than just a physical mountain on which they live in this story they were also on a spiritual mountain where they were not supposed to come down to the valley. Once the Lord God had removed the physical snake that had been possessed by Satan eventually the attacks of Satan against mankind after Adam and Eve was much more subtle and from the invisible realm.

1 Peter 5.8 'Be sober, be vigilant, because your adversary the Devil as a roaring lion walketh about seeking whom he may devour'.

3 Then Adam and Eve worshipped before God 'and gave Him thanks and praised Him for having delivered them from death.

CHAPTER 21

Adam and Eve 'as dead'

THEN Adam and Eve went in search of the Garden.

2 And the heat beat like a flame on their faces; and they sweated from the heat and wept before the Lord.

3 But the place where they wept was nigh unto a high mountain, facing the western gate of the garden.

4 Then Adam threw himself down from the top of that mountain; his face was torn and his flesh was flayed; much blood flowed from him, and he was nigh unto death.

5 Meanwhile Eve remained standing on the mountain weeping over him, thus lying.

6 And she said, "I wish not to live after him; for all that he did to himself was through me."

7 Then she threw herself after him; and was torn and scotched by stones; and remained lying as dead.

8 But the merciful God, who looks upon His creatures, looked upon Adam and Eve as they lay dead, and He sent His Word unto them, and raised them.

9 And said to Adam, "O Adam, all this misery which thou hast wrought upon thyself, will not avail against My rule, neither will it alter the covenant of the 5500 years."

C.1 Was it true that Adam and Eve threw themselves off the mountain and killed themselves as in this Book of the Lost books of Adam and Eve? I think that is highly unlikely, and we certainly do not find that in the Bible. What could the meaning be? It would appear that the religious influence of ascetics has been introduced into this story, although I would suspect that it certainly would not have been in the original 'Story of Adam and Eve': **Ascetics:** Def: Ascetic | Definition of Ascetic at Dictionary.com

C.2 ORIGIN OF THE **LOST BOOKS OF ADAM AND EVE**? Leonhard Rost writes: "There can be no doubt that the lost original can be ascribed to a Jewish author who probably lived in Palestine—possibly toward the end of the first century B.C. The year A.D. 70 is the *terminus ante quem* since the Temple—of Herod? — is still standing. The author may have had affinities with Essene circles, as the ascetic features (especially the Apocalypse's description of the physical separation of the sexes, even for animals) suggest." (*Judaism Outside the Hebrew Canon*, p. 154) Life of Adam and Eve (earlyjewishwritings.com)

C.3 I do not think that that Adam and Eve would be continually committing suicide. After all, as God was sending His Word to them repeatedly, they would have had plenty of faith in God's protection and provision. Not to mention the protection of the angels of God who certainly would not allow God's very first creations to meet death right away!

C.4 However I think that one of the points of this story is that the changes that Adam and Eve were compelled to have to go through were both 'drastic and sudden'. The way they behaved initially as in the first 50 days or so of leaving the Garden of Eden were such a contrast - in moving from the celestial paradise of the Garden of Eden to our physical dimension, that it was almost too much for them to bear.

C.5 The story is a bit repetitive on this point and yet I suppose it is trying to slowly but surely bring out the many different things that now affected them very differently now that they were no longer in the Garden of Eden.

C.6 The story mentions how it was difficult for them. In reality it would seem that they were merely in a new stage of growth like a small child. They were slowly but surely having to learn to trust God that He knew best and that all their frantic actions or even their pious actions and even what some would call ascetic behaviour was not going to allow them to go back to the Garden of Eden.

C.7 They would not be able to 'force the hand of God' by their actions no matter what they did as God does not operate man's way. Adam and Eve could not re-enter the Garden of Eden because of their sins until the time in which the Lord had promised his covenant of 5 and a half days or 5500 years.

C.8 We should not be condescending towards this story of Adam and Eve as none of us have had to exactly experience what they went through in 'falling from grace' and being kicked out of the Garden of Eden. In some ways it was like the birth of a baby. Everyone knows that babies often cry when they are born. Probably because of having to come into a whole new world of strange sights and sounds and many unknowns. The birth of a baby is I think the best comparison to Adam and Eve's experience of being 'kicked out' of the Garden of Eden in this version of Adam and Eve of the Lost books of Adam and Eve 1.

C.9 Adam and Eve came into the physical realm to learn. There are apparently many things that humans can only learn whilst in the physical plane that would be difficult to learn in the spirit world.

C.10 This physical life is about exploring and learning new things and new ways even in adversity. Endurance and difficulty teach us to grow physically, mentally, emotionally, and spiritually. Without difficulties we could not mature.

C.11 God knew all that mankind would 'fall from Grace', but he has been there ever since for those who are 'listening'.

C.12 As has been wisely stated 'When we all get back to the spiritual realm - we will find that all our life-experiences have served us well and we will continue to use much of our earth-life training in the heavenly life - if what we have done has been loving, positive and helpful to others'.

C.13 The beauty of this story of the 'Lost Book of Adam and Eve book 1' is that it is similar in some ways to the case of a new-born baby. The new-born baby has parents to lovingly take care for it when it is born and in the case of Adam and Eve it was no different.

C.14 Their spiritual parents were no longer visible it was true, but they were very much still there in the background in the form of the Word of God and His Holy Spirit. To my understanding the Holy Spirit is female which makes a lot more sense* (See the Appendix) and is the wife of God the Father. Jesus is their son and is also the Word of God – the creator of our physical realm.

C.15 At first, I thought that there was too much 'weeping' and crying and too many emotional outbursts - like jumping off mountains. However, in putting 'my feet' in the 'shoes of Adam and Eve' so to speak, I see that it is important to have lots of emotions and to cry out for understanding in many situations and for what we need - especially unto the Lord God Himself as he is our true parent. God has lots of feelings and emotions and we are made in His image.

CHAPTER 22

Adam cries for help!

THEN Adam said to God, "I wither in the heat; I am faint from walking and am loth of this world. And I know not when Thou wilt bring me out of it, to rest."

2 Then the Lord God said unto him, "O Adam, it cannot be at present, not until thou hast ended thy days. Then shall I bring thee out of this wretched land."

3 And Adam said to God, "While I was in the garden, I knew neither heat, nor languor, neither moving about, nor trembling, nor fear; but now since I came to this land, all this affliction has come upon me."

C.1 Here Adam is stating that whilst in the Garden of Eden he did not have to move about and was not subject to fear nor trembling or heat and other afflictions, oppression, and a sort of languor (lethargy) that existed in the physical realm.

C.2 This is interesting as it is showing a great difference between the Garden of Eden and the earth life. The physical life is full of labour and sweat, toil and great difficulties, pains, and sorrows.

C.3 The spiritual realm of Heaven is totally different in that there is no 'heavy weight' and gravity pushing you down. There are no afflictions being bothersome. There are no sorrows and frustrations.

C.4 No Satan around to attack people and destroy them in accidents, wars, murders or cancers and other illnesses. The physical realm is totally limited by Death and Time.

C.5 Both the Garden of Eden and Heaven do not know death and they are not limited by Time. In heaven people move around in a quite different way apparently by gliding by or floating or softly walking but there is no sense of weight and pain and tiredness. They can also fly and move amazingly fast when it is necessary like the angels, but almost effortlessly. Heaven and a return to the Garden of Eden is something to look forward to for all those who have received Jesus into their hearts. [See Salvation on my website: SALVATION - www.outofthebottomlesspit.co.uk]

4 Then God said to Adam, "So long as thou wast keeping My commandment, My light and My grace rested on thee. But when thou didst transgress My commandment, sorrow and misery befell thee in this land."

> 5 And Adam wept and said, "O Lord, do not cut me off for this, neither smite me with heavy plagues, nor yet repay me according to my sin; For we, of our own will, did transgress Thy commandment, and forsook Thy law, and sought to become gods like unto Thee, when Satan the enemy deceived us."

C.6 Adam confesses that both Eve and he transgressed God's commandment. What commandment in particular? Just eating an apple or other fruit from a forbidden tree or is there a whole lot more to what happened in the Garden of Eden?

C.7 Adam also states that of their own free will they also forsook God's law and wanted to 'become as gods' like unto the Lord Himself, as tempted by Satan. The real issue is what is Satan's price for helping humans to become 'gods' throughout history? [See the **APPENDIX** for more on this topic.]

> 6 Then God said again unto Adam, "Because thou hast borne fear and trembling in this land, languor and suffering treading and walking about, going upon this mountain, and dying from it, I will take all this upon Myself in order to save thee."

C.8 The Lord Creator is stating that He will come to earth and give his life as a sacrifice to save all of mankind.

CHAPTER 23

The First Altar

THEN Adam wept more and said, "O God, have mercy on me, so far as to take upon Thee, that which I will do."

2 But God took His Word from Adam and Eve.

3 Then Adam and Eve stood on their feet; and Adam said to Eve "Gird thyself, and I also will gird myself." And she girded herself, as Adam told her.

4 Then Adam and Eve took stones and placed them in the shape of an altar; and they took leaves from the trees outside the garden, with which they wiped, from the face of the rock, the blood they had spilled.

5 But that which had dropped on the sand, they took together with the dust wherewith it was mingled and offered it upon the altar as an offering unto God.

6 Then Adam and Eve stood under the altar and wept, thus entreating God, "Forgive us our trespass and our sin, and look upon us with Thine eye of mercy. For when we were in the garden our praises and our hymns went up before Thee without ceasing.

7 "But when we came into this strange land, pure praise was no longer ours, nor righteous prayer, nor understanding hearts, nor sweet thoughts, nor just counsels, nor long discernment, nor upright feelings, neither is our bright nature left us. But our body is changed from the similitude in which it was at first, when we were created.

8 "Yet now look upon our blood which is offered upon these stones, and accept it at our hands, like the praise we used to sing unto Thee at first, when in the garden."

9 And Adam began to make more requests unto God.

C.1 I find it very odd that Adam and Eve would think to offer their 'own blood' as an offering or sacrifice unto God?

C.2 Killing oneself or even attempting to do so and then trying to offer one's spilt blood as 'an offering' unto God to our 'modern understanding' is simply not scriptural. It sounds like something ungodly.

I Sam 15.22 'And Samuel said, Hath the LORD *as great* delight in burnt offerings and sacrifices, as in obeying the voice of the LORD? Behold, to obey *is* better than sacrifice, *and* to hearken than the fat of rams.

C.3 The only one who was pure enough to be able to give His blood as a sacrifice unto God was Jesus, the Son of God, for the sake of redeeming the sins of all mankind.

Hebrews 9.14 How much more shall the blood of Christ, who through the eternal Spirit offered himself without spot to God, purge your conscience from dead works to serve the living God?

C.4 If this part of the story is to be believed, then it must simply be that as everything was so new to Adam and Eve, they didn't know that what they were doing was not what was the normal thing to do.

C.5 No laws and ordinances or scriptures had yet been 'written down' by mankind as everything was so new, with only Adam and Eve present on the earth to represent mankind.

C.6 You notice in this story that God is very patient with Adam and Eve, and initially He has to send 'His Word' and angels to instruct Adam and Eve more directly than most of us today, in that sometimes it would appear that they could see spiritual things.

C.7 As time went by, the visible sight of the Son of God as the Word of God, and sent by God the Father, seem to fade more into the realm of the spirit. Adam and Eve had to learn to live by faith, and not by sight, which is the whole purpose of all of us being here on earth. In other words, to learn to connect with God, even if you can't see Him for the present time on earth.

Hebrews 10:38 – "Now the just shall live by faith: but if any man draw back, My soul shall have no pleasure in him."

C.8 Even though Adam and Eve seem to *not* get the point, that no matter what they do or what sacrifices that they make or how many days that they fast for or how many hours that they pray, the fact is that they are not going to be allowed to get back into the Garden of Eden. They had to learn to move on to new pastures and at the same time get to know God in new ways. In otherwards by faith and not by sight.

Hebrews 11:1 says, "Now faith is the substance of things hoped for, the evidence of things not seen."

CHAPTER 24

Life and Death of Christ

THEN the merciful God, good and 'lover of men', looked upon Adam and Eve, and upon their blood, which they had held up as an offering unto Him; without an order from Him for so doing. But He wondered at them; and accepted their offerings.

2 And God sent from His presence a bright fire, that consumed their offering.

3 He smelt the sweet savour of their offering and showed them mercy.

4 Then came the Word of God to Adam, and said unto him, "O Adam, as thou hast shed thy blood, so will I shed My own blood when I become flesh of thy seed; and as thou didst die, O Adam, so also will I die. And as thou didst build an altar, so also will I make for thee an altar on the earth; and as thou didst offer thy blood upon it, so also will I offer My blood upon an altar on the earth.

5 "And as thou didst sue for forgiveness through that blood, so also will I make My blood forgiveness of sins and blot out transgressions in it".

Romans 5.19 For as by one man's disobedience many were made sinners, so by the obedience of one (Christ) shall many be made righteous.

1 Jn 1.7 "But if we walk in the light, as he is in the light, we have fellowship one with another, and the blood of Jesus Christ his Son cleanses us from all sin."

6 "And now, behold, I have accepted thy offering, O Adam, but the days of the covenant, wherein I have bound thee, are not fulfilled. When they are fulfilled, then will I bring thee back into the garden.

7 "Now, therefore, strengthen thy heart; and when sorrow comes upon thee, make Me an offering, and I will be favourable to thee."

Book of Jubilees: 16.22,31 And during those seven days he brought each day to the altar a burnt offering to the Lord, two oxen, two rams, seven sheep, one he-goat, for a sin offering, that he might atone thereby for himself and for his seed. And Abraham took branches of palm trees, and fruit of goodly trees, and every day going around the altar with the branches seven times in the morning he praised and gave thanks to his God for all things in joy.

CHAPTER 25

God the Merciful

1 BUT God knew that Adam had in his thoughts, that he should often kill himself and make an offering to Him of his blood.

2 Therefore did He say unto him, "O Adam, do not again kill thyself as thou didst, by throwing thyself down from that mountain."

3 But Adam said unto God, "It was in my mind to put an end to myself at once, for having transgressed Thy commandments, and for my having come out of the beautiful garden; and for the bright light of which Thou hast deprived me; and for the praises which poured forth from my mouth without ceasing, and for the light that covered me.

4 "Yet of Thy goodness, O God, do not do away with me altogether; but be favourable to me every time I die, and bring me to life.

5 "And thereby it will be made known that Thou art a merciful God, who willest not that one should perish; who love not that one should fall; and who dost not condemn any one cruelly, badly, and by whole destruction."

6 Then Adam remained silent.

7 And the Word of God came unto him, and blessed him, and comforted him, and covenanted with him, that He would save him at the end of the days determined upon him.

8 This, then, was the first offering Adam made unto God; and so, it became his custom to do.

C.1 Here the Lord God makes it noticeably clear that Adam does not have to make a human sacrifice of himself and to spill his own blood. That was initially done by Adam in ignorance of God's ways in this story.

CHAPTER 26

Eternal Life

THEN Adam took Eve, and they began to return to the Cave of Treasures where they dwelt. But when they neared it and saw it from afar, heavy sorrow fell upon Adam and Eve when they looked at it.

2 Then Adam said to Eve, "When we were on the mountain, we were comforted by the Word of God that conversed with us; and the light that came from the east, shone over us.

3 "But now the Word of God is hidden from us; and the light that shone over us is so changed as to disappear, and let darkness and sorrow come upon us.

4 "And we are forced to enter this cave, which is like a prison, wherein darkness covers us, so that we are parted from each other; and thou canst not see me, neither can I see thee."

5 When Adam had said these words, they wept and spread their hands before God; for they were full of sorrow.

6 And they entreated God to bring the sun to them, to shine on them, so that darkness return not upon them, and they come not again under this covering of rock. And they wished to die rather than see the darkness.

7 Then God looked upon Adam and Eve and upon their great sorrow, and upon all they had done with a fervent heart, on account of all the trouble they were in, instead of their former well-being, and on account of all the misery that came upon them in a strange land.

8 Therefore God was not wroth with them; nor impatient with them; but He was longsuffering and forbearing towards them, as towards the children He had created.

9 Then came the Word of God to Adam, and said unto him, "Adam, as for the sun, if I were to take it and bring it to thee, days, hours, years

and months would all come to naught, and the covenant I have made with thee, would never be fulfilled.

10 "But thou shouldest then be turned and left in a long plague, and no salvation would be left to thee for ever.

11 "Yea, rather, bear long and calm thy soul while thou abide night and day; until the fulfilment of the days, and the time of My covenant is come.

12 "Then shall I come and save thee, O Adam, for I do not wish that thou be afflicted.

13 "And when I look at all the good things in which thou didst live, and why thou came out of them, then would I willingly show thee mercy.

14 "But I cannot alter the covenant that has gone out of My mouth; else would I have brought thee back into the garden.

15 "When, however, the covenant is fulfilled, then shall I show thee and thy seed mercy, and bring thee into a land of gladness, where there is neither sorrow nor suffering; but abiding joy and gladness, and light that never fails, and praises that never cease; and a beautiful garden that shall never pass away."

C.1 Eternal values shall be how it is on the earth in the future, once the Saviour returns. At present the world is bound by day and night and by time, distance, and size.

Revelations 10.6 "And sware by him that lives for ever and ever, who created heaven, and the things that therein are, and the earth, and the things that therein are, and the sea, and the things which are therein, that there should be time no longer:"

16 And God said again unto Adam, "Be long-suffering and enter the cave, for the darkness, of which thou wast afraid, shall only be twelve hours long; and when ended, light shall arise."

17 Then when Adam heard these words from God, he and Eve worshipped before Him, and their hearts were comforted. They returned into the cave after their custom, while tears flowed from their eyes, sorrow and wailing came from their hearts, and they wished their

81

soul would leave their body.

C.2 Adam and Eve are conscious of the fact that they have a spiritual body inside a physical body. They wanted their soul to leave their body but that could not happen unless it was the exact time ordained by God.

18 And Adam and Eve stood praying, until the darkness of night came upon them, and Adam was hid from Eve, and she from him.

19 And they remained standing in prayer.

CHAPTER 27

Tempted

WHEN Satan, the hater of all good, saw how they continued in prayer, and how God communed with them, and comforted them, and how He had accepted their offering--Satan made an apparition.

What the Bible says about Satan's Nature (bibletools.org)

2 He began with transforming his hosts; in his hands was a flashing fire, and they were in a great light.

C.1 The Bible says that Satan, who is a fallen angel can appear even as an angel of light. So, he can take the form he wants.

C.2 The Devil has made appearances to people usually as a very well-dressed man most of the time. But he can also take another form, including that of an animal. The Bible also said to treat every people well as they can be angels of God. [See the movie: The Devil's Advocate: https://youtu.be/IBxD1qZnJzw?t=6

Hebrews 13.2: Be not forgetful to entertain strangers: for thereby some have entertained angels unawares.

3 He then placed his throne near the mouth of the cave because he could not enter into it by reason of their prayers. And he shed light into the cave, until the cave glistened over Adam and Eve; while his hosts began to sing praises.

4 And Satan did this, in order that when Adam saw the light, he should think within himself that it was a heavenly light, and that Satan's hosts were angels; and that God had sent them to watch at the cave, and to give him light in the darkness.

5 So that when Adam came out of the cave and saw them, and Adam and Eve bowed to Satan, then he would overcome Adam thereby, and a second time humble him before God.

6 When, therefore, Adam and Eve saw the light, fancying it was real, they strengthened their hearts; yet, as they were trembling, Adam said to Eve:

7 "Look at that great light, and at those many songs of praise, and at that host standing outside that do not come into us, do not tell us what they say, or whence they come, or what is the meaning of this light; what those praises are; wherefore they have been sent hither, and why they do not come in.

8 "If they were from God, they would come to us in the cave, and would tell us their errand."

9 Then Adam stood up and prayed unto God with a fervent heart, and said:

10 "O Lord, is there in the world another god than Thou, who created angels and filled them with light, and sent them to keep us, who would come with them?

11 "But, lo, we see these hosts that stand at the mouth of the cave; they are in a great light; they sing loud praises. If they are of some other god than Thou, tell me; and if they are sent by Thee, inform me of the reason for which Thou hast sent them."

12 No sooner had Adam said this, than an angel from God appeared unto him in the cave, who said unto him, "O Adam, fear not. This is Satan and his hosts; he wishes to deceive you as he deceived you at first. For the first time, he was hidden in the serpent; but this time he is come to you in the similitude of an angel of light; in order that, when you worshipped him, he might enthrall you, in the very presence of God."

2 Cor 11.14 And no marvel, for Satan himself is transformed into an angel of light.

13 Then the angel went from Adam, and seized Satan at the opening of the cave, and stripped him of the feint he had assumed, and brought him in his own hideous form to Adam and Eve; who were afraid of him when they saw him.

C.3 Apparently, Satan after the 'Fall of man' became hideous' as some type of reptilian form - sometimes as a dragon and other times as a serpent or snake. He can also appear in his original form upon occasion as evidenced by some people. He can disguise himself as other people as well when it suits his purpose both male and female.

84

14 And the angel said to Adam, "This hideous form has been his ever since God made him fall from heaven. He could not have come near you in it; therefore, did he transform himself into an angel of light."

15 Then the angel drove away Satan and his hosts from Adam and Eve, and said unto them, "Fear not; God who created you, will strengthen you."

16 And the angel went from them.

17 But Adam and Eve remained standing in the cave; no consolation came to them; they were divided in their thoughts.

18 And when it was morning they prayed; and then went out to seek the garden. For their hearts were towards it, and they could get no consolation for having left it.

C.4 Adam and Eve are finding it very hard to live without the Garden of Eden. They act like children who are crying because they got lost and are continually seeking out the Garden of Eden, as they think it is the only way of becoming happy and inspired again.

C.5 It takes them quite some time before they finally realise that they now need to move on and face the new challenges of life which the earth life is providing for them. God is still with them even outside the Garden though now mostly hidden.

C.6 In the Garden of Eden, Adam and Eve had the ecstasy of being very close to God. Now, outside the Garden, they hard to learn to obey and listen, in order to get much closer to God. It took them quite some time to learn these basics.

C.7 It is beautiful story as it shows God's infinite love for His children and that He is always there for all of us. Sure, life is full of troubles, and yes, we do have to confront Satan quite frequently, and tell him where to get off in the name of Jesus, but it is important to learn to fight for the truth and against the Lies of Satan. Opposition and not too much comfort, is what makes a warrior!

CHAPTER 28

Satan The Deceiver

BUT when the wily Satan saw them, that they were going to the garden, he gathered together his host, and came in appearance upon a cloud, intent on deceiving them.

2 But when Adam and Eve saw him thus in a vision, they thought they were angels of God come to comfort them about their having left the garden, or to bring them back again into it.

3 And Adam spread his hands unto God, beseeching Him to make him understand what they were.

4 Then Satan, the hater of all good, said unto Adam, "O Adam, I am an angel of the great God; and behold the hosts that surround me.

5 "God has sent me and them to take thee and bring thee to the border of the garden northwards; to the shore of the clear sea, and bathe thee and Eve in it, and raise you to your former gladness, that ye return again to the garden."

6 These words sank into the heart of Adam and Eve.

7 Yet God withheld His Word from Adam, and did not make him understand at once, but waited to see his strength; whether he would be overcome as Eve was when in the garden, or whether he would prevail.

8 Then Satan called to Adam and Eve, and said, "Behold, we go to the sea of water," and they began to go.

9 And Adam and Eve followed them at some little distance.

10 But when they came to the mountain to the north of the garden, a very high mountain, without any steps to the top of it, the Devil drew near to Adam and Eve, and made them go up to the top in reality, and not in a vision; wishing, as he did, to throw them down and kill them, and to wipe off their name from the earth; so that this earth should

remain to him and his hosts alone.

Matthew 4.6 "Satan talking to Jesus -the Word of God '**If** you are **the Son of God**," he said, "throw yourself **down**. For it is written: "'He will command his angels concerning you, and they will lift you up in their hands, so that you will not strike your foot against a stone.'"

CHAPTER 29

Devil Exposed

1 BUT when the merciful God saw that Satan wished to kill Adam with his manifold devices, and saw that Adam was meek and without guile, God spake unto Satan in a loud voice, and cursed him.

Ephesians 5.11 Have no fellowship with the unfruitful works of darkness but rather reprove them.

2 Then he and his hosts fled, and Adam and Eve remained standing on the top of the mountain, whence they saw below them the wide world, high above which they were. But they saw none of the host which anon were by them.

3 They wept, both Adam and Eve, before God, and begged for forgiveness of Him.

4 Then came the Word from God to Adam, and said unto him, "Know thou and understand concerning this Satan, that he seeks to deceive thee and thy seed after thee."

2 Cor 11.13-15 For such men are false apostles, deceitful workmen, disguising themselves as apostles of Christ. And no wonder, for even Satan disguises himself as an angel of light. So, it is no surprise if his servants, also, disguise themselves as servants of righteousness. Their end will correspond to their deeds.

5 And Adam wept before the Lord God and begged and entreated Him to give him something from the garden, as a token to him, wherein to be comforted.

6 And God looked upon Adam's thought, and sent the angel Michael as far as the sea that reaches unto India, to take from thence golden rods and bring them to Adam.

7 This did God in His wisdom, in order that these golden rods, being with Adam in the cave, should shine forth with light in the night around him, and put an end to his fear of the darkness.

8 Then the angel Michael went down by God's order, took golden rods, as God had commanded him, and brought them to God.

CHAPTER 30

3 Special Presents

AFTER these things, God commanded the angel Gabriel to go down to the garden, and say to the cherub who kept it, "Behold, God has commanded me to come into the garden, and to take thence sweet-smelling incense, and give it to Adam."

2 Then the angel Gabriel went down by God's order to the garden and told the cherub as God had commanded him.

3 The cherub then said, "Well." And Gabriel went in and took the incense.

4 Then God commanded His angel Raphael to go down to the garden, and speak to the cherub about some myrrh, to give to Adam.

5 And the angel Raphael went down and told the cherub as God had commanded him, and the cherub said, "Well." Then Raphael went in and took the myrrh.

6 The golden rods were from the Indian sea, where there are precious stones. The incense was from the eastern border of the garden; and the myrrh from the western border, whence bitterness came upon Adam.

7 And the angels brought these three things to God, by the Tree of Life, in the garden.

8 Then God said to the angels, "Dip them in the spring of water; then take them and sprinkle their water over Adam and Eve, that they be a little comforted in their sorrow, and give them to Adam and Eve.

9 And the angels did as God had commanded them, and they gave all those things to Adam and Eve on the top of the mountain upon which Satan had placed them, when he sought to make an end of them.

10 And when Adam saw the golden rods, the incense, and the myrrh, he was rejoiced and wept because he thought that the gold was a token

of the kingdom whence, he had come, that the incense was a token of the bright light which had been taken from him, and that the myrrh was a token of the sorrow in which he was.

Matthew 2.11 'And when they had come into the house, they saw the young Child with Mary His mother, and fell down and worshiped Him. And when they had opened their treasures, they presented gifts to Him: gold, frankincense, and myrrh.

C.1 What is the **symbolism** of **gold, frankincense,** and **myrrh**? Myrrh being commonly used as an anointing oil, frankincense as a perfume, and gold as a valuable. The three gifts had a spiritual meaning: **gold** as a **symbol** of kingship on earth, **frankincense** (an incense) as a symbol of deity, and **myrrh** (an embalming oil) as a symbol of death. That Christ would die for the sins of all mankind. What is the symbolism of gold frankincense and myrrh? (askinglot. com)

Exodus 30.34-38 Then the LORD said to Moses, "Take fragrant spices-gum resin, onycha and galbanum-and pure **frankincense,** all in equal amounts, ³⁵and make a fragrant blend of incense, the work of a perfumer. It is to be salted and pure and sacred. ³⁶Grind some of it to powder **and** place it in front of the ark of the covenant law in the tent of meeting, where I will meet with you. It shall be most holy to you.

C.2 In the Old Testament gold, frankincense and myrrh come together in one place when the priest offers incense and prayers on the altar of incense. The altar of incense was made of gold (Ex. 30:1-10). A special blend of incense, including frankincense, was to be burned upon the altar of gold (Ex. 30:34-38). And myrrh was used in the anointing oil that was poured out on the priests and upon the tabernacle and its furniture (Ex. 30:22-33). Thus, the gifts of the magi were not only kingly gifts, but priestly gifts as well as was also our High Priest. Biblical Horizons » No. 12: Gold, Incense, and Myrrh

Hebrews 7.3, 21: Without father, without mother, without descent, having neither beginning of days, nor end of life; but made like unto the Son of God; abides a priest continually. 21 Thou art a high priest for ever after the order of Melchisedec:)

CHAPTER 31

Three Tokens

AFTER these things God said unto Adam, "Thou didst ask of Me something from the garden, to be comforted therewith, and I have given thee these three tokens as a consolation to thee; that thou trust in Me and in My covenant with thee.

2 "For I will come and save thee; and kings shall bring me when in the flesh, gold, incense and myrrh; gold as a token of My kingdom; incense as a token of My divinity; and myrrh as a token of My suffering and of My death.

3 "But, O Adam, put these by thee in the cave; the gold that it may shed light over thee by night; the incense, that thou smell its sweet savour; and the myrrh, to comfort thee in thy sorrow."

4 When Adam heard these words from God, he worshipped before Him. He and Eve worshipped Him and gave Him thanks because He had dealt mercifully with them.

5 Then God commanded the three angels, Michael, Gabriel, and Raphael, each to bring what he had brought, and give it to Adam. And they did so, one by one.

C.1 These same 3 angels are mentioned in the Book of Enoch chapter 9.

6 And God commanded Suriyel and Salathiel to bear up Adam and Eve and bring them down from the top of the high mountain, and to take them to the Cave of Treasures.

C.2 Salathiel is mentioned as a powerful archangel in the book of 2nd Esdras and is also mentioned by the Eastern Orthodox church. Suriyel is mentioned as being a powerful archangel not to be confused with Sariel, who is a fallen angel and mentioned in the Book of Enoch.

7 There they laid the gold on the south side of the cave, the incense on the eastern side, and the myrrh on the western side. For the mouth of the cave was on the north side.

8 The angels then comforted Adam and Eve and departed.

9 The gold was seventy rods; the incense, twelve pounds; and the myrrh, three pounds.

10 These remained by Adam in the House of Treasures; therefore, was it called "of concealment." But other interpreters say it was called the "Cave of Treasures," by reason of the bodies of righteous men that were in it.

11 These three things did God give to Adam, on the third day after he had come out of the garden, in token of the three days the Lord should remain in the heart of the earth.

C.3 The 3 days that the Lord Jesus remained in the heart of the earth is an interesting topic indeed.

Matt. 12:40 For as Jonah was three days and three nights in the belly of a huge fish, so the Son of Man will be **three days and three nights in the heart of the earth.** **[See Chapter 42 of this same book for more on this topic.]**

12 And these three things, as they continued with Adam in the cave, gave him light by night; and by day they gave him a little relief from his sorrow.

CHAPTER 32

Prayer

AND Adam and Eve remained in the Cave of Treasures until the seventh day; they neither ate of the fruit of the earth, nor drank water.

2 And when it dawned on the eighth day, Adam said to Eve, "O Eve, we prayed God to give us somewhat from the garden, and He sent His angels who brought us what we had desired.

3 "But now, arise, let us go to the sea of water we saw at first, and let us stand in it, praying that God will again be favourable to us and take us back to the garden; or give us something; or that He will give us comfort in some other land than this in which we are."

C.1 Adam and Eve's mistake is that they do *not* accept God's will, that they are not allowed back into the Garden of Eden after they had been banished from it.

C.2 They continually seek to find a way 'by hook or by crook' to get back into the Garden of Eden when God has already closed the door and told them many times.

4 Then Adam and Eve came out of the cave, went, and stood on the border of the sea in which they had before thrown themselves, and Adam said to Eve:

5 "Come, go down into this place, and come not out of it until the end of thirty days, when I shall come to thee. And pray to God with fervent heart and a sweet voice, to forgive us.

6 "And I will go to another place, and go down into it, and do like thee."

7 Then Eve went down into the water, as Adam had commanded her. Adam also went down into the water; and they stood praying; and besought the Lord to forgive them their offence, and to restore them to their former state.

8 And they stood thus praying, unto the end of the five-and-thirty days.

C.3 It does not matter if Adam and Eve had fasted 30 days or even more, or

94

if they had prayed incessantly, if they are refusing to listen to God's Spirit and obey God's voice and do exactly what He says.

Proverbs 28.9 He that turns away his ear from hearing the law, even his prayer *shall be* abomination.

C.4 They simply needed to accept God's will and move on.

CHAPTER 33

Satan's Lies

BUT Satan, the hater of all good, sought them in the cave, but found them not, although he searched diligently for them.

2 But he found them standing in the water praying and thought within himself, "Adam and Eve are thus standing in that water beseeching God to forgive them their transgression, and to restore them to their former estate, and to take them from under my hand.

Luke 4.6 'And the Devil (Satan) said unto him (Jesus), All this power will I give thee, and the glory of them: for that is delivered unto me; and to whomsoever I will I give it.' 4.7 If thou therefore wilt worship me, all shall be thine.

3 "But I will deceive them so that they shall come out of the water, and not fulfil their vow."

4 Then the hater of all good, went not to Adam, but be went to Eve, and took the form of an angel of God, praising and rejoicing, and said to her--

5 "Peace be unto thee! Be glad and rejoice! God is favourable unto you, and He sent me to Adam. I have brought him the glad tidings of salvation, and of his being filled with bright light as he was at first.

C.1 If Satan can't directly persuade you to do evil, he will try to get you to compromise. To not live up to your convictions, as to what is right and wrong.

6 "And Adam, in his joy for his restoration, has sent me to thee, that thou come to me, in order that I crown thee with light like him.

7 "And he said to me, 'Speak unto Eve; if she does not come with thee, tell her of the sign when we were on the top of the mountain; how God sent His angels who took us and brought us to the Cave of Treasures; and laid the gold on the southern side; incense, on the eastern side; and myrrh on the western side.' Now come to him."

8 When Eve heard these words from him, she rejoiced greatly. And thinking that Satan's appearance was real, she came out of the sea.

9 He went before, and she followed him until they came to Adam. Then Satan hid himself from her, and she saw him no more.

10 She then came and stood before Adam, who was standing by the water and rejoicing in God's forgiveness.

11 And as she called to him, he turned round, found her there and wept when he saw her, and smote upon his breast; and from the bitterness of his grief, he sank into the water.

12 But God looked upon him and upon his misery, and upon his being about to breathe his last. And the Word of God came from heaven, raised him out of the water, and said unto him, "Go up the high bank to Eve." And when he came up to Eve he said unto her, "Who said to thee 'come hither'?"

13 Then she told him the discourse of the angel who had appeared unto her and had given her a sign.

14 But Adam grieved, and gave her to know it was Satan. He then took her, and they both returned to the cave.

2 Cor 2.11 'Lest Satan should take advantage of us. For we are not ignorant of his devices'.

15 These things happened to them the second time they went down to the water, seven days after their coming out of the garden.

16 They fasted in the water thirty-five days; altogether forty-two days since they had left the garden.

Daniel 9.3-5 So, I turned to the Lord God and pleaded with him in prayer and petition, in fasting, and in sackcloth and ashes. I prayed to the LORD my God and confessed: "Lord, the great and awesome God, who keeps his covenant of love with those who love him and keep his commandments, we have sinned and done wrong. We have been wicked and have rebelled; we have turned away from your commands and laws."

CHAPTER 34

Food and Drink

> 1 AND on the morning of the forty-third day, they came out of the cave, sorrowful and weeping. Their bodies were lean, and they were parched from hunger and thirst, from fasting and praying, and from their heavy sorrow on account of their transgression.

Joel 2:12-13 "Even now," declares the Lord, "return to me with all your heart, with fasting and weeping and mourning." Rend your heart and not your garments. Return to the Lord your God, for he is gracious and compassionate, slow to anger and abounding in love, and he relents from sending calamity.

> 2 And when they had come out of the cave, they went up the mountain to the west of the garden.
>
> 3 There they stood and prayed and besought God to grant them forgiveness of their sins.
>
> 4 And after their prayers Adam began to entreat 'God, saying, "O my Lord my God, and my Creator, thou didst command the four elements to be gathered together, and they were gathered together by Thine order.

C.1 What are the 4 elements mentioned in this story. It is not talking about the 'Element Table' of metals, liquids and gases known to man, but about something more basic, which modern science loves to dismiss as mere superstition of the Middle Ages. The 4 elements are: Fire, Water, Air, Earth. We have the same elements in the Star Signs of the Zodiac.

C.2 However, after investigating, we find that the 4 elements are mentioned not just in the Middle-Ages but millennia ago in the Book of II Esdras and other apocryphal books.

II Esdras 3.12 'And God passed through the 4 gates of fire and earthquake and wind and ice, to give the law to the descendants of Jacob, and thy commandments to the posterity of Israel, yet thou didst not take away from it their evil heart, so that thy law might bring forth fruit in them.

C.3 See my book '**Ezdras Insights**' for much more on this topic. That book gives insight into the book of **II Esdras,** which describes the times in Israel in circa 450-500 BC.

C.4 Modern man tends to boast that he is so smart today and has 'evolved'. The truth is that mankind is fast descending into ignorance, apostasy, and spiritual darkness.

---

5 "Then Thou spread Thy hand and didst create me out of one element, that of dust of the earth; and Thou didst bring me into the garden at the third hour, on a Friday, and didst inform me of it in the cave.

6 "Then, at first, I knew neither night nor day, for I had a bright nature; neither did the light in which I lived ever leave me to know night or day.

7 "Then, again, O Lord, in that third hour in which Thou didst create me, Thou brought to me all beasts, and lions, and ostriches, and fowls of the air, and all things that move in the earth, which you had created at the first hour before me of the Friday.

C.5 Why is it stated in this book that Adam was born on a Friday? It also states later that Adam died on a Friday. Why the specific day of a Friday? It is said that this book was influenced by Arabic in the 5th century AD, and we can see evidence of this.

C.6 Although, the Arabic influence has not taken away anything important from these 'Lost Books of Adam and Eve'.

C.7 These 'Lost books of Adam and Eve' were translated into Arabic from the original Hebrew. It is my opinion that they simplified parts of the books in order to make it easier for children to understand it. You will see in Book II of the Lost Books of Adam and Eve that some Arabic names are given which were obviously not part of the original Hebrew copy of these books.

C.8 Just to summarise. In my opinion, the **Lost Books of Adam and Eve**, just like the **Book of Enoch,** were originally written in Pre-Flood times.

C.9 They were then assembled and re-written in around 100 BCE by a Jewish writer. Later in time or around 500 AD the Hebrew copy was translated into Arabic.

C.10 Much later in time this same story was translated from Arabic into English.

C.11 There are many different copies of these **Lost books of Adam and Eve** in many languages. This would seem to verify their authenticity, by the fact that so many peoples have highly valued these Lost Books of Adam and Eve.

---

8 "And Thy will was that I should name them all, one by one, with a suitable name. But Thou gave me understanding and knowledge, and a pure heart and a right mind from Thee, that I should name them after Thine own mind regarding the naming of them.

---

9 "O God, You made them obedient to me, and did order that not one of them break from my sway, according to your commandment, and to the dominion which You hast given me over them. But now they are all estranged from me.

10 "Then it was in that third hour of Friday, in which you did create me, and didst command me concerning the tree, to which I was neither to draw near, nor to eat thereof; for you said to me in the garden, 'When you eat of it, of death you shall die.'

11 "And if Thou hardest punished me as Thou saidst, with death, I should have died that very moment.

12 "Moreover, when Thou commanded me regarding the tree, I was neither to approach nor to eat thereof, Eve was not with me; Thou had not Yet created her, neither had Thou yet taken her out of my side; nor had she yet heard this order from Thee.

13 "Then, at the end of the third hour of that Friday, O Lord, Thou didst cause a slumber and a sleep to come over me, and I slept, and was overwhelmed in sleep.

14 "Then Thou didst draw a rib out of my side and created it after my own similitude and image. Then I awoke; and when I saw her and knew who she was, I said, 'This is bone of my bones, and flesh of my flesh; henceforth she shall be called woman.'

Genesis 2.23 The man said, "**This** is now bone of my bones and **flesh of my** flesh; **she shall be called 'woman**,' for she was taken out of man."

15 "It was of Thy good will, O God, that Thou brought a slumber and a sleep over me, and that Thou didst forthwith bring Eve out of my side, until she was out, so that I did not see how she was made; neither could I witness, O my Lord, how awful and great are Thy goodness and glory.

16 "And of Thy goodwill, O Lord, Thou made us both with bodies of a bright nature, and Thou made us two, one; and Thou gave us Thy grace, and didst fill us with praises of the Holy Spirit; that we should be

> neither hungry nor thirsty, nor know what sorrow is, nor yet faintness of heart; neither suffering, fasting, nor weariness.

C.12 This is both beautiful and romantic. I love the way how Adam and Eve talk about each other. Eve states that she simply cannot live without Adam, and he says the same. Just beautiful.

C.13 There is a deeper love between a man and woman which is way beyond the 'eros' or physical passion of youthfulness.

C.14 Marriage was originally instituted by God, in the hope that couples would stay together for His Glory. Marriage is supposed to provide a safe and enduring environment for the resultant children to feel happy and loved.

C.15 It is when you want to care for each other through thick and thin, and when you are willing to give unselfishly for your mate asking no reward. Now that is oneness. It is a deeper love that nothing can break! A true marriage.

C.16 This book is beautiful in showing that marriage is really the joining of a man and woman in such a way that they are truly **one** as Adam stated in the above verse.

> 17 "But now, O God, since we transgressed Thy commandment and broke Thy law, Thou hast brought us out into a strange land, and has caused suffering, and faintness, hunger and thirst to come upon us.
>
> 18 "Now, therefore, O God, we pray Thee, give us something to eat from the garden, to satisfy our hunger with it; and something wherewith to quench our thirst.
>
> 19 "For, behold, many days, O God, we have tasted nothing and drunk nothing, and our flesh is dried up, and our strength is wasted, and sleep is gone from our eyes from faintness and weeping.
>
> 20 "Then, O God, we dare not gather aught of the fruit of trees, from fear of Thee. For when we transgressed at first, Thou didst spare us, and didst not make us die.
>
> 21 "But now, we thought in our hearts, if we eat of the fruit of trees, without God's order, He will destroy us this time, and will wipe us off from the face of the earth.
>
> 22 "And if we drink of this water, without God's order, He will make an end of us, and root us up at once.

23 "Now, therefore, O God, that I am come to this place with Eve, we beg Thou wilt give us of the fruit of the garden, that we may be satisfied with it.

24 "For we desire the fruit that is on the earth, and all else that we lack in it."

CHAPTER 35

The Word of God

THEN God looked again upon Adam and his weeping and groaning, and the Word of God came to him, and said unto him:

2 "O Adam, when thou was in My garden, thou knew neither eating nor drinking; neither faintness nor suffering; neither leanness of flesh, nor change; neither did sleep depart from thine eyes. But since you transgressed, and came into this strange land, all these trials are come upon thee."

CHAPTER 36

Figs

THEN God commanded the cherub, who kept the gate of the garden with a sword of fire in his hand, to take some of the fruit of the fig-tree, and to give it to Adam.

2 The cherub obeyed the command of the Lord God, and went into the garden and brought two figs on two twigs, each fig hanging to its leaf; they were from two of the trees among which Adam and Eve hid themselves when God went to walk in the garden, and the Word of God came to Adam and Eve and said unto them, "Adam, Adam, where art thou?"

3 And Adam answered, "O God, here am I. When I heard the sound of Thee and Thy voice, I hid myself, because I am naked."

4 Then the cherub took two figs and brought them to Adam and Eve. But he threw them to them from afar; for they might not come near the cherub by reason of their flesh, that could not come near the fire.

5 At first, angels trembled at the presence of Adam and were afraid of him. But now Adam trembled before the angels and was afraid of them.

C.1 This is interesting, as it states that at one time the angels trembled at the presence of Adam and that they were afraid of him, but that now Adam trembled and was afraid of the angels.

C.2 Why the big change? When Adam and Eve were in the Garden they were seen as the 'image of God' and had immortal bodies that shone with light. They had powers that we simply don't have today. Those powers and 'bright nature' have been forfeited due to the Fall, man's disobedience, and rebellion.

1 Cor 6.3 'Know ye not that we shall judge angels? How much more things that pertain to this life?'

6 Then Adam drew near and took one fig, and Eve also came in turn and took the other.

7 And as they took them up in their hands, they looked at them, and knew they were from the trees among which they had hidden themselves.

CHAPTER 37

Self-Works Cannot Redeem

THEN Adam said to Eve, "See thou not these figs and their leaves, with which we covered ourselves when we were stripped of our bright nature? But now, we know not what misery and suffering may come upon us from eating them.

Genesis 3.7 Then the eyes of both of them were opened, and they realized they were naked; so, they sewed fig leaves together and made coverings for themselves.

2 "Now, therefore, O Eve, let us restrain ourselves and not eat of them, thou and I; and let us ask God to give us of the fruit of the Tree of Life."

3 Thus did Adam and Eve restrain themselves, and did not eat of these figs.

4 But Adam began to pray to God and to beseech Him to give him of the fruit of the Tree of Life, saying thus: "O God, when we transgressed Thy commandment at the sixth hour of Friday, we were stripped of the bright nature we had, and did not continue in the garden after our transgression, more than three hours.

C.1 I think it unlikely that the Friday was mentioned in the original book, but this is a tampering with the original text for religious reasons.

5 "But on the evening Thou made us come out of it. O God, we transgressed against Thee one hour, and all these trials and sorrows have come upon us until this day.

6 "And those days together with this the forty-third day, do not redeem that one hour in which we transgressed!

7 "O God, look upon us with an eye of pity, and do not requite us according to our transgression of Thy commandment, in presence of Thee.

8 "O, God, give us of the fruit of the Tree of Life, that we may eat of it, and live, and turn not to see sufferings and other trouble, in this earth; for Thou art God.

C.2 Why are Adam and eve insisting on asking for fruit from the Tree of Life, when one of the reasons that they originally got kicked out of the Garden of Eden was:

Genesis 3.22-23 And the LORD GOD SAID, 'BEHOLD, THE MAN IS BECOME AS ONE OF US, TO KNOW GOOD AND EVIL': AND NOW, LEST he put forth his hand, and take also of the tree of life, and eat, and live for ever:

[23] Therefore the Lord God sent him FORTH FROM THE GARDEN OF EDEN, TO TILL THE GROUND FROM WHENCE HE WAS TAKEN.

9 "When we transgressed Thy commandment, Thou made us come out of the garden, and didst send a cherub to keep the Tree of Life, lest we should eat thereof, and live; and know nothing of faintness after we transgressed.

10 "But now, O Lord, behold, we have endured all these days, and have borne sufferings. Make these forty-three days an equivalent for the one hour in which we transgressed."

C.3 Here is a link to a comprehensive excellent explanation about all the many things that the Fig Tree symbolizes. It mentions the many times figs and the Fig Tree are mentioned in the Bible. The Fig Tree became the symbol of Judah the leading tribe of Israel: **The symbolism of the Fig Tree**: The Symbolism of the Fig Tree (hope-of-israel.org)

CHAPTER 38

The Fulfilment of 5500 Years

AFTER these things, the Word of God came to Adam, and said unto him:

2 "O Adam, as to the fruit of the Tree of Life, for which thou ask, I will not give it thee now, but when the 5500 years are fulfilled. Then will I give thee of the fruit of the Tree of Life, and thou shalt eat, and live for ever, thou, and Eve, and thy righteous seed.

3 "But these forty-three days cannot make amends for the hour in which thou didst transgress My commandment.

4 "O Adam, I gave thee to eat of the fig-tree in which thou didst hide thyself. Go and eat of it, thou, and Eve.

5 "I will not deny thy request, neither will I disappoint thy hope; therefore, bear up unto the fulfilment of the covenant I made with thee."

6 And God withdrew His Word from Adam.

C.1 These **good** and **evil figs** also hark back to the Tree of the Knowledge of Good and Evil in the Garden, showing that the link of the fig with that tree is correct. I believe that *in symbol* (while the *actual tree* was an almond) it was this tree on which the Messiah was crucified, as it was the Judean leaders of his day, the bad figs, who incited the populous and persuaded the Roman governor, Pilate, to hand the Messiah over to the Temple authorities for his execution. The Symbolism of the Fig Tree (hope-of-israel.org)

CHAPTER 39

Adam and Eve Fear to Eat

THEN Adam returned to Eve, and said to her, "Arise, and take a fig for thyself, and I will take another; and let us go to our cave."

C.1 The Fig tree, which was one of the most important trees in Israel. Its fruit was a staple food, and it is very rich in symbolism throughout Scripture. The story of the fig tree begins in the Garden of Eden, where YEHOVAH God had placed in the midst of the Garden two special trees: the Tree of Life and the Tree of the Knowledge of Good and Evil: The Symbolism of the Fig Tree (hope-of-israel.org)

2 Then Adam and Eve took each a fig and went towards the cave; the time was about the setting of the sun; and their thoughts made them long to eat of the fruit.

3 But Adam said to Eve, "I am afraid to eat of this fig. I know not what may come upon me from it."

4 So Adam wept, and stood praying before God, saying, "Satisfy my hunger, without my having to eat this fig; for after I have eaten it, what will it profit me? And what shall I desire and ask of Thee, O God, when it is gone?"

5 And he said again, "I am afraid to eat of it; for I know not what will befall me through it."

CHAPTER 40

Adam and Eve suffer Hunger

THEN the Word of God came to Adam, and said unto him, "O, Adam, why hadst thou not this dread, neither this fasting, nor this care ere this? And why hadst thou not this fear before thou didst transgress?

2 "But when thou camest to dwell in this strange land, thy animal body could not be on earth without earthly food, to strengthen it and to restore its powers."

C.1 Is it correct to state that Adam and Eve had an animal body? As it is suggesting that man is no more than a beast. I think A better definition for Adam and Eve's new bodies would have been 'carnal body' or 'physical body'.

C.2 It is true that some scriptures mention than some men do behave as beasts. However, God's intent was for mankind to rise above the cruel nature of the Beast as shown clearly in the story of Nebuchadnezzar the emperor of Babylon who was turned into a Beast for 7 years by God and then it is stated 'A man's heart was given unto it – the Beast', meaning that Nebuchadnezzar finally turned to God in his great affliction and became righteous. So, there is hope for the 'beast' to yet become a man with a 'heart for God.'

Daniel 4.16 'Let his mind be changed from that of a man and let him be given the mind of an animal, till seven times pass by for him'.

Daniel 4.25 'You will be driven away from people and will live with the wild animals; you will eat grass like the ox and be drenched with the dew of heaven. Seven times will pass by for you until you acknowledge that the Most High is sovereign over all kingdoms on earth and gives them to anyone, he wishes'. [33] Immediately what had been said about Nebuchadnezzar was fulfilled. He was driven away from people and ate grass like the ox. His body was drenched with the dew of heaven until his hair grew like the feathers of an eagle and his nails like the claws of a bird. [34] At the end of that time, I, Nebuchadnezzar, raised my eyes toward heaven, and my sanity was restored. Then I praised the Most High; I honoured and glorified him who lives forever. [37] Now I, Nebuchadnezzar, praise and exalt and glorify the King of heaven, because everything he does is right, and all his ways are just. And those who walk in pride he is able to humble.

3 And God withdrew His Word from Adam.

CHAPTER 41

Adam and Eve suffer Thirst

THEN Adam took the fig and laid it on the golden rods. Eve also took her fig and put it upon the incense.

2 And the weight of each fig was that of a watermelon; for the fruit of the garden was much larger than the fruit of this land.

3 But Adam and Eve remained standing and fasting the whole of that night, until the morning dawned.

4 When the sun rose, they were at their prayers, and Adam said to Eve, after they had done praying:

5 "O Eve, come, let us go to the border of the garden looking south; to the place whence the river flows, and is parted into four heads. There we will pray to God and ask Him to give us to drink of the Water of Life.

6 "For God has not fed us with the Tree of Life, in order that we may not live. We will, therefore, ask him to give us of the Water of Life, and to quench our thirst with it, rather than with a drink of water of this land."

7 When Eve heard these words from Adam, she agreed; and they both arose and came to the southern border of the garden, upon the brink of the river of water at some little distance from the garden.

8 And they stood and prayed before the Lord, and asked Him to look upon them this once, to forgive them, and to grant them their request.

9 After this prayer from both of them, Adam began to pray with his voice before God, and said:

10 "O Lord, when I was in the garden and saw the water that flowed from under the Tree of Life, my heart did not desire, neither did my body require to drink of it; neither did I know thirst, for I was living;

and above that which I am now.

11 "So that in order to live I did not require any Food of Life, neither did I drink of the Water of Life.

12 "But now, O God, I am dead; my flesh is parched with thirst. Give me of the Water of Life that I may drink of it and live.

13 "Of Thy mercy, O God, save me from these plagues and trials, and bring me into another land different from this, if Thou wilt not let me dwell in Thy garden."

CHAPTER 42

3rd prophecy About Christ

1 THEN came the Word of God to Adam, and said unto him:

John 1.1 ‹In the beginning was the Word and the word was with God and the Word was God, the same was in the beginning with God'.

2 "O Adam, as to what thou sayest, 'Bring me into a land where there is rest,' it is not another land than this, but it is the kingdom of heaven where alone there is rest.

C.1 In this amazing book the ‹**Lost Book of Adam and Eve Book 1**' it is like adding to the story in the Bible of Adam and Eve from the time that they got kicked out of the Garden until Cain slew his brother Abel. This book gives a little more 'insight' and colour to the biblical story of both Creation and Adam and Eve and their descendants.

Hebrews 4.11 Let us labour therefore to enter into that rest, lest any man fall after the same example of unbelief.

Psalm 37.7 "Rest in the LORD and wait patiently for him: fret not thyself because of him who prospers in his way, because of the man who bringeth wicked devices to pass."

3 "But thou canst not make thy entrance into it at present; but only after thy judgment is past and fulfilled.

1 Cor.11.31-32 For if we would judge ourselves, we should not be judged. But when we are judged, we are chastened of the Lord, that we should not be condemned with the world.

4 "Then will I make thee go up into the kingdom of heaven, thee and thy righteous seed; and I will give thee and them the rest you ask for at present.

Matthew 7.21"Not everyone who says to me, 'Lord, Lord,' will enter the kingdom of heaven, but the one who does the will of my Father who is in heaven.

5 "And if you said, 'Give me of the Water of Life that I may drink and live' - it cannot be this day, but on the day that I shall descend into hell, and break the gates of brass, and bruise in pieces the kingdoms of iron.

C.2 Such love is manifested by Jesus the 'Word of God' in willing to suffer and die for all the sins of mankind whilst on the cross and immediately afterwards descend into hell to preach to the souls in Hell that many might get saved as spoken of in the scriptures very clearly.

John 3.16 For God so loved the world that he gave his only begotten Son that whosoever believes on him should not perish but have everlasting life.

Philippians 2:10-11 That at the name of Jesus every knee **should bow**, of things in heaven, and things in earth, and things under the earth; [11]And that every tongue should confess that Jesus Christ is LORD, to the glory of God the Father.

Romans 14:11 For it is written, As I live, saith **the** LORD, every knee shall **bow** to me, and every tongue shall confess to God.

John 10.1 Verily, verily, I say unto you, He that enters not by the door into the sheepfold, but climbs up some other way, the same is a thief and a robber.

C.3 'descend into hell, and break the gates of brass, and bruise in pieces the kingdoms of iron'. [See Daniel 2 - The Image dream of all the empires of man from 600 BC until the Anti-Christ End-time worldwide empire of the Beast **(Rev 13).**

C.4 Rome was a kingdom of **iron** and so will the coming worldwide **Anti-Christ kingdom** also be as a re-birth of the Roman empire in fierceness. (**Daniel 7.7**)]

C.5 Here is an amazing verse. Why? Because some of the Christian world is in denial that Christ went down to Hell for 3 days and nights, giving the excuse that there was not enough time between Good Friday and Easter Sunday.

C.6 However, you will find by doing a little calculating that Jesus must have died on the Thursday before Easter Sunday as it states in scripture that Christ spent 3 days and 3 nights in the heart of the earth - so counting three days back from Easter Sunday we arrive at the Thursday and not the Friday as the date for his death, and then he arose on the Sunday.

C.7 He, Jesus - the 'Word of God' clearly stated that He would spend some time in the 'heart of the earth' as that in the above verse 5 of this 'Lost Book of Adam and Eve Book 1' [Note: some hold to the view that Jesus died on the Wednesday and that he was resurrected on the Saturday, rather than the Sunday: source Was Jesus dead for three days and three nights? (biblestudy. org)]

Matthew 12.40 For as Jonah was three days and three nights in the belly of a huge fish, so the Son of Man will be three days and three nights in the heart of the earth.

C.8. '*I shall descend into hell, and break the gates of brass, and bruise in pieces the kingdoms of iron*'. Why did Jesus descend into Hell for 3 days and three nights according to the Bible scriptures?

C.9 As it clearly states in this 5th verse of this chapter Jesus descended into hell to 'break the gates of brass' which represents the gates of both Death and Hell, and smash all of Satan's fleshly worldly powers which fulfils what Jesus Himself also state in the book of Revelation chapter 1:

Revelation 1:18 'I am he that lives and was dead, and behold I am alive for evermore, Amen; and have the keys of Hell and Death.

C.10 Well, what is clear is that Jesus must have gone down into hell and fought against Satan and his fallen angels and took away the 'keys of hell and death' from Him right after He died and before He was resurrected on Easter Sunday.

1 Peter 4.6 For this cause was the gospel peached unto the dead.. [1 Peter 3.19-20 ‹By which also he went and preached unto the spirits in prison, which sometime were disobedient, when once the longsuffering of God waited in the days of Noah, while the ark was a preparing, wherein few, that is, eight souls were saved by water›.]

Ephesians 4.9-10 Now that he ascended, what is it but that he also descended first into the lower parts of the earth? He that descended is the same also that ascended up far above all heavens, that he might fulfil all things.

Acts 2.31 He (King David in1000 BC) seeing this before spake of the resurrection of Christ, that **his soul was not left in hell**, neither his flesh did see corruption.

1 Cor 15.4 And that he was buried, and that he rose again the third day according to the scriptures:

1 Cor 15.21-22 For since by man came death, by man also came the resurrection of the dead. For as in Adam all die, even so in Christ shall all be made alive.

1 Cor 15.25-26 For he must reign, till he hath put all enemies under his feet. The last enemy that shall be destroyed is death.

Revelations 20.14 And Death and Hell were cast into the Lake of Fire. This is the second death.

> 6 "Then will I in mercy save thy soul and the souls of the righteous, to give them rest in My garden. And that shall be when the end of the world is come.

1 Cor 15.42-47 So also is the resurrection of the dead. It is sown in corruption; it is raised in incorruption:[43] It is sown in dishonour; it is raised in glory: it is sown in weakness; it is raised in power:[44] It is sown a natural body; it is raised a spiritual body. There is a natural body, and there is a spiritual body.[45] And so it is written, The first man Adam was made a living soul; the last Adam was made a quickening spirit.[47] The first man is of the earth, earthy; the second man is the Lord from heaven.

> 7 "And again, as regards the Water of Life thou seek, it will not be granted thee this day; but on the day that I shall shed My blood upon

> thy head in the land of Golgotha.

C.11 What an amazing prophecy giving even the name 'Golgotha' some almost 6000 years ago just after Creation, if we can fully rely on the source of the ‹Lost books of Adam and Eve›?

Mark 15.22 'And they bring him unto the place Golgotha, which is, being interpreted, The place of a skull'.

C.12 For the crucifixion: See Matthew 27: 32-44; Luke 23:26-43, John 19: 16-27. More about Christ the Messiah and his sufferings Psalm 22, Psalm 69, Isaiah 53

> 8 "For My blood shall be the Water of Life unto thee, at that time, and not to thee alone, but unto all those of thy seed who shall believe in Me; that it be unto them for rest for ever."

Jn 1.37 He that believes in Me as the scripture has said 'Out of his belly shall flow rivers of Living Waters.

Rev.22.1-2 And he showed me a pure river of the Water of Life, clear as crystal, proceeding out of the throne of God and of the Lamb. [2] In the midst of the street of it, and on either side of the river, there was the Tree of Life, which bore twelve kinds of fruit and yielded her fruit every month; and the leaves of the tree were for the healing of the nations.

> 9 The Lord said again unto Adam, "O Adam, when you were in the garden, these trials did not come to you.
>
> 10 "But since you did transgress My commandment, all these sufferings have come upon you.
>
> 11. "Now, also, does your flesh require food and drink; drink then of that water that flows by you on the face of the earth."
>
> 12 Then God withdrew His Word from Adam.
>
> 13 And Adam and Eve worshipped the Lord and returned from the river of water to the cave. It was noonday; and when they drew near to the cave, they saw a large fire by it.

C.13 Just an idea, but the fact that this book is stating that Adam and Eve originally lived in the 'Cave of Treasures' after having been booted out of the 'Garden of Eden' could have been the concept that led to evolutionists believing that man used to be a 'cave-man'. Well, here we are only talking about around 6000 years ago, and not millions of years ago. It is quite easy to prove that the age of the earth is very young by many different methods, which I have covered before. Many honest scientists can testify to the young age of the earth.

C.14 Notice how that Easter always falls in a different week each year according to the cycles of the moon - and can vary from late March to around the middle of April - i.e., around a 1 month of fluctuations in the timing of Easter.

C.15 Easter happened at the same time as the Jewish celebrations of the **Passover** which was governed by the cycles of the moon! Why was that?

C.16 When we think about it, Jesus was born on a **specific day & DATE** - so why celebrate it on a different day each year? The **day will fluctuate** so would not it be better to celebrate the **exact date** on which Christ was **resurrected** or has that info been lost to time itself?

Is the fact that Easter is on some random date -decided by whom -that I do not yet know - to minimize the date; or better said to make **'important dates'** seem random which is the way of modern man in his unbelief and worshipping the idol of evolution with all its randomness and so-called co-incidences.

C.17 Were dates and time erratic in the far past or even Pre-Flood times or perhaps not? I leave it up to **you** to decide: Which is the most important - the actual **date** as to when God did something or the exact day?

I mean which is the most useful information in the long run. I would personally reckon that the actual **date is** more important to know than a fluctuating **day** like a Friday for example.

C.18 According to these interesting books of the Lost Book of Adam and Eve Pt 1 and 2 - Adam was born on a Friday and 930 years later he also died on a Friday.

Is this true? If so, why? I will investigate that topic more in the future.

C.19 For more on **'real time'** as created by God in the beginning - see my new book '**Jubilees Insights**', as believe it or not, man has **interfered with the times** and seasons by **altering the original number of days** in the **year**...How and when was the *time* altered?

Isn't it true that the number of degrees in a circle is exactly 360 - A perfect number in ancient maths - a constant?

C.20 Shouldn›t we have **360** days in a **year** like the good old fashioned **prophetic year** has in both the **Books of Daniel and Revelations.**

The big question is why and when has time been changed?...

CHAPTER 43

Arson

THEN Adam and Eve were afraid and stood still. And Adam said to Eve, "What is that fire by our cave? We did nothing in it to bring about this fire.

2 "We neither have bread to bake therein, nor broth to cook there. As to this fire, we know not the like, neither do we know what to call it.

3 "But ever since God sent the cherub with a sword of fire that flashed and lightened in his hand, from fear of which we fell down and were like corpses, have we not seen the like.

4 "But now O Eve, behold, this is the same fire that was in the cherub's hand, which God has sent to keep the cave in which we dwell.

5 "O Eve, it is because God is angry with us, and will drive us from it.

6 "O Eve, we have again transgressed His commandment in that cave, so that He had sent this fire to burn around it, and to prevent us from going into it.

7 "If this be really so, O Eve, where shall we dwell? And whither shall we flee from before the face of the Lord? Since, as regards the garden, He will not let us abide in it, and He has deprived us of the good things thereof; but He has placed us in this cave, in which we have borne darkness, trials and hardships, until at last we found comfort therein.

8 "But now that He has brought us out into another land, who knows what may happen in it? And who knows but that the darkness of that land may be far greater than the darkness of this land?

9 "Who knows what may happen in that land by day or by night? And who knows whether it will be far or near, O Eve? Where it will please God to put us, may be far from the garden, O Eve! or where God will prevent us from beholding Him, because we have transgressed His commandment, and because we have made requests unto Him at all

times?

10 "O Eve, if God will bring us into a strange land other than this, in which we find consolation, it must be to put our souls to death, and blot out our name from the face of the earth.

11 "O Eve, if we are farther estranged from the garden and from God, where shall we find Him again, and ask Him to give us gold, incense, myrrh, and some fruit of the fig-tree?

12 "Where shall we find Him, to comfort us a second time? Where shall we find Him, that He may think of us, as regards the covenant He has made on our behalf.

13 Then Adam said no more. And they kept looking, he and Eve, towards the cave, and at the fire that flared up around it.

14 But that fire was from Satan. For he had gathered trees and dry grasses, and had carried and brought them to the cave, and had set fire to them, to consume the cave and what was in it.

15 So that Adam and Eve should be left in sorrow, and he should cut off their trust in God, and make them deny Him.

16 But by the mercy of God he could not burn the cave, for God sent His angel round the cave to guard it from such a fire, until it went out.

17 And this fire lasted from noonday until the break of day. That was the forty-fifth day.

CHAPTER 44

Fire

YET Adam and Eve were standing and looking at the fire, and unable to come near the cave from their dread of the fire.

2 And Satan kept on bringing trees and throwing them into the fire, until the flame thereof rose up on high, and covered the whole cave, thinking, as he did in his own mind, to consume the cave with much fire. But the angel of the Lord was guarding it.

3 And yet he could not curse Satan, nor injure him by word, because he had no authority over him, neither did he take to doing so with words from his mouth.

4 Therefore did the angel bear with him, without saying one bad word until the Word of God came who said to Satan, "Go; hence, once before didst thou deceive My servants, and this time thou seek to destroy them.

5 "Were it not for My mercy I would have destroyed thee and thy hosts from off the earth. But I have had patience with thee, unto the end of the world."

6 Then Satan fled from before the Lord. But the fire went on burning around the cave like a coal-fire the whole day; which was the forty-sixth day Adam and Eve had spent since they came out of the garden.

7 And when Adam and Eve saw that the heat of the fire had somewhat cooled down, they began to walk towards the cave to get into it as they were wont; but they could not, by reason of the heat of the fire.

8 Then they both took to weeping because of the fire that made separation between them and the cave, and that drew towards them, burning. And they were afraid.

9 Then Adam said to Eve, "See this fire of which we have a portion in us: which formerly yielded to us, but no longer does so, now that we have transgressed the limit of creation, and changed our condition,

> and our nature is altered. But the fire is not changed in its nature, nor altered from its creation. Therefore, has it now power over us; and when we come near it, it scorches our flesh."

C.1 Another Key verse in the story, as saying *"'See this fire of which we have a portion in us: which formerly yielded to us, but no longer does so, now that we have transgressed the limit of creation, and changed our condition, and our nature is altered".*

C.2 How is it possible that Adam is stating that when they were in the Garden of Eden they had 'fire in their bodies' that they were able to control but that now outside the Garden of Eden they no longer have any control over fire but that it now both burns and harms them?

C.3 It find quite remarkable as it was not until the **Book of Enoch** that Enoch mentioned beings of fire. It was later mentioned in different books about people or angels of fire.

Enoch 17.1 'And they took and brought me to a place in the which those who were there were like flaming fire, and when they wished they appeared as men'.

Enoch 71.1 'And it came to pass after this that my spirit was translated and it ascended into the heavens, and I saw the holy sons of God. They were stepping on flames of fire.'

Hebrews 1.7 And of the angels he says, 'Who makes his angels spirits and his ministers a flame of fire.'

Daniel 12.3 'And they that be wise shall shine as the brightness of the firmament; and they that turn many to righteousness as the stars for ever and ever.'

Revelation 1.13-15 And in the midst of the seven candlesticks one like unto the Son of man, clothed with a garment down to the foot, and girt about the paps with a golden girdle.

[14] His head and his hairs were white like wool, as white as snow; and his eyes were as a flame of fire;

[15] And his feet like unto fine brass, as if they burned in a furnace; and his voice as the sound of many waters.

C.4 In the New Testament there is a symbolic return to the fire mentioned by Adam and Eve - 'Fire of the Holy Spirit' manifested in 'cloven tongues of fire.'

Acts 2.3 'Then there appeared to them divided tongues, as of fire, and *one* sat upon each of them.'

C.5 I think that we can deduce that Adam and Eve really did have a 'bright nature' whilst they were in the Garden of Eden and were like unto the angels of God.

CHAPTER 45

Hell

THEN Adam rose and prayed unto God, saying, "See, this fire has made separation between us and the cave in which Thou hast commanded us to dwell; but now, behold, we cannot go into it."

C.1 Here is a symbolism in this story about Hell and being separated from God and Heaven. What separates us is our sins. Sin is snot just doing something inherently wrong or evil it is by definition 'Missing the mark' of what God has told one to do.

2 Then God heard Adam, and sent him His Word, that said:

3 "O Adam, see this fire! how different the flame and heat thereof are from the garden of delights and the good things in it!

4 "When thou was under My control, all creatures yielded to thee; but after thou hast transgressed My commandment, they all rise over thee."

5 Again said God unto him, "See, O Adam, how Satan has exalted thee! He has deprived thee of the Godhead, and of an exalted state like unto Me, and has not kept his word to thee; but, after all, is become thy foe. It is he who made this fire in which he meant to burn thee and Eve.

C.2 Fire represents Hell and the fruit of sin.

Psalm 68.21 "But God shall wound the head of his enemies: and the hairy scalp of such a one as goes on still in his trespasses."

C.3 God is pointing out to both Adam and Eve that Satan is a big liar and that he never keeps his word but is only a deceiver and destroyer of man.

C.4 Mankind has been dumb enough to listen to Satan ever since the times of Adam and Eve, and that is why our world is now on the brink of destruction, one way or another.

C.5 Only God himself can rescue this usurped planet. Who has usurped it? Well, the Devil and his angels for one. Evil ruling merchants for another. The good news is that both of their times is almost up, thank God.

6 "Why, O Adam, has he not kept his agreement with thee, not even one day; but has deprived thee of the glory that was on thee--when thou didst yield to his command?

7 "Thinkest thou, Adam, that he loved thee when he made this agreement with thee? Or, that he loved thee and wished to raise thee on high?

8 "But no, Adam, he did not do all that out of love to thee; but he wished to make thee come out of light into darkness, and from an exalted state to degradation; from glory to abasement; from joy to sorrow; and from rest to fasting and fainting."

9 God said also to Adam, "See this fire kindled by Satan around thy cave; see this wonder that surrounds thee; and know that it will encompass about both thee and thy seed, when ye hearken to his behest; that he will plague you with fire; and that ye shall go down into hell after ye are dead.

10 "Then shall ye see the burning of his fire, that will thus be burning around you and your seed. There shall be no deliverance from it for you, but at My coming; in like manner as thou canst not now go into thy cave, by reason of the great fire around it; not until My Word shall come that will make a way for thee on the day My covenant is fulfilled.

11 "There is no way for thee at present to come from hence to rest, not until My Word comes, who is My Word. Then will He make a way for thee, and thou shalt have rest." Then God called with His Word to that fire that burned around the cave, that it part itself asunder, until Adam had gone through it. Then the fire parted itself by God's order, and a way was made for Adam.

12 And God withdrew His Word from Adam.

CHAPTER 46

Deliverance

THEN Adam and Eve began again to come into the cave. And when they came to the way between the fire, Satan blew into the fire like a whirlwind, and made on Adam and Eve a burning coal-fire; so that their bodies were singed; and the coal-fire scorched them.

2 And from the burning of the fire Adam and Eve cried aloud, and said, "O Lord, save us! Leave us not to be consumed and plagued by this burning fire; neither require us for having transgressed Thy commandment."

3 Then God looked upon their bodies, on which Satan had caused fire to burn, and God sent His angel that stayed the burning fire. But the wounds remained on their bodies.

4 And God said unto Adam, "See Satan's love for thee, who pretended to give thee the Godhead and greatness; and behold, he burns thee with fire, and seeks to destroy thee from off the earth.

5 "Then look at Me, O Adam; I created thee, and how many times have I delivered thee out of his hand? If not, would he not have destroyed thee?"

6 God said again to Eve, "What is that he promised thee in the garden, saying, 'At the time ye shall eat of the tree, your eyes will be opened, and you shall become like gods, knowing good and evil.' But lo! he has burnt your bodies with fire, and has made you taste the taste of fire, for the taste of the garden; and has made you see the burning of fire, and the evil thereof, and the power it has over you.

7 "Your eyes have seen the good he has taken from you, and in truth he has opened your eyes; and you have seen the garden in which ye were with Me, and ye have also seen the evil that has come upon you from Satan. But as to the Godhead he cannot give it you, neither fulfil his speech to you. Nay, he was bitter against you and your seed, that will come after you."

8 And God withdrew His Word from them.

CHAPTER 47

The Devil's Tricks

THEN Adam and Eve came into the cave yet trembling at the fire that had scorched their bodies. So, Adam said to Eve:

2 "Lo, the fire has burnt our flesh in this world; but how will it be when we are dead, and Satan shall punish our souls? Is not our deliverance long and far off, unless God come, and in mercy to us fulfil His promise?"

3 Then Adam and Eve passed into the cave, blessing themselves for coming into it once more. For it was in their thoughts, that they never should enter it, when they saw the fire around it.

4 But as the sun was setting the fire was still burning and nearing Adam and Eve in the cave, so that they could not sleep in it. After the sun had set, they went out of it. This was the forty-seventh day after they came out of the garden.

5 Adam and Eve then came under the top of hill by the garden to sleep, as they were wont.

6 And they stood and prayed God to forgive them their sins, and then fell asleep under the summit of the mountain.

7 But Satan, the hater of all good, thought within himself: Whereas God has promised salvation to Adam by covenant, and that He would deliver him out of all the hardships that have befallen him-but has not promised me by covenant, and will not deliver me out of my hardships; nay, since He has promised him that He should make him and his seed dwell in the kingdom in which I once was--I will kill Adam.

8 The earth shall be rid of him; and shall be left to me alone; so that when he is dead he may not have any seed left to inherit the kingdom that shall remain my own realm; God will then be in want of me, and He will restore me to it with my hosts.

CHAPTER 48

5ᵗʰ Apparition of Satan

> AFTER this Satan called to his hosts, all of which came to him, and said unto him:
>
> 2 "O, our Lord, what wilt thou do?"

Revelation 12.9 And the great dragon was cast out, that old serpent, called the Devil, and Satan, which deceives the whole world: he was cast out into the earth, and his angels were cast out with him.

> 3 He then said unto them, "Ye know that this Adam, whom God created out of the dust, is he who has taken our kingdom. Come, let us gather together and kill him; or hurl a rock at him and at Eve, and crush them under it."

C.1 These Lost Books of Adam and Eve do a very good job of explaining how Evil came into the world. Not only that, but they clearly show that the fight with Satan is a daily one for each one of us.

2 Cor. 11:3 But I fear, lest by any means, as the serpent beguiled Eve through his subtilty, so your minds should be corrupted from the simplicity that is in Christ.

C.2 Satan hated Adam and Eve, because in his warped mind 'they' caused him to fall. It was all Adam and Eve's fault when it was Satan himself, who was the guiltiest in tempting both Adam and Eve to disobey God in the Garden of Eden.

John 8.44 'Ye are of your father the devil, and the lusts of your father ye will do. He was a murderer from the beginning, and abode not in the truth, because there is no truth in him. When he speaks a lie, he speaks of his own: for he is a liar, and the father of it.'

C.3 Satan really has a twisted sense of 'right and wrong'. Not that he cares about the truth. He does not believe in the Truth as he is a liar and a father of it as Jesus clearly stated. Satan is the Accuser of the saints in the courts of heaven as shown clearly in the Book of Job.

Job 1.6-8 Now there was a day when the sons of God came to present themselves before the LORD, AND SATAN CAME ALSO AMONG THEM.

⁷And the LORD SAID UNTO SATAN, WHENCE COMEST THOU? THEN SATAN ANSWERED THE LORD, AND SAID, FROM GOING TO AND FRO IN THE EARTH, AND FROM WALKING UP AND DOWN IN IT.

⁸And the LORD SAID UNTO SATAN, HAST THOU CONSIDERED MY SERVANT JOB, THAT THERE IS

C.4 There is no truth in Satan. He behaves just like many merchants today. They commit a crime and then blame it on someone else.

Revelation 18.23-24 For thy merchants were the great men of the earth; for by thy sorceries were all nations deceived. And in her was found the blood of prophets, and of saints, and of all that were slain upon the earth.

---

4 When Satan's hosts heard these words, they came to the part of the mountain where Adam and Eve were asleep.

5 Then Satan and his hosts took a huge rock, broad and even, and without blemish, thinking within himself, "If there should be a hole in the rock, when it fell on them, the hole in the rock might come upon them, and so they would escape and not die."

6 He then said to his hosts, "Take up this stone, and throw it flat upon them, so that it roll not from them to somewhere else. And when ye have hurled it, flee and tarry not."

7 And they did as he bid them. But as the rock fell down from the mountain upon Adam and Eve, God commanded it to become a kind of shed over them, that did them no harm. And so it was by God's order.

8 But when the rock fell, the whole earth quaked with it, and. was shaken from the size of the rock.

9 And as it quaked and shook, Adam and Eve awoke from sleep, and found themselves under a rock like a shed. But they knew not how it was; for when they fell asleep they were under the sky, and not under a shed; and when they saw it, they were afraid.

10 Then Adam said to Eve, "Wherefore has the mountain bent itself, and the earth quaked and shaken on our account? And why has this rock spread itself over us like a tent?

11 "Does God intend to plague us and to shut us up in this prison? Or will He close the earth upon us?

---

12 "He is angry with us for our having come out of the cave without His order; and for our having done so of our own accord, without consulting Him, when we left the cave and came to this place."

13 Then Eve said, "If, indeed, the earth quaked for our sake, and this rock forms a tent over us because of our transgression, then woe be to us, O Adam, for our punishment will be long.

14 "But arise and pray Ito God to let us know concerning this, and what this rock is, that is spread over us like a tent."

15 Then Adam stood up and prayed before the Lord, to let him know about this strait. And Adam thus stood praying until the morning.

Ephesians 6.16 Above all, taking the shield of faith, wherewith ye shall be able to quench all the fiery darts of the wicked.

C.5 Satan always tries to take the blame away from himself and pin it on some unsuspecting innocent people. Satan is a trickster. He tempts people to do evil and then accuses them once they have given into his tricks.

Revelation 12.10 'And I heard a loud voice saying in heaven, Now is come salvation, and strength, and the kingdom of our God, and the power of his Christ: for the accuser of our brethren is cast down, which accused them before our God, day and night'.

C.6 The good news is one of these days Satan is going to get locked up in the Bottomless Pit for a 1000-years. Good riddance to bad rubbish when that happens.

Revelation 20.1 And I saw an angel coming down out of heaven, having the key to the Abyss and holding in his hand a great chain. [2]He seized the dragon, that ancient serpent, who is the devil, or Satan, and bound him for a thousand years. [3]He threw him into the Abyss, and locked and sealed it over him, to keep him from deceiving the nations anymore until the thousand years were ended.

CHAPTER 49

Resurrection

THEN the Word of God came and said:

2 "O Adam, who counselled thee, when thou earnest out of the cave, to come to this place?"

3 And Adam said unto God, "O Lord, we came to this place because of the heat of the fire, that came upon us inside the cave."

4 Then the Lord God said unto Adam, "O Adam, you dread the heat of fire for one night, but how will it be when thou dwellest in hell?

C.1 Why would Adam have to descend into hell? Those who are saved by Jesus do not go into the fires of hell. That is simply a 'works trip' false doctrine.

C.2 The 'Word of God' in this story has told Adam many times that He would come and be born on earth and would save mankind from his sins, so why on earth would Adam be going down to hell? That sounds just like the eternal insecurity of some of the churches who teach such nauseating doctrines.

C.3 The truth is that once you are saved then you are saved for ever and no ands, if's or buts added. Jesus died for every man who will willingly reach out and whole-heartedly receive him into his heart and believe that Jesus is the Son of God who died for their Salvation.

Jn 3.36 'He that believes on the son has everlasting life but he that believes not shall not see life, but the wrath of God abides upon him' Hell is for the unbelievers and not the believers.

C.4 Organized religions will be going to Hell for sure - for deceiving the people. People do not need religions and church buildings and hocus-pocus traditions and ceremonies of the 'man-made' religions to get saved.

C.5 God does not need buildings to live in:

Isaiah 66.1 Heaven is My Throne and the earth is My footstool what building can contain me saith the Lord

Acts 7.48 Howbeit the Most High dwelleth not in temples built with hands as saith the prophet

C.6 Organized religions are normally 'clap-traps of control' and 'money making rackets' specially to favour the rich and rob the poor. Many churches try to scare people into going to church with their instilling fear of 'going to hell' if you do not attend church every Sunday.

C.7 The word 'disciple' means 'follower'. A disciple of Christ is supposed to be a follower of Christ and to follow in his footsteps. It is important not believe such awful lies such as the 'prosperity' doctrine and yet another church doctrines which state that 'those who are poor' have a 'poverty demon'. How convenient a doctrine for a rich established church system! Such utter nonsense!

Titus 3.5 Not by works of righteousness which we have done but according to his mercy he saved us.

Ephesians 2.8-9 'For by Grace are ye saved by faith and that NOT of yourselves, it is the gift of God and not of works lest any man should boast.

Revelation 3.17 Because thou sayest I am rich and in need of nothing and know not that thou are poor and naked and wretched .(in the sight of God)

C.8 The first disciples of 'Christ' or the 'Word of God' did not need churches and synagogues. They certainly did not build any of them. They went into those places to witness to the people in them. Some few people listened and followed them, and the vast majority rejected them, and they left the buildings and moved on to another location to be a witness to those who would listen.

C.9 The organized religions themselves in general never listen as they are part of the 'status quo' like the government - as they are more interested in buildings and ceremonies and making money, controlling the people, and certainly not interested in genuinely loving God and learning true mercy and forgiveness and charity. The organized churches certainly do not teach people to obey Christ's teachings which say:

Luke 14.33 Whosoever he be of you that forsakes not all that he hath he cannot be my disciple.

---

5 "Yet, O Adam, fear not, neither say in thy heart that I have spread this rock as an awning over thee, to plague thee therewith.

6 "It came from Satan, who had promised thee the Godhead and majesty. It is he who threw down this rock to kill thee under it, and Eve with thee, and thus to prevent you from living upon the earth.

7 "But, in mercy for you, just as that rock was falling down upon you, I commanded it to form an awning over you; and the rock under you, to lower itself.

8 "And this sign, O Adam, will happen to Me at My coming upon earth: Satan will raise the people of the Jews to put Me to death; and they will lay Me in a rock, and seal a large stone upon Me, and I shall remain

---

within that rock three days and three nights.

9 "But on the third day I shall rise again, and it shall be salvation to thee, O Adam, and to thy seed, to believe in Me. But, O Adam, I will not bring thee from under this rock until three days and three nights are passed."

10 And God withdrew His Word from Adam.

11 But Adam and Eve abode under the rock three days and three nights, as God had told them.

12 And God did so to them because they had left their cave and had come to this same place without God's order.

13 But, after three days and three nights, God opened the rock and brought them out from under it. Their flesh was dried up, and their eyes and their hearts were troubled from weeping and sorrow.

CHAPTER 50

Nakedness

THEN Adam and Eve went forth and came into the Cave of Treasures, and they stood praying in it the whole of that day, until the evening.

2 And this took place at the end of fifty days after they had left the garden.

3 But Adam and Eve rose again and prayed to God in the cave the whole of that night and begged for mercy from Him.

4 And when the day dawned, Adam said unto Eve, "Come! let us go and do some work for our bodies."

5 So they went out of the cave, and came to the northern border of the garden, and they sought something to cover their bodies withal. But they found nothing and knew not how to do the work. Yet their bodies were stained, and they were speechless from cold and heat.

6 Then Adam stood and asked God to show him something wherewith to cover their bodies.

7 Then came the Word of God and said unto him, "O Adam, take Eve and come to the seashore, where ye fasted before. There ye shall find skins of sheep, whose flesh was devoured by lions, and whose skins were left. Take them and make raiment for yourselves and clothe yourselves withal."

C.1 Most of the content of this book of the 'Lost Book of Adam and Eve Book I' is exceptionally good and understandable.

C.2 I think there was original content, and much later things were added which were both deeply religious and ascetic. With the long time period since the book was originally written errors crept in. (See more about this in the Appendix)

C.3 Whoever wrote this last verse 7 does not know their Bible, as it is stated that before the Great Flood the normal humans and animals were herbivores and not meat eaters/carnivores. So, this verse is incorrect. The Bible states:

Genesis 1.29 Then God said, "I give you every seed-bearing plant on the face of the whole earth and every tree that has fruit with seed in it. They will be yours for food.

C.4 It is probable that 'Adam and Eve were not originally completely naked as most people assume but had 'garments of light' on like the 'righteous' in heaven - which they lost when they disobeyed. It was then that they noticed that they were naked. I know that the Bible states 'And Adam and Eve were naked and were not ashamed:

Genesis 2.25 "The man and his wife were both **naked**, but they were not ashamed."

C.5 If we look at the original Hebrew language, we find that the word naked can sometimes mean having only an undergarment on. The same is the case in the New Testament where it states that Peter went on the water to meet Jesus and he throw a garment on him for he was 'naked'. In that case also it did not mean 'naked as we do today i.e., 'stark naked' but Peter was in his underwear. Same with Adam and Eve.

[See: garments of light – from '**Corrupting the Image'** book 1 by **Douglas Hamp]**

Isaiah 11:6 The wolf also shall dwell with the lamb, and the leopard shall lie down with the kid; and the calf and the young lion and the fatling together; and a little child shall lead them.

Book of Jasher 6.2-3 All the animals came unto Noah and encompassed the Ark. Notice none of them was devouring each other that would happen if it was today. Today, the moment a lion sees a sheep or goat. chomp.

C.6 After the Great Flood God specially told Noah that from that time onwards, he would have to eat meat for strength. Now why would God make this point if Noah was already used to eating meat before the great Flood? Eating meat for strength could also apply to the carnivores after the Great Flood.

Genesis 9.3 Every moving thing that lives shall be meat for you; even as the green herb have I given you all things.

C.7 There were 'meat eaters' before the Great Flood but not ones created by God...but by the Fallen angels creating hybrids through altering the DNA of both humans and animals and other creatures.

CHAPTER 51

Sheep Skins

WHEN Adam heard these words from God, he took Eve and removed from the northern end of the garden to the south of it, by the river of water, where they once fasted.

2 But as they were going in the way, and before they reached that place, Satan, the wicked one, had heard the Word of God communing with Adam respecting his covering.

3 It grieved him, and he hastened to the place where the sheepskins were, with the intention of taking them and throwing them into the sea, or of burning them with fire, that Adam and Eve should not find them.

4 But as he was about to take them, the Word of God came from heaven, and bound him by the side of those skins until Adam and Eve came near him. But as they neared him, they were afraid of him, and of his hideous look.

5 Then came the Word of God to Adam and Eve, and said to them, "This is he who was hidden in the serpent, and who deceived you, and stripped you of the garment of light and glory in which you were.

6 "This is he who promised you majesty and divinity. Where, then, is the beauty that was on him? Where is his divinity? Where is his light? Where is the glory that rested on him?

7 "Now his figure is hideous; he is become abominable among angels; and he has come to be called Satan.

8 "O Adam he wished to take from you this earthly garment of sheep-skins, and to destroy it, and not let you be covered with it.

9 "What, then, is his beauty that you should have followed him? And what have you gained by hearkening to him? See his evil works and then look at Me; at Me, your Creator, and at the good deeds I do you.

10 "See, I bound him until you came and saw him and beheld his weakness, that no power is left with him."

11 And God released him from his bonds.

CHAPTER 52

To Sew a Shirt

AFTER this Adam and Eve said no more, but wept before God on account of their creation, and of their bodies that required an earthly covering.

2 Then Adam said unto Eve, "O Eve, this is the skin of beasts with which we shall be covered. But when we have put it on, behold, a token of death shall have come upon us, inasmuch as the owners of these skins have died, and have wasted away. So also, shall we die, and pass away."

3 Then Adam and Eve took the skins and went back to the Cave of Treasures; and when in it, they stood and prayed as they were wont.

4 And they thought how they could make garments of those skins; for they had no skill for it.

5 Then God sent to them His angel to show them how to work it out. And the angel said to Adam, "Go forth, and bring some palm-thorns." Then Adam went out, and brought some, as the angel had commanded him.

6 Then the angel began before them to work out the skins, after the manner of one who prepares a shirt. And he took the thorns and stuck them into the skins before their eyes.

7 Then the angel again stood up and prayed God that the thorns in those skins should be hidden, so as to be, as it were, sewn with one thread.

8 And so it was, by God's order; they became garments for Adam and Eve, and He clothed them withal.

9 From that time the nakedness of their bodies was covered from the sight of each other's eyes.

10 And this happened at the end of the fifty-first day.

11 Then when Adam's and Eve's bodies were covered, they stood and prayed, and sought mercy of the Lord, and forgiveness, and gave Him thanks for that He had had mercy on them and had covered their nakedness. And they ceased not from prayer the whole of that night.

12 Then when the day dawned at the rising of the sun, they said their prayers after their custom; and then went out of the cave.

13 And Adam said unto Eve, "Since we know not what there is to the westward of this cave, let us go forth and see it to-day." Then they came forth and went towards the western border.

CHAPTER 53

The Great Flood

> THEY were not very far from the cave, when Satan came towards them, and hid himself between them and the cave, under the form of two ravenous lions three days without food, that came towards Adam and Eve, as if to break them in pieces and devour them.

C.1 Satan disguises himself as two ravenous lions with the intent of attacking and killing Adam and Eve.

1 Peter 5:8-9 Be sober, be vigilant; because your adversary the devil, as a roaring lion, walketh about, seeking whom he may devour: 9 Whom resist steadfast in the faith, knowing that the same afflictions are accomplished in your brethren that are in the world.

> 2 Then Adam and Eve wept and prayed God to deliver them from their paws.
>
> 3 Then the Word of God came to them and drove away the lions from them.

Isaiah 59:19 'When the **enemy** shall come in like a flood, the Spirit of the LORD shall lift up a standard against him'.

> 4 And God said unto Adam, "O Adam, what seek thou on the western border? And why hast thou left of thine own accord the eastern border, in which was thy dwelling-place?
>
> 5 "Now, then, turn back to thy cave, and remain in it, that Satan do not deceive thee, nor work his purpose upon thee.

Ephesians 4:27 'Neither give place to the devil'.

> 6 "For in this western border, O Adam, there will go from thee a seed, that shall replenish it; and that will defile themselves with their sins, and with their yielding to the behests of Satan, and by following his works.
>
> 7 "Therefore will I bring upon them the waters of a flood and over-whelm them all. But I will deliver what is left of the righteous among them; and I will bring them to a distant land, and the land in which

> thou dwellest now shall remain desolate and without one inhabitant in it."

C.2 This verse 7 is a jewel because it reveals several things that only God Himself could have known in the time of Adam and Eve. First, it is a prophecy given by the Lord that He would bring the waters of the Great Flood upon the whole world. That is a marvellous prophecy, but there is something even more revealing in this verse as it states 'I will bring them to a distant land, and the land in which thou now dwellest shall remain desolate and without one inhabitant within it.

C.3 If we take the traditional stance that the earth is solid, and that Noah started his journey some place close to Israel today and he landed after the Great Flood on Mt Ararat in the mountains of Turkey then the above verse could not have been fulfilled as it clearly states, 'and I will bring them to a distant land'.

C.4 From the traditional viewpoint one could not justify that Noah had moved to a distant land after the Great Flood as the mountains of Ararat are not far away from Israel.

C.5 Also we know that Noah and his descendants came down from Mount Ararat and from thence they populated the earth so how would it be possible that *'land in which thou dwellest now shall remain desolate and without one inhabitant in it?"*

C.6 Here is my take on the situation: 1) If the earth is in fact hollow, what if Noah started on the inside of the earth before the Great Flood 2) He travelled an exceptionally long distance 'to a faraway land' being the outer surface of the planet where man had in general not been living before until after the Great Flood. 3) Mankind came to live on the outer surface of the planet and the inner surface became without inhabitant and desolate at least for a very long time.

C.7 Inner earth eventually became the domain of evil spirits and demons as they were already in a lower dimension in the inner earth. Apart from the evil spirits eventually different people migrated to inner earth since the Great Flood for different reasons.

C.8 Strangely enough, there is a very odd verse in the apocryphal book of 2nd Esdras which sounds like the above verse in reverse. In other words, some representatives of the 10 Lost Tribes of Israel made a pact with God to go to a distant land where man had supposedly not been to before…

II Esdras 13.17-18 'But they formed this plan for themselves that they would leave the multitude of the nations and go to a more distant region, where mankind had never lived; that there at least they might keep their statutes which they had not kept in their own land; and they went <u>in</u> by the narrow passages of the Euphrates River. **18** For at that time the Most High performed signs for them and stopped the channels of the river until they had passed over through that region there was a long way to go, a journey of a year and a half; and that country is called Arzareth. They dwelt there until the 'Last times' and now when they are about to come again.

C.9 You can read a lot more about this intriguing story in my book '**Ezdras Insights**'. Here is the source reference from that book concerning the **INNER EARTH:**

Merton, Loner Nikolai

– BEYOND ARZARETH: A STORY OF THE LOST TEN TRIBES., Article in THE RELIEF SOCIETY MAGAZINE., Oct. 1919 – July 1920., Salt Lake City, Utah; Reprinted in SEARCH magazine., Palmer Publications., Summer 1980, Fall 1980, & Winter 1980-1981, under the title: "ARZARETH – LAND BEYOND THE POLE" (Forwarded by John Bringingham, who allegedly discovered this manuscript-diary telling of the experiences of the author, the sole survivor of a wrecked whaling vessel in the Arctic Ocean, and his encounter with the Lost Tribes of Israel, who reside in a hidden Polar country in the extreme north.

SOURCE: A Guide to the Inner Earth: M – Subterranean Bases (thinkaboutit. site)

---

8 After God had thus discoursed to them, they went back to the Cave of Treasures. But their flesh was dried up, and their strength failed from fasting and praying, and from the sorrow they felt at having trespassed against God.

CHAPTER 54

Adam and Eve go Exploring

THEN Adam and Eve stood up in the cave and prayed the whole of that night until the morning dawned. And when the sun was risen they both went out of the cave; their heads wandering from heaviness of sorrow, and they not knowing whither they went.

2 And they walked thus unto the southern border of the garden. And they began to go up that border until they came to the eastern border beyond which there was no farther space.

3 And the cherub who guarded the garden was standing at the western gate, and guarding it against Adam and Eve, lest they should suddenly come into the garden. And the cherub turned round, as if to put them to death; according to the commandment God had given him.

4 When Adam and Eve came to the eastern border of the garden-- thinking in their hearts that the cherub was not watching--as they were standing by the gate as if wishing to go in, suddenly came the cherub with a flashing sword of fire in his hand; and when he saw them, he went forth to kill them. For he was afraid lest God should destroy him if they went into the garden without His order.

5 And the sword of the cherub seemed to flame afar off. But when he raised it over Adam and Eve, the flame thereof did not flash forth.

6 Therefore did the cherub think that God was favourable to them and was bringing them back into the garden. And the cherub stood wondering.

7 He could not go up to Heaven to ascertain God's order regarding their getting into the garden; he therefore abode standing by them, unable as he was to part from them; for he was afraid lest they should enter the garden without leave from God, who then would destroy him.

8 When Adam and Eve saw the cherub coming towards them with a flaming sword of fire in his hand, they fell on their faces from fear, and

were as dead.

9 At that time the heavens and the earth shook; and other cherubim came down from heaven to the cherub who guarded the garden and saw him amazed and silent.

10 Then, again, other angels came down nigh unto the place where Adam and Eve were. They were divided between joy and sorrow.

11 They were glad, because they thought that God was favourable to Adam, and wished him to return to the garden; and wished to restore him to the gladness he once enjoyed.

12 But they sorrowed over Adam, because he was fallen like a dead man, he, and Eve; and they said in their thoughts, "Adam has not died in this place; but God has put him to death, for his having come to this place, and wishing to get into the garden without His leave."

CHAPTER 55

God versus Satan

THEN came the Word of God to Adam and Eve, and raised them from their dead state, saying unto them, "Why came ye up hither? Do you intend to go into the garden, from which I brought you out? It cannot be today; but only when the covenant I have made with you is fulfilled."

2 Then Adam, when he heard the Word of God, and the fluttering of the angels whom he did not see, but only heard the sound of them with his ears, he and Eve wept, and said to the angels:

C.1 Adam and Eve are clearly stating that they could still hear the sound of the 'fluttering of the wings' of the angels but that they could no longer see the angels.

3 "O Spirits, who wait upon God, look upon me, and upon my being unable to see you! For when I was in my former bright nature) then I could see you. I sang praises as you do; and my heart was far above you.

C.2 'Then I could see you' and my heart was far above you. What does that mean that Adam and Eve's hearts were far above the angels when they were yet in the Garden of Eden? I think that whilst in the Garden of Eden as Adam and Eve had been fully protected by God and that they were waited on by the angels they were in their element and for the first 7 years after Creation they praised God like unto the angels and had the privilege of being able to the see the angels all the time.

4 "But now, that I have transgressed, that bright nature is gone from me, and I am come to this miserable state. And now am I come to this, that I cannot see you, and you do not serve me as you were wont. For I am become animal flesh.

C.3 'I have transgressed' and that 'bright nature' is gone from me. Adam and Eve were only good whilst in the Garden of Eden until they were allowed to be tested by Satan and they readily fell. Why was that? There is a very good verse in the Bible which states:

'Not a novice lest being lifted up in pride he falls into the condemnation of the devil' -**I Tim 3.6**

5 "Yet now O angels of God, ask God with me, to restore me to that wherein I was formerly; to rescue me from this misery, and to remove from me the sentence of death He passed upon me, for having tres-

passed against Him."

C.4 Sin has brought with it misery and sorrow and the 'sentence of death' upon Adam and Eve.

6 Then, when the angels heard these words, they all grieved over him; and cursed Satan who had beguiled Adam, until he came from the garden to misery; from life to death; from peace to trouble; and from gladness to a strange land.

7 Then the angels said unto Adam, "Thou didst hearken to Satan, and didst forsake the Word of God who created thee; and thou didst believe that Satan would fulfil all he had promised thee.

8 "But now, O Adam, we will make known to thee, what came upon us through him, before his fall from heaven.

9 "He gathered together his hosts, and deceived them, promising them to give them a great kingdom, a divine nature; and other promises he made them.

10 "His hosts believed that. his word was true, so they yielded to him, and renounced the glory of God.

11 "He then sent for us according to the orders in which we were-to come under his command, and to hearken to his vain promise. But we would not, and we took not his advice.

C.5 The time of the Great Rebellion in Heaven happened long before God created the physical Creation. It was a great testing time for God's angels, to see who would follow Satan and who would remain true to God and resist the temptation of pride.

C.6 'Taunting condemnation rained down upon those who remained faithful and who were not accustomed to the ways of war and having to face their former companions, who were intoxicated with the spirit of defiance and rebellion. Many of those Fallen Angels collapsed inwardly, and because of their self-love, and for having worshipped the creature Satan rather than the Creator'. [Except from the book '**Journey to Gragau**' – by Alan W Trenholm]

Peter 2:4 For if God spared not the angels that sinned, but cast them down to

hell, and delivered them into chains of darkness, to be reserved unto judgment.

144

Jude 1:6 And the angels which kept not their first estate, but left their own habitation, he hath reserved in everlasting chains under darkness unto the judgment of the great day.

Matthew 25:41 Then shall he say also unto them on the left hand, 'Depart from me, ye cursed, into everlasting fire, prepared for the devil and his angels.'

---

12 "Then after he had fought with God, and had dealt forwardly with Him, he gathered together his hosts, and made war with us. And if it had not been for God's strength that was with us, we could not have prevailed against him to hurl him from heaven.

13 "But when he fell from among us, there was great joy in heaven, because of his going down from us. For had he continued in heaven, nothing, not even one angel would have remained in it.

C.7 This verse is shocking whether true or not only God knows, but it is stating that if God had not cast out Satan from heaven with his Fallen angels when he did that most of the angels would have ended up falling and that would have been a disaster for us all.

C.8 Strictly speaking, according to the Bible the Devil and his Fallen angels do not get cast out until the end of the game so to speak as it talks about Michael the archangel both in the books of Daniel and Revelations standing up against Satan and his forces in the End-time.

Daniel 12.1 'And at that time shall Michael stand up, the great prince which stands for the children of thy people: and there shall be a time of trouble, such as never was since there was a nation even to that same time: and at that time thy people shall be delivered, every one that shall be found written in the book.

Revelations 12.3-4 'And there appeared another wonder in heaven; and behold a great red dragon, having seven heads and ten horns, and seven crowns upon his heads.

And his tail drew the third part of the stars of heaven, and did cast them to the earth: and the dragon stood before the woman which was ready to be delivered, for to devour her child as soon as it was born.

---

14 "But God in His mercy, drove him from among us to this dark earth; for he had become darkness itself and a worker of unrighteousness.

15 "And he has continued, O Adam, to make war against thee, until he beguiled thee and made thee come out of the garden, to this strange land, where all these trials have come to thee. And death, which God brought upon him he has also brought to thee, O Adam, because thou

---

didst obey him, and didst transgress against God."

16 Then the angels rejoiced and praised God, and asked Him not to destroy Adam this time, for his having sought to enter the garden; but to bear with him until the fulfilment of the promise; and to help him in this world until he was free from Satan's hand.

CHAPTER 56

Divine Comfort

THEN came the Word of God to Adam, and said unto him:

2 "O Adam, look at that garden of joy and at this earth of toil, and behold the angels who are in the garden-that is full of them, and see thyself alone on this earth, with Satan whom thou didst obey.

3 "Yet, if thou had submitted, and been obedient to Me, and had kept My Word, thou wouldst be with My angels in My garden.

4 "But when thou didst transgress and hearken to Satan, thou didst become his guest among his angels, that are full of wickedness; and thou came to this earth, that brings forth to thee thorns and thistles.

5 "O Adam, ask him who deceived thee, to give thee the divine nature he promised thee, or to make thee a garden as I had made for thee; or to fill thee with that same bright nature with which I had filled thee.

6 "Ask him to make thee a body like the one I made thee, or to give thee a day of rest as I gave thee; or to create within thee a reasonable soul, as I did create for thee; or to remove thee hence to some other earth than this one which I gave thee. But, O Adam, he will not fulfil even one of the things he told thee.

7 "Acknowledge, then, My favour towards thee, and My mercy on thee, My creature; that I have not requited thee for thy transgression against Me, but in My pity for thee I have promised thee that at the end of the great five days and a half I will come and save thee."

8 Then God said again to Adam and Eve, "Arise, go down hence, lest the cherub with a sword of fire in his hand destroy you."

9 But Adam's heart was comforted by God's words to him, and he worshipped before Him.

10 And God commanded His angels to escort Adam and Eve to the

cave with joy, instead of the fear that had come upon them.

11 Then the angels took up Adam and Eve and brought them down from the mountain by the garden, with songs and psalms, until they brought them to the cave. There the angels began to comfort and to strengthen them, and then departed from them towards heaven, to their Creator, who had sent them.

12 But, after the angels were gone from Adam and Eve, came Satan, with shamefacedness, and stood at the entrance of the cave in which were Adam and Eve. He then called to Adam, and said, "O Adam, come, let me speak to thee."

13 Then Adam came out of the cave, thinking he was one of God's angels that was come to give him some good counsel.

CHAPTER 57

The Hideous form of Satan

> BUT when Adam came out and saw this hideous figure, he was afraid of him, and said unto him, "Who art thou?"

C.1 Our enemy is a hideous Beast and an indefatigable Warmonger; and he is a snake, sometimes a dragon and extremely cunning, ruthless, fox-like, and is anything and everything else wicked that exists. He is, for the most part, totally unseen (at least in modern times), a spirit, and much more lethal than any human enemy can ever be - Satan our Enemy: the relentless killer of souls.

C.2 Satan, full of vengeful Hatred and Evil, has been waging war on humanity ever since the creation of Adam and Eve. Satan is Disorder, Chaos, and Destruction, all of which, just before being kicked out of Heaven and into the fires of Hell, he threatened he would do to Creation at the time of his rebellion against Jesus.

C.3 Satan's orders to his devils: 'Sow horror, despair, and errors so that the peoples will separate themselves from God, cursing Him'." Source: Satan our Enemy: the relentless killer of souls. By Joseph Costa (pakistanchristianpost. com)

> 2 Then Satan answered and said unto him, "It is I, who hid myself within the serpent, and who talked to Eve, and beguiled her until she hearkened to my command. I am he who sent her, through the wiles of my speech, to deceive thee, until thou and she ate of the fruit of the tree, and ye came away from under the command of God."
>
> 3 But when Adam heard these words from him, he said unto him, "Canst thou make me a garden as God made for me? Or canst thou clothe me in the same bright nature in which God had clothed me?
>
> 4 "Where is the divine nature thou didst promise to give me? Where is that fair speech of thine, thou didst hold with us at first, when we were in the garden?"

C.4 Here is a notable verse as Adam is acknowledging that he was there together with Eve when she was tempted by the serpent at the Tree of the Knowledge of Good and Evil.

C.5 According to this chapter in verse 4 of these Lost books of Adam and Eve, Adam was just as guilty as Eve in the sin of disobedience of God's command to not take fruit from the Tree of the Knowledge of Good and evil. Well, at least it could be argued from this verse that Adam was at least close to the Tree when Satan promised Adam and eve that they would be as gods. Contradictions: Who Gets the Blame for Original Sin—Adam or Eve? | Answers in Genesis

1 Tim 2.14 'And Adam was not deceived, but the woman being deceived was in the transgression.'

> 5 Then Satan said unto Adam, "Thinkest thou, that when I have spoken to one about anything, I shall ever bring it to him or fulfil my word? Not so. For I myself have never even thought of obtaining what I asked.
>
> 6 "Therefore did I fall, and did I make you fall by that for which I myself fell; and with you also, whosoever accepts my counsel, falls thereby.

Genesis 3:5 For God doth know that in the day ye eat thereof, then your eyes shall be opened, and **ye shall be as gods**, knowing good and evil.

> 7 "But now, O Adam, by reason of thy fall thou art under my rule, and I am king over thee; because thou hast hearkened to me, and hast transgressed against thy God. Neither will there be any deliverance from my hands until the day promised thee by thy God."
>
> 8 Again he said, "Inasmuch as we do not know the day agreed upon with thee by thy God, nor the hour in which thou shalt be delivered, for that reason will we multiply war and murder upon thee and thy seed after thee.

C.6 Here, right in the beginning of time itself Satan is threatening to multiply war and murder upon mankind as shown clearly as the 4th Horsemen in Revelations 6. In fact, not only the 4th Horseman of Death followed by the Hell rider, but all the other 3 Horsemen are also bringing with them devastation.

Revelation 6.8 'And I looked and behold a pale horse: and his name that sat on him was Death, and Hell followed with him. And power was given unto them over the fourth part of the earth, to kill with sword, and with hunger, and with death, and with the beasts of the earth.'

> 9 "This is our will and our good pleasure, that we may not leave one of the sons of men to inherit our orders in heaven.
>
> 10 "For as to our abode, O Adam, it is in burning fire; and we will not cease our evil doing no, not one day nor one hour. And I, O Adam, shall

sow fire upon thee when thou comest into the cave to dwell there."

C.7 Satan is promising that he and his fallen angels will not cease to cause trouble for humanity for as long that the earth exists, and this has indeed proven to be true with millions slaughtered by wars and by abortion and by every means possible. Satan is indeed a monster that needs to be locked up, which will soon happen according to Revelations 20.

11 When Adam heard these words he wept and mourned, and said unto Eve, "Hear what he said; that he will not fulfil aught of what he told thee in the garden. Did he then become king over us?

Job.41.30 "He beholds all high *things*: he *is* a king over all the children of pride."

12 "But we will ask God, who created us, to deliver us out of his hands."

C.8 Satan has the enormous power to transform himself and appear to man as an angel of light, luminous as if he were a true angel of God, as if he had been sent to man as a messenger of God. And countless men, throughout the ages, have been beguiled by him in this way, and countless men continue to be beguiled by him to this very day, every day.

II Corinthians 11.14-15 And no marvel; for Satan himself is transformed into an angel of light. [15] Therefore it is no great thing if his ministers also be transformed as the ministers of righteousness; whose end shall be according to their works.

C.9 Satan himself can pass for an angel of light, and his servants have no difficulty in passing for servants of holiness."

151

CHAPTER 58

53rd Day

THEN Adam and Eve spread their hands unto God, praying and entreating Him to drive Satan away from them; that he do them no violence, and do not force them to deny God.

2 Then God sent to them at once His angel, who drove away Satan from them. This happened about sunset, on the fifty-third day after they had come out of the garden.

3 Then Adam and Eve went into the cave and stood up and turned their faces to the earth, to pray to God.

4 But ere they prayed Adam said unto Eve, "Lo, thou hast seen what temptations have befallen us in this land. Come, let us arise, and ask God to forgive us the sins we have committed; and we will not come out until the end of the day next to the fortieth. And if we die herein, He will save us."

James 1.12-16 Blessed is the man that endures temptation: for when he is tried, he shall receive the crown of life, which the Lord hath promised to them that love him.

[13] Let no man say when he is tempted, I am tempted of God: for God cannot be tempted with evil, neither tempts he any man:

[14] But every man is tempted, when he is drawn away of his own lust, and enticed.

[15] Then when lust hath conceived, it bringeth forth sin: and sin, when it is finished, bringeth forth death.

5 Then Adam and Eve arose and joined together in entreating God.

6 They abode thus praying in the cave; neither did they come out of it, by night or by day, until their prayers went up out of their mouths, like a flame of fire.

CHAPTER 59

Eighth apparition of Satan

BUT Satan, the hater of all good, did not allow them to end their prayers. For he called to his hosts, and they came, all of them. He then said to them, "Since Adam and Eve, whom we beguiled, have agreed together to pray to God night and day, and to entreat Him to deliver them, and since they will not come out of the cave until the end of the fortieth day.

2 "And since they will continue their prayers as they have both agreed to do, that He will deliver them out of our hands, and restore them to their former state, see what we shall do unto them." And his hosts said unto him, "Power is thine, O our Lord, to do what thou listest."

3 Then Satan, great in wickedness, took his hosts and came into the cave, in the thirtieth night of the forty days and one; and he smote Adam and Eve, until he left them dead.

C.1 As I have mentioned before, Satan cannot go around beating God's people up without permission from God. Some would argue, 'Well what about poor old Job'? Satan still had to have permission.

Job 1.12 And the LORD said unto Satan, 'Behold, all that he hath is in thy power; only upon himself put not forth thine hand'. So, Satan went forth from the presence of the LORD.

C.2 Why didn't God's angels intervene in this chapter? Sometimes this story of Adam and Eve is making out that Satan can do anything he wants to Adam and Eve, but this simply is not true, or even scriptural. Well, as long as Adam and Eve stay under the shelter of God's wings.

Psalm 91.10-11 There shall no evil befall thee, neither shall any plague come nigh thy dwelling.

[11] For he shall give his angels charge over thee, to keep thee in all thy ways.

C.3 As Jesus said to the Pharisees who murdered him. Forty years after Jesus' death Israel was destroyed by the romans in 70 AD.

Matthew 23:38 "Behold, your house is left unto you desolate." Jesus prophesied the city and the temple's destruction. To His own disciples, He said just three verses later, "There shall not be left here one stone upon another, that shall not be thrown down" (Matthew 24:2).

C.4 Satan does not have the power to randomly attack those who love God.

C.5 God normally warns His children of eminent attacks by the Enemy in the form of Satan or of persecution from the ungodly. God sends his angels and spirit helpers to warn his people of danger as shown clearly in the scriptures. The following verse shows how God protected Joseph and Mary and baby Jesus.

Matthew 1.20 And when they were departed, behold, the angel of the Lord appeared to Joseph in a dream, saying, Arise, and take the young child and his mother, and flee into Egypt, and be thou there until I bring thee word: for Herod will seek the young child to destroy him.

> 4 Then came the Word of God unto Adam and Eve, who raised them from their suffering, and God said unto Adam, "Be strong, and be not afraid of him who has just come to thee."
>
> 5 But Adam wept and said, "Where wast Thou, O my God, that they should smite me with such blows, and that this suffering should come upon us; upon me and upon Eve, Thy handmaid?"

C.6 Do we really think that God is going to let Satan have the upper hand and beat up Eve? That is something that wicked people do to the women and certainly not the righteous.

C.7 It is indeed sadly clear that many women and children are cruelly treated on this planet and probably have been since near to the beginning of the Creation.

Psalm 58:3 [3]The wicked are estranged from the womb: they go astray as soon as they be born, speaking lies.

> 6 Then God said unto him, "O Adam, see, he is lord and master of all thou hast, he who said, he would give thee divinity. Where is this love for thee? And where is the gift he promised?

C.8 There have been millions of human sacrifices by Satan's seed throughout time. Wars, forced abortions, paedophilia, sex-slaves, children sex traffic, forced imprisonment of millions of souls throughout time. Wanton violence and slaughter of innocent peoples or genocides.

C.9 Those who perpetrate those sorts of actions are in modern times described in the Book of revelations as the Merchants of the Earth and are indeed children of Satan or even demons, which continue to lead mankind to his ultimate destruction.

Hosea 12.7 'He is a merchant, the balances of deceit are in his hand: he loveth to oppress'.

154

C.10 One can see many of these types in the world today that are easily identifiable. They are extraordinarily rich and 'uncaring' souls many of whom often talk about eugenics and getting rid of most of the peoples on the earth. The Lost Books of Adam and Eve clearly show repeatedly how evil took over in all of its forms.

---

7 "For once has it pleased him, O Adam, to come to thee, to comfort thee, and to strengthen thee, and to rejoice with thee, and to send his hosts to guard thee; because thou hast hearkened to him, and hast yielded to his counsel; and hast transgressed My commandment but has followed his behest?"

8 Then Adam wept before the Lord, and said, "O Lord because I transgressed a little, Thou hast sorely plagued me in return for it, I ask Thee to deliver me out of his hands; or else have pity on me and take my soul out of my body now in this strange land."

9 Then God said unto Adam, "If only there had been this sighing and praying before, ere thou didst transgress! Then wouldst thou have rest from the trouble in which thou art now."

10 But God had patience with Adam and let him and Eve remain in the cave until they had fulfilled the forty days.

11 But as to Adam and Eve, their strength and flesh withered from fasting and praying, from hunger and thirst; for they had not tasted either food or drink since they left the garden; nor were the functions of their bodies yet settled; and they had no strength left to continue in prayer from hunger, until the end of the next day to the fortieth. They were fallen down in the cave; yet what speech escaped from their mouths, was only in praises.

Matthew 24.26-27 And as it was in the days of Noe, so shall it be also in the days of the Son of man.

27 They did eat, they drank, they married wives, they were given in marriage, until the day that Noah entered into the ark, and the flood came, and destroyed them all.

155

CHAPTER 60

The Devil in Disguise

THEN on the eighty-ninth day, Satan came to the cave, clad in a garment of light, and girt about with a bright girdle.

2 Corinthians 11:14 And no marvel; for Satan himself is transformed into an angel of light.

2 In his hands was a staff of light, and he looked most awful: but his face was pleasant, and his speech was sweet,

3 He thus transformed himself in order to deceive Adam and Eve, and to make them come out of the cave, ere they had fulfilled the forty days.

4 For he said within himself, "Now that when they had fulfilled the forty days' fasting and praying, God would restore them to their former estate; but if He did not do so, He would still be favourable to them; and even if He had not mercy on them, would He yet give them something from the garden to comfort them; as already twice before."

C.1 A staff represented power. Moses was commanded to take a staff (or rod), with which he was to do miracles; and that he took the rod of God in his hand (*Exod.* 4:17).

5 Then Satan drew near the cave in this fair appearance, and said:

6 "O Adam, rise ye, stand up, thou and Eve, and come along with me, to a good land; and fear not. I am flesh and bones like you; and at first, I was a creature that God created.

C.2 The key was that Adam and Eve should not have even listened to the Devil in the first place. Never mind listening to his evil machinations and temptations. As has been said by others, 'If the Devil comes to your door, 'slam the door so hard even if it cuts his nose off'.

James 4.7 'Submit yourselves therefore to God. Resist the devil, and he will flee from you.

7 "And it was so, that when He had created me, He placed me in a garden in the north, on the border of the world.

> 8 "And He said to me, 'Abide here!' And I abode there according to His Word, neither did I transgress His commandment.

C.3 Satan sometimes behaves like that horrible 'Joker' character in the Dark Knight in one of the Batman movies.

Ephesians 6.11 'Put on the whole armour of God, that you may be able to stand against the schemes of the devil'.

> 9 "Then He made a slumber to come over me, and He brought thee, O Adam, out of my side, but did not make thee abide by me.
>
> 10 "But God took thee in His divine hand and placed thee in a garden to the eastward.
>
> 11 "Then I grieved because of thee, for that while God had taken thee out of my side, He had not let thee abide with me.
>
> 12 "But God said unto me: 'Grieve not because of Adam whom I brought out of thy side; no harm will come to him.
>
> 13 "'For now I have brought out of his side a help-meet for him; and I have given him joy by so doing.'"
>
> 14 Then Satan said again, "I did not know how it is ye are in this cave, nor anything about this trial that has come upon you until God said to me, 'Behold, Adam has transgressed, he whom I had taken out of thy side, and Eve also, whom I took out of his side; and I have driven them out of the garden; I have made them dwell in a land of sorrow and misery, because they transgressed against Me, and have hearkened to Satan. And lo, they are in suffering unto this day, the eightieth.'
>
> 15 "Then God said unto me, 'Arise, go to them, and make them come to thy place, and suffer not that Satan come near them, and afflict them. For they are now in great misery; and lie helpless from hunger.'
>
> 16 "He further said to me, 'When thou hast taken them to thyself, give them to eat of the fruit of the Tree of Life, and give them to drink of the water of peace; and clothe them in a garment of light, and restore them to their former state of grace, and leave them not in misery, for

they came from thee. But grieve not over them, nor repent of that which has come upon them.'

17 "But when I heard this, I was sorry; and my heart could not patiently bear it for thy sake, O my child.

18 "But, O Adam, when I heard the name of Satan, I was afraid, and I said within myself, I will not come out, lest he ensnare me, as he did my children, Adam and Eve.

19 "And I said, 'O God, when I go to my children, Satan will meet me in the way, and war against me, as he did against them.'

20 "Then God said unto me, 'Fear not; when thou find him, smite him with the staff that is in thine hand, and be not afraid of him for thou art of old standing, and he shall not prevail against thee.'

21 "Then I said, 'O my Lord, I am old, and cannot go. Send Thy angels to bring them.'

22 "But God said unto me, 'Angels, verily, are not like them; and they will not consent to come with them. But I have chosen thee, because they are thy offspring, and like thee, and will hearken to what thou sayest.'

23 "God said further to me, 'If thou hast not strength to walk, I will send a cloud to carry thee and alight thee at the entrance of their cave; then the cloud will return and leave thee there.

24 "'And if they will come with thee, I will send a cloud to carry thee and them.'

25 "Then He commanded a cloud, and it bare me up and brought me to you; and then went back.

26 "And now O my children, Adam and Eve, look at my hoar hairs and at my feeble estate, and at my coming from that distant place. Come, come with me, to a place of rest."

27 Then he began to weep and to sob before Adam and Eve, and his tears poured upon the earth like water.

28 And when Adam and Eve raised their eyes and saw his beard, and heard his sweet talk, their hearts softened towards him; they hearkened unto him, for they believed he was true.

29 And it seemed to them that they really were his offspring, when they saw that his face was like their own; and they trusted him.

C.4 Satan even utilises verses from the Holy Bible whenever they may prop up or enhance his cause.

Matthew 4.5-6 Then the devil taketh him up into the holy city, and setteth him on a pinnacle of the temple, 6 And saith unto him, if thou be the Son of God, cast thyself down: for it is written, He shall give his angels charge concerning thee: and in their hands they shall bear thee up, lest at any time thou dash thy foot against a stone. –

C.5 He thus quotes holy verses from the Holy Bible to beguile his followers, to paralyse them into believing that he comes from God, as a messenger of God; and, without them realising it, having already been benumbed by his fake holiness are led astray.

C.6 Too many men simply cannot fully imagine or comprehend the cunning power and subtle intricacies of Satan's covert cunning methods. And many of Satan's followers, devil-men, reflect those covert cunning methods in their own daily lives.

C.7 Satan is not called Snake for nothing. But he once got too smart by half, really, as he got kicked out of glorious Heaven and cast down into the tortures and fires of dark Hell.

C.8 "Among the many things which the world denies, swollen as it is with pride and with today's incredulity, is the power and the presence of the demon.

C.9 Atheism which denies God, logically also denies Lucifer: created by God, the rebel of God, the adversary of God, the Tempter, the Envier, the Cunning, the Tireless, the Imitator of God. Source: Satan our Enemy: the relentless killer of souls. By Joseph Costa (pakistanchristianpost.com)

CHAPTER 61

Led Astray

THEN he took Adam and Eve by the hand and began to bring them out of the cave.

2 But when they were come a little way out of it, God knew that Satan had overcome them, and had brought them out ere the forty days were ended, to take them to some distant place, and to destroy them.

3 Then the Word of the Lord God again came and cursed Satan and drove him away from them.

John 12.31 'Now is the judgment of this world; now will the ruler of this world be cast out'.

4 And God began to speak unto Adam and Eve, saying to them, "What made you come out of the cave, unto this place?"

5 Then Adam said unto God, "Didst thou create a man before us? For when we were in the cave there suddenly came unto us a good old man who said to us, 'I am a messenger from God unto you, to bring you back to some place of rest.'

C.1 Adam and Eve keep making the same mistake of wanting to go backwards instead of forwards. They keep looking for ways to get back into the Garden of Eden, but God has already said 'no' many times, so why do they blindly keep going in the same direction?

C.2 They act like little children in this story at least for the first few months, until they started to have a family and learnt some responsibility.

C.3 Desiring to go backwards makes them easy prey for Satan to come along with his many disguises and to tempt them in to believing that they could possibly get back into the Garden. That is naïve, as Satan was the one who got them kicked out of the Garden of Eden or the place of rest in the first place.

C.4 It reminds me of most people today in our Western world. They do what they are told without questioning whether it is right or wrong morally speaking? Is what people do: 'To follow the truth of God's Word', like God required Adam and Eve to do?

C.5 The governments of this world are plainly following Satan's ways and most people do not even blink an eyelid in opposition to all the evils around them.

C.6 Most people are more interested in 'settling down' into some comfort zone of money, success, or popularity especially when young. Not realizing that one's life is very short and could be over tomorrow.

Ps. 103:15–16 "As for man, his days are as grass: as a flower of the field, so he flourishes. "For the wind passes over it, and it is gone; and the place thereof shall know it no more.".) "All flesh is grass, and all the goodliness thereof is as the flower of the field:

C.7 What is really worth living for if not to seek God and find His ways and forsake the ways of this world or Satan's usurped world as it now stands today.

---

6 "And we did believe, O God, that he was a messenger from Thee; and we came out with him; and knew not whither we should go with him."

7 Then God said unto Adam, "See, that is the father of evil arts, who brought thee and Eve out of the Garden of Delights. And now, indeed, when he saw that thou and Eve both joined together in fasting and praying, and that you came not out of the cave before the end of the forty days, he wished to make your purpose vain, to break your mutual bond; to cut off all hope from you, and to drive you to some place where he might destroy you.

8 "Because he was unable to do aught to you unless he showed himself in the likeness of you.

9 "Therefore did he come to you with a face like your own and began to give you tokens as if they were all true.

10 "But I in mercy and with the favour I had unto you, did not allow him to destroy you; but I drove him away from you.

11 "Now, therefore, O Adam, take Eve, and return to your cave, and remain in it until the morrow of the fortieth day. And when ye come out, go towards the eastern gate of the garden."

12 Then Adam and Eve worshipped God and praised and blessed Him for the deliverance that had come to them from Him. And they returned towards the cave. This happened at eventide of the thirty-ninth day.

---

13 Then Adam and Eve stood up and with great zeal, prayed to God, to be brought out of their want for strength; for their strength had departed from them, through hunger and thirst and prayer. But they watched the whole of that night praying, until morning.

14 Then Adam said unto Eve, "Arise, let us go towards the eastern gate of the garden as God told us."

15 And they said their prayers as they were wont to do every day; and they went out of the cave, to go near to the eastern gate of the garden.

16 Then Adam and Eve stood up and prayed, and besought God to strengthen them, and to send them something to satisfy their hunger.

17 But when they had ended their prayers, they remained where they were by reason of their failing strength.

18. Then came the Word of God again, and said unto them, "O Adam, arise, go and bring hither two figs."

19 Then Adam and Eve arose and went until they drew near to the cave.

Ecclesiastes 12:13 'Let us hear the conclusion of the whole matter: Fear God and keep his commandments: for this is the whole duty of man. Let us hear the conclusion of the whole matter: Fear God and keep his commandments: for this is the whole duty of man'.

CHAPTER 62

Fruit trees

BUT Satan the wicked was envious, because of the consolation God had given them.

2 So he prevented them and went into the cave and took the two figs, and buried them outside the cave, so that Adam and Eve should not find them. He also had in his thoughts to destroy them.

3 But by God's mercy, as soon as those two figs were in the earth, God defeated Satan's counsel regarding them; and made them into two fruit-trees, that overshadowed the cave. For Satan had buried them on the eastern side of it.

4 Then when the two trees were grown, and were covered with fruit, Satan grieved and mourned, and said, "Better were it to have left those figs as they were; for now, behold, they have become two fruit-trees, whereof Adam will eat all the days of his life. Whereas I had in mind, when I buried them, to destroy them entirely, and to hide them for eye.

5 "But God has overturned my counsel; and would not that this sacred fruit should perish; and He has made plain my intention and has defeated the counsel I had formed against His servants."

6 Then Satan went away ashamed of not having wrought out his design.

C.1 It always amazes me how that Satan has always been such a bad loser and is always whining and whimpering like a spoilt baby, when he simply can't get his way. He is often feeling sorry for himself.

C.2 The 7 World Empires of Man. Just look at history and the **6 world empires** that have already passed: 1) Egypt 2) Assyria 3) Babylon 4) Medio-Persia, 5) Greece, 6) Rome and their dictators and how wantonly they behaved.

C.3 The 7th World empire will be that of the satanic Anti-Christ and his minions. He will be mentored by his father Satan directly according to scripture.

2 Thessalonians 2.3-4 Let no man deceive you by any means: for that day shall not come, except there come a falling away first, and that man of sin be revealed, the son of perdition; [4] Who opposes and exalts himself above all that is called God, or that is worshipped; so that he as God sits in the temple of God, shewing himself that he is God.

C.4 Satan is full of fury and vengeance, as well as hatred and insane violence, and has all the traits of a psychopath, both unpredictable and also a very dangerous monster.

C.5 The Great Tribulation of the Future Anti-Christ world empire: **Retaliation:** When Satan seems to be losing, he often 'flies into a rage' and takes out his anger on the innocent.

Revelations 12.12-14 Therefore rejoice, ye heavens, and ye that dwell in them. Woe to the inhabitants of the earth and of the sea! for the Devil is come down unto you, having great wrath, because he knows that he hath but a short time.

[13] And when the Dragon saw that he was cast unto the earth, he persecuted the woman which brought forth the man child.

[14] And to the woman were given two wings of a great eagle, that she might fly into the wilderness, into her place, where she is nourished for a time, and times, and half a time, from the face of the Serpent.

CHAPTER 63

Two Fig Trees

BUT Adam and Eve, as they drew near to the cave, saw two fig-trees, covered with fruit, and overshadowing the cave.

2 Then Adam said to Eve, "It seems to me we have gone astray. When did these two trees grow here? It seems to me that the enemy wishes to lead us astray, Sayest thou that there is in the earth another cave than this?

3 "Yet, O Eve, let us go into the cave, and find in it the two figs; for this is our cave, in which we were. But if we should not find the two figs in it, then it cannot be our cave."

4 They went then into the cave, and looked into the four corners of it, but found not the two figs.

5 And Adam wept and said to Eve, "Are we come to a wrong cave, then, O Eve? It seems to me these two fig-trees are the two figs that were in the cave." And Eve said, "I, for my part, do not know."

6 Then Adam stood up and prayed and said, "O God, Thou didst command us to come back to the cave, to take the two figs, and then to return to Thee.

7 "But now, we have not found them. O God, hast Thou taken them, and sown these two trees, or have we gone astray in the earth; or has the enemy deceived us? If it be real, then, O God, reveal to us the secret of these two trees and of the two figs."

8 Then came the Word of God to Adam, and said unto him, "O Adam, when I sent thee to fetch the figs, Satan went before thee to the cave, took the figs, and buried them outside, eastward of the cave, thinking to destroy them; and not sowing them with good intent.

9 "Not for his mere sake, then, have these trees grown up at once; but I had mercy on thee and I commanded them to grow. And they grew

165

to be two large trees, that you be overshadowed by their branches, and find rest; and that I make you see My power and My marvellous works.

10 "And, also, to show you Satan's meanness, and his evil works, for ever since ye came out of the garden, he has not ceased, no, not one day, from doing you some harm. But I have not given him power over you."

11 And God said, "Henceforth, O Adam, rejoice on account of the trees, thou and Eve; and rest under them when ye feel weary. But eat not of their fruit, nor come near them."

12 Then Adam wept, and said, "O God, wilt Thou again kill us, or wilt Thou drive us away from before Thy face, and cut our life from off the face of the earth?

13 "O God, I beseech Thee, if Thou knowest that there be in these trees either death or some other evil, as at the first time, root them up from near our cave, and wither them; and leave us to die of the heat, of hunger and of thirst.

14 "For we know Thy marvellous works, O God, that they are great, and that by Thy power Thou canst bring one thing out of another, without one's wish. For Thy power can make rocks to become trees, and trees to become rocks."

C.1 Fig Trees are mentioned many times in the Bible. But there is another secret held in this parable of the figs in Jeremiah 24. To repeat, one basket had particularly good figs, and the other had very evil figs that could not be eaten, they were so evil. These good and evil figs also hark back to the Tree of the Knowledge of Good and Evil in the Garden, showing that the link of the fig with that tree is correct. The Symbolism of the Fig Tree (hope-of-israel.org)

CHAPTER 64

Earthly Food

THEN God looked upon Adam and upon his strength of mind, upon his endurance of hunger and thirst, and of the heat. And he changed the two fig-trees into two figs, as they were at first, and then said to Adam and to Eve, "Each of you may take one fig." And they took them, as the Lord commanded them.

2 And he said to them, "Go ye into the cave, and eat the figs, and satisfy your hunger, lest ye die."

3 So, as God commanded them, they went into the cave, about the time when the sun was setting. And Adam and Eve stood up and prayed at the time of the setting sun.

4 Then they sat down to eat the figs; but they knew not how to eat them; for they were not accustomed to eat earthly food. They feared also lest, if they ate, their stomach should be burdened and their flesh thickened, and their hearts take to liking earthly food.

5 But while they were thus seated, God, out of pity for them, sent them His angel, lest they should perish of hunger and thirst.

6 And the angel said unto Adam and Eve, "God says to you that ye have not strength to fast until death; eat, therefore, and strengthen your bodies; for ye are now animal flesh, that cannot subsist without food and drink."

7 Then Adam and Eve took the figs and began to eat of them. But God had put into them a mixture as of savoury bread and blood.

8 Then the angel went from Adam and Eve, who ate of the figs until they had satisfied their hunger. Then they put by what remained; but by the power of God, the figs became full as before, because God blessed them.

C.1 The **fig** tree became a metaphor for Israel the **fig** tree is also **symbolic** of

Israel itself – It often **symbolized** the health of the nation both spiritually and physically.

Hosea 9:10 says, "When I found Israel, it was like finding grapes in the desert; when I saw your ancestors, it was like seeing the early fruit on the **fig** tree."

9 After this Adam and Eve arose, and prayed with a joyful heart and renewed strength, and praised and rejoiced abundantly the whole of that night. And this was the end of the eighty-third day.

CHAPTER 65

The Garden is Lost

AND when it was day, they rose and prayed, after their custom, and then went out of the cave.

2 But as they felt great trouble from the food they had eaten, and to which they were not used, they went about in the cave saying to each other:

3 "What has happened to us through eating, that this pain should have come upon us? Woe be to us, we shall die! Better for us to have died than to have eaten; and to have kept our bodies pure, than to have defiled them with food."

4 Then Adam said to Eve, "This pain did not come to us in the garden, neither did we eat such bad food there. Thinkest thou, O Eve, that God will plague us through the food that is in us, or that our inwards will come out; or that God means to kill us with this pain before He has fulfilled His promise to us?"

C.1 I think it highly unlikely that God would have made a mistake in the way that he had created Adam and Eve. Just because they had left the Garden of Eden didn't mean that God had forgotten to give them internal organs to help them digest the physical food. It is possible that eating physical food was something new to them and something that they were unaccustomed to doing, because they had just left the Garden of Eden where their bodies had been more of a spiritual nature.

C.2 Another explanation - as to their sudden discomfort? Well, Adam and Eve who had never eaten physical food before, like a baby had to be careful what they ate and how they ate so that they would not get Indigestion.

C.3 Introduce a baby to simple foods and not complex foods. Perhaps Adam and Eve, not being accustomed to physical food got pains in their stomachs and thought that they were in serious trouble when it was simply indigestion? It was a gradual learning process for Adam and Eve.

5 Then Adam besought the Lord and said, "O Lord, let us not perish through the food we have eaten. O Lord, smite us not; but deal with us according to Thy great mercy, and forsake us not until the day of the promise Thou hast made us."

6 Then God looked upon them, and at once fitted them for eating food; as unto this day; so that they should not perish.

7 Then Adam and Eve came back into the cave sorrowful and weeping because of the alteration in their nature. And they both knew from that hour that they were altered beings, that their hope of returning to the garden was now cut off; and that they could not enter it.

8 For that now their bodies had strange functions; and all flesh that requires food and drink for its existence, cannot be in the garden.

C.4 This proves that the Garden of Eden was on a higher plane.

9 Then Adam said to Eve, "Behold, our hope is now cut off; and so is our trust to enter the garden. We no longer belong to the inhabitants of the garden; but henceforth we are earthy and of the dust, and of the inhabitants of the earth. We shall not return to the garden, until the day in which God has promised to save us, and to bring us again into the garden, as He promised us."

10 Then they prayed to God that He would have mercy on them; after which, their mind was quieted, their hearts were broken, and their longing was cooled down; and they were like strangers on earth. That night Adam and Eve spent in the cave, where they slept heavily by reason of the food they had eaten.

CHAPTER 66

Adam to start work

WHEN it was morning, the day after they had eaten food, Adam and Eve prayed in the cave, and Adam said unto Eve, "Lo, we asked for food of God, and He gave it. But now let us also ask Him to give us a drink of water."

2 Then they arose and went to the bank of the stream of water, that was on the south border of the garden, in which they had before thrown themselves. And they stood on the bank and prayed to God that He would command them to drink of the water.

3 Then the Word of God came to Adam, and said unto him, "O Adam, thy body is become brutish, and requires water to drink. Take ye, and drink, thou and Eve; give thanks and praise."

I Cor 10.31 Whatsoever Ye eat or drink or whatsoever Ye do it all for the glory of God.

4 Adam and Eve then drew near, and drank of it, until their bodies felt refreshed. After having drunk, they praised God, and then returned to their cave, after their former custom. This happened at the end of eighty-three days.

5 Then on the eighty-fourth day, they took two figs and hung them in the cave, together with the leaves thereof, to be to them a sign and a blessing from God. And they placed them there until there should arise a posterity to them, who should see the wonderful things God had done to them.

6 Then Adam and Eve again stood outside the cave, and besought God to show them some food wherewith to nourish their bodies.

7 Then the Word of God came and said unto him, "O Adam, go down to the westward of the cave, as far as a land of dark soil, and there thou shalt find food."

8 And Adam hearkened unto the Word of God, took Eve, and went down to a land of dark soil, and found there wheat growing, in the ear and ripe, and figs to eat; and Adam rejoiced over it.

9 Then the Word of God came again to Adam, and said unto him, "Take of this wheat and make thee bread of it, to nourish thy body withal." And God gave Adam's heart wisdom, to work out the corn until it became bread.

10 Adam accomplished all that, until he grew very faint and weary. He then returned to the cave; rejoicing at what he had learned of what is done with wheat, until it is made into bread for one's use.

CHAPTER 67

More Tricks

BUT when Adam and Eve went down to the land of black mud and came near to the wheat God had showed them, and saw it ripe and ready for reaping, as they had no sickle to reap it withal, they girt themselves, and began to pull up the wheat, until it was all done.

2 Then they made it into a heap; and faint from heat and from thirst, they went under a shady tree, where the breeze fanned them to sleep.

3 But Satan saw what Adam and Eve had done. And he called his hosts, and said to them, "Since God has shown to Adam and Eve all about this wheat, wherewith to strengthen their bodies, and, lo, they are come and have made a heap of it, and faint from the toil are now asleep, come, let us set fire to this heap of corn, and burn it, and let us take that bottle of water that is by them, and empty it out, so that they may find nothing to drink, and we kill them with hunger and thirst.

C.1 This part of the story reminds me of the 4 Horsemen of Revelations chapter 6.

Revelation 6:8 'So I looked, and behold, a pale horse. And the name of him who sat on it was Death, and Hades followed with him. And power was given to them over a fourth of the earth, to kill with sword, with hunger, with death, and by the beasts of the earth'.

C.2 When I first read this part of the story about Adam and Eve learning to use wheat to make flour and bread, I wondered why the writer kept changing from wheat to corn and back again, as if there was no difference between them. I thought I would investigate this exact point and the following surprisingly is what I discovered:

***To **Americans**, 'corn' means only maize which, while sweetcorn is maize, is mostly used as an ingredient in other foods. When you see 'corn' in the list of ingredients, that's maize.*

*In **Britain**, corn is wheat or barley or perhaps oats; it's a general term, and a field of corn could be any of those. When a farmer talks of a cornfield, he means a field where any of those are grown, since the same field may not always have the same grain crop grown in it. Collins Dictionary says 'corn' was applied to the predominant crop in an area; well, once maybe, but there is no predominant crop in most fertile places in the UK. We grow wheat or barley in East Anglia, for example, and some oats are grown (mostly for local horses!) **SOURCE:** What's the difference between corn and wheat? in The*

4 "Then, when they wake up from their sleep, and seek to return to the cave, we will come to them in the way, and will lead them astray; so that they die of hunger and thirst; when they may, perhaps, deny God, and He destroy them. So shall we be rid of them."

5 Then Satan and his hosts threw fire upon the wheat and consumed it. Most Americans Have No Idea How Close They are to Poverty, Starvation, and Death - Survival Dan 101

C.3 Another point is that this book is often introducing new concepts and conditions into the lives of Adam and Eve, the very first humans to walk the planet. Now they are learning to sow crops that could benefit mankind, for both themselves and their descendants.

C.4 This story vividly shows how dangerous Satan really is, and that he is a nasty character bent of destroying God's creation and Adam and Eve and the rest of humanity that would soon follow after them.

C.5 The tragedy today is that so many people believe the Devil's lies, such as: 'There is no God and Satan does not exist'. Nothing could be further from the truth. As the story of the wise little girl's answer to the sceptic when she was told 'There is no Devil' she said 'Well, someone is certainly doing his dirty-work for him'.

C.6 Satan and his minions 'setting fire to the crops', has been a common occurrence in times of war throughout history ever since the ancient pre-Flood times of Adam and Eve.

6 But from the heat of the flame Adam and Eve awoke from their sleep, and saw the wheat burning, and the bucket of water by them, poured out.

7 Then they wept and went back to the cave.

8 But as they were going up from below the mountain where they were, Satan and his hosts met them in the form of angels, praising God.

9 Then Satan said to Adam, "O Adam, why art thou so pained with hunger and thirst? It seems to me that Satan has burnt up the wheat." And Adam said to him, "Ay."

10 Again Satan said to Adam, "Come back with us; we are angels of God. God sent us to thee, to show thee another field of corn, better

than that; and beyond it is a fountain of good water, and many trees, where thou shalt dwell near it, and work the corn-field to better purpose than that which Satan has consumed."

11 Adam thought that he was true, and that they were angels who talked with him; and he went back with them.

12. Then Satan began to lead astray Adam and Eve eight days, until they both fell down as if dead, from hunger, thirst, and faintness. Then he fled with his hosts and left them.

CHAPTER 68

Satan the Destructive Master

THEN God looked upon Adam and Eve, and upon what had come upon them from Satan, and how he had made them perish.

2 God, therefore, sent His Word, and raised up Adam and Eve from their state of death.

3 Then, Adam, when he was raised, said, "O God, Thou hast burnt and taken from us the corn Thou had given us, and Thou hast emptied out the bucket of water. And Thou hast sent Thy angels, who have waylaid us from the cornfield. Wilt Thou make us perish? If this be from Thee, O God, then take away our souls; but punish us not."

James 1.13 Let no man say when he is tempted, that he is tempted of God. For God tempts no man, neither can He be tempted of evil.

4 Then God said to Adam, "I did not burn down the wheat, and I did not pour the water out of the bucket, and I did not send My angels to lead thee astray.

5 "But it is Satan, thy master who did it; he to whom thou hast subjected thyself; My commandment being meanwhile set aside. He it is, who burnt down the corn, and poured out the water, and who has led thee astray; and all the promises he has made you, verily are but feint, and deceit, and a lie.

James 1:14-15 But every man is tempted, when he is drawn away of his own lust, and enticed. 15Then when lust hath conceived, it bringeth forth sin: and sin, when it is finished, bringeth forth death.

C.1 'Well said' or written about Satan. He *is* both dangerous, highly deceptive, and insidious.

C.2 In modern times, rather than directly attack people, Satan often attacks people in their thoughts with constant doubts about themselves, others, life, God, and the spirit world. He loves to get people all confused and messed-up in their hearts and minds.

Romans 8.6-7 For to be carnally minded is **death**, but to be spiritually minded is life and peace. "Because the carnal mind *is* enmity against God: for it is not subject to the law of God, neither indeed can be."

Luke 12:29-31 And seek not ye what ye shall eat, or what ye shall drink, neither be ye of doubtful mind. For all these things do the nations of the world seek after: and your Father knows that ye have need of these things. But rather seek ye the kingdom of God; and all these things shall be added unto you.

C.3 The reason why it would seem that most people more readily listen to the Devil's lies, in all forms, rather that the simple truth that 'God is Love', is simple. It's Pride.

I Peter 5.6 Humble yourselves therefore under the mighty hand of God, that he may exalt you in due season.

C.4 There is an excellent story in the Book of Job talking about Satan, as Leviathan an exceptionally large scaly sea monster, that cannot be killed, and that breathes fire underwater heating up the very waters. It ends up with this remarkable verse:

Job 41.34 "He beholds all high *things*: he *is* a **king** over all the **children of pride**."

---

6 "But now, O Adam, thou shalt acknowledge My good deeds done to thee."

7 And God told His angels to take Adam and Eve, and to bear them up to the field of wheat, which they found as before, with the bucket full of water.

8 There they saw a tree and found on it solid manna; and wondered at God's power. And the angels commanded them to eat of the manna when they were hungry.

Exodus 16.43 And the children of Israel ate manna forty years, till they came to a habitable land: with this meat were they fed, until they reached the borders of the land of Canaan.

---

9 And God adjured Satan with a curse, not to come again, and destroy the field of corn.

Matthew 4.4 But He answered, "It is written: **Man** must **not live** on **bread alone** but on every word that comes from the mouth **of God."**

---

10 Then Adam and Eve took of the corn, and made of it an offering, and took it and offered it up on the mountain, the place where they had offered up their first offering of blood.

11 And they offered this oblation again on the altar they had built at

---

first. And they stood up and prayed, and besought the Lord saying, "Thus, O God, when we were in the garden, did our praises go up to Thee, like this offering; and our innocence went up to thee like incense. But now, O God, accept this offering from us, and turn us not back, bereft of Thy mercy."

Genesis 12.8 And he (Abraham) removed from thence unto a mountain on the east of Bethel, and pitched his tent, having Bethel on the west, and Hai on the east: and there he built an altar unto the LORD, and called upon the name of the LORD.

12 Then God said to Adam and Eve, "Since ye have made this oblation and have offered it to Me, I shall make it My flesh, when I come down upon earth to save you; and I shall cause it to be offered continually upon an altar, for forgiveness and for mercy, unto those who partake of it duly."

1 Jn 2.2 Christ is the atoning sacrifice for our sins, and not only for ours but also for the sins of the whole world.

13 And God sent a bright fire upon the offering of Adam and Eve, and filled it with brightness, grace, and light; and the Holy Ghost came down upon that oblation.

14 Then God commanded an angel to take fire-tongs, like a spoon, and with it to take an offering and bring it to Adam and Eve. And the angel did so, as God had commanded him, and offered it to them.

15 And the souls of Adam and Eve were brightened, and their hearts were filled with joy and gladness and with the praises of God.

16 And God said to Adam, "This shall be unto you a custom, to do so, when affliction and sorrow come upon you. But your deliverance and your entrance into the garden, shall not be until the days are fulfilled, as agreed between you and Me; were it not so, I would, of My mercy and pity for you, bring you back to My garden and to My favour for the sake of the offering you have just made to My name."

17 Adam rejoiced at these words which he heard from God; and he and Eve worshipped before the altar, to which they bowed, and then went back to the Cave of Treasures.

18 And this took place at the end of the twelfth day after the eightieth day, from the time Adam and Eve came out of the garden.

19 And they stood up the whole night praying until morning; and then went out of the cave.

1 Thessalonians 5:16–18 Rejoice always, pray without ceasing, in everything give thanks; for this is the will of God in Christ Jesus for you.

20 Then Adam said to Eve, with joy of heart, because of the offering they had made to God, and that had been accepted of Him, "Let us do this three times every week, on the fourth day Wednesday, on the preparation day Friday, and on the Sabbath Sunday, all the days of our life."

21 And as they agreed to these words between themselves, God was pleased with their thoughts, and with the resolution they had each taken with the other.

22 After this, came the Word of God to Adam, and said, "O Adam, thou hast determined beforehand the days in which sufferings shall come upon Me, when I am made flesh; for they are the fourth Wednesday, and the preparation day Friday.

23 "But as to the first day, I created in it all things, and I raised the heavens. And, again, through My rising again on this day, will I create joy, and raise them on high, who believe in Me; O Adam, offer this oblation, all the days of thy life."

Acts 16:31 - And they said, 'Believe on the Lord Jesus Christ, and thou shalt be saved, and thy house'.

John 5:24 - Verily, verily, I say unto you, 'He that heareth my word, and believeth on him that sent me, hath everlasting life, and shall not come into condemnation; but is passed from death unto life.'

24 Then God withdrew His Word from Adam.

25 But Adam continued to offer this oblation thus, every week three times, until the end of seven weeks. And on the first day, which is the fiftieth, Adam made an offering as he was wont, and he and Eve took it and came to the altar before God, as He had taught them.

CHAPTER 69

12th Apparition of Satan

THEN Satan, the hater of all good, envious of Adam and of his offering through which he found favour with God, hastened, and took a sharp stone from among sharp ironstones; appeared in the form of a man, and went and stood by Adam and Eve.

2 Adam was then offering on the altar, and had begun to pray, with his hands spread unto God.

3 Then Satan hastened with the sharp ironstone he had with him, and with it pierced Adam on the right side, when flowed blood and water, then Adam fell upon the altar like a corpse. And Satan fled.

C.1 I would say that this part of the story of Satan being able to kill Adam and Eve is totally false and is but fantasy. Satan does not have the power to randomly do things. He must get permission from God himself directly to do anything drastic in the lives of one of his servants such as Adam.

C.2 Again, this part of the story would appear to be a 'religious' works trip of either killing oneself or being killed by Satan as some sort of sacrifice. In my opinion these ascetic parts of the story have been deliberately added by 'religionists' to gain merit for human sacrifices which are actually an abomination to God.

I Cor 6.19 'What know ye not that your body is the temple of the Holy Ghost which is in you, which ye have of God, and ye are not your own?'

I Cor 6.20 '"For ye are bought with a price therefore glorify God in your body, and in your spirit, which are God's."

C.3 Suicide is obviously destructive like unto murder and is inspired by Satan himself' Satan was the first murderer. Killing oneself or being killed have no merit as a human sacrifice before God, especially when God did not order it.

C.4 The following is what Jesus said to the 'religious' leaders the Pharisees who in his time or 2000 years ago ended up murdering him:

Jn 8.44 'Ye are of *your* father the devil, and the lusts of your father ye will do. He was a murderer from the beginning, and abode not in the truth, because there is no truth in him. When he speaks a lie, he speaks of his own: for he is a liar, and the father of it.

C.5 Only Christ was pure and worthy enough to 'give his life' as a sacrifice for souls of others.

I Peter 3.18 'For Christ also hath once suffered for sins, the just for the unjust, that he might bring us to God, being put to death in the flesh, but quickened by the Spirit:

---

4 Then Eve came and took Adam and placed him below the altar. And there she stayed, weeping over him while a stream of blood flowed from Adam's side upon his offering.

5 But God looked upon the death of Adam. He then sent His Word, and raised him up and said unto him, "Fulfil thy offering, for indeed, Adam, it is worth much, and there is no shortcoming in it."

6 God said further unto Adam, "Thus will it also happen to Me, on the earth, when I shall be pierced and blood shall flow blood and water from My side and run over My body, which is the true offering; and which shall be offered on the altar as a perfect offering."

7 Then God commanded Adam to finish his offering, and when he had ended it he worshipped before God and praised Him for the signs He had showed him.

8 And God healed Adam in one day, which is the end of the seven weeks; and that is the fiftieth day.

9 Then Adam and Eve returned from the mountain, and went into the Cave of Treasures, as they were used to do. This completed for Adam and Eve, one hundred and forty days since their coming out of the garden.

10 Then they both stood up that night and prayed to God. And when it was morning, they went out, and went down westward of the cave, to the place where their corn was, and there rested under the shadow of a tree, as they were wont.

11 But when there a multitude of beasts came all round them. It was Satan's doing, in his wickedness, to wage war against Adam through marriage.

CHAPTER 70

13th Apparition of Satan

AFTER this Satan, the hater of all good, took the form of an angel, and with him two others, so that they looked like the three angels who had brought to Adam gold, incense, and myrrh.

2 They passed before Adam and Eve while they were under the tree and greeted Adam and Eve with fair words that were full of guile.

3 But when Adam and Eve saw their comely mien, and heard their sweet speech, Adam rose, welcomed them, and brought them to Eve, and they remained all together; Adam's heart the while, being glad because he thought concerning them, that they were the same angels, who had brought him gold, incense, and myrrh.

Ephesians 2.2 In which you once walked, following the course of this world, following the prince of the power of the air, the spirit that is now at work in the sons of disobedience.

4 Because, when they came to Adam the first time, there came upon him from them, peace, and joy, through their bringing him good tokens; so, Adam thought that they were come a second time to give him other tokens for him to rejoice withal. For he did not know it was Satan therefore did he receive them with joy and companied with them.

5 Then Satan, the tallest of them, said, "Rejoice, O Adam, and be glad. Lo, God has sent us to thee to tell thee something."

6 And Adam said, "What is it?" Then Satan answered, "It is a light thing, yet it is a word of God, wilt thou hear it from us and do it? But if thou hearest not, we will return to God, and tell Him that thou wouldest not receive His word."

Ephesians 6.12 'For we wrestle not against flesh and blood, but against principalities, against powers, against the rulers of darkness of this world, against spiritual wickedness in high places.

7 And Satan said again to Adam, "Fear not, neither let a trembling

come upon thee; dost not thou know us?"

8 But Adam said, "I know you not."

9 Then Satan said to him, "I am the angel who brought thee gold, and took it to the cave; this other one is he who brought thee incense; and that third one, is he who brought thee myrrh when thou wast on the top of the mountain, and who carried thee to the cave.

10 "But as to the other angels our fellows, who bare you to the cave, God has not sent them with us this time; for He said to us, 'You suffice.'"

11 So when Adam heard these words he believed them, and said to these angels, "Speak the word of God, that I may receive it."

12 And Satan said unto him "Swear and promise me that thou wilt receive it."

13 Then Adam said, "I know not how to swear and promise."

Matthew 5.34-35 But I say unto you, 'Swear not at all; neither by heaven; for it is God's throne:

[35] Nor by the earth; for it is his footstool: neither by Jerusalem; for it is the city of the great King'.

14 And Satan said to him, "Hold out thy hand, and put it inside my hand."

15 Then Adam held out his hand, and put it into Satan's hand; when Satan said unto him, "Say, now--so true as God is living, rational, and speaking, who raised the heavens in the space, and established the earth upon the waters, and has created me out of the four elements, and out of the dust of the earth--I will not break my promise, nor renounce my word."

16 And Adam swore thus.

17 Then Satan said to him, "Lo, it is now some time since thou came out of the garden, and thou know neither wickedness nor evil. But now

God says to thee, to take Eve who came out of thy side, and to wed her, that she bear thee children, to comfort thee, and to drive from thee trouble and sorrow; now this thing is not difficult, neither is there any scandal in it to thee."

CHAPTER 71

Adam and Eve to Marry

BUT when Adam heard these words from Satan, he sorrowed much, because of his oath and of his promise, and said, "Shall I commit adultery with my flesh and my bones, and shall I sin against myself, for God to destroy me, and to blot me out from off the face of the earth?

2 "Since, when at first, I ate of the tree, He drove me out of the garden into this strange land, and deprived me of my bright nature, and brought death upon me. If, then, I should do this, He will cut off my life from the earth, and He will cast me into hell, and will plague me there a long time.

3 "But God never spoke the words thou hast told me; and ye are not God's angels, nor yet sent from Him. But ye are devils, come to me under the false appearance of angels. Away from me; ye cursed of God!"

4 Then those devils fled from before Adam. And he and Eve arose, and returned to the Cave of Treasures, and went into it.

1 Peter 5.8 'Be sober-minded; be watchful. Your adversary the devil prowls around like a roaring lion, seeking someone to devour.

5 Then Adam said to Eve, "If thou saw what I did, tell it not; for I sinned against God in swearing by His great name, and I have placed my hand another time into that of Satan." Eve, then, held her peace, as Adam told her.

6 Then Adam arose, and spread his hands unto God, beseeching and entreating Him with tears, to forgive him what he had done. And Adam remained thus standing and praying forty days and forty nights. He neither ate nor drank until he dropped down upon the earth from hunger and thirst.

7 Then God sent His Word unto Adam, who raised him up from where he lay, and said unto him, "O Adam, why hast thou sworn by My name,

and why hast thou made agreement with Satan another time?"

8 But Adam wept, and said, "O God, forgive me, for I did this unwittingly; believing they were God's angels."

9 And God forgave Adam, saying, to him, "Beware of Satan."

10 And He withdrew His Word from Adam.

11 Then Adam's heart was comforted; and he took Eve, and they went out of the cave, to make some food for their bodies.

12 But from that day Adam struggled in his mind about his wedding Eve; afraid as he was to do it, lest God should be wroth with him.

13 Then Adam and Eve went to the river of water, and sat on the bank, as people do when they enjoy themselves.

14 But Satan was jealous of them; and would destroy them.

1 John 3.12 By this it is evident who are the children of God, and who are the children of the devil: whoever does not practice righteousness is not of God, nor is the one who does not love his brother.

CHAPTER 72

Tempting Maidens

THEN Satan, and ten from his hosts, transformed themselves into maidens, unlike any others in the whole world for grace.

2 They came up out of the river in presence of Adam and Eve, and they said among themselves, "Come, we will look at the faces of Adam and of Eve, who are of the men upon earth. How beautiful they are, and how different is their look from our own faces." Then they came to Adam and Eve and greeted them; and stood wondering at them.

3 Adam and Eve looked at them also, and wondered at their beauty, and said, "Is there, then, under us, another world, with such beautiful creatures as these in it?"

4 And those maidens said to Adam and Eve, "Yes, indeed, we are an abundant creation."

5 Then Adam said to them, "But how do you multiply?"

6 And they answered him, "We have husbands who wedded us, and we bear them children, who grow up, and who in their turn wed and are wedded, and also bear children; and thus we increase. And if so be, O Adam, thou wilt not believe us, we will show thee our husbands and our children."

C.1 God's very first commandment according to the Bible was that Adam and Eve marry and make love and multiply and fill the earth with their offspring.

Genesis 1:28 God blessed them and said to them, «Be fruitful and multiply, and fill the earth and subdue it; rule over the fish of the sea and the birds of the air and every creature that crawls upon the earth.» God blessed them and said to them, «Be fruitful and increase in number; fill the earth and subdue it.

7 Then they shouted over the river as if to call their husbands and their children, who came up from the river, men, and children; and everyone came to his wife, his children being with him.

8 But when Adam and Eve saw them, they stood dumb, and wondered

at them.

9 Then they said to Adam and Eve, "You see our husbands and our children, wed Eve as we wed our wives, and you shall have children the same as we." This was a device of Satan to deceive Adam.

10 Satan also thought within himself, "God at first commanded Adam concerning the fruit of the tree, saying to him, 'Eat not of it; else of death thou shalt die.' But Adam ate of it, and yet God did not kill him; He only decreed upon him death, and plagues and trials, until the day he shall come out of his body.

11 "Now, then, if I deceive him to do this thing, and to wed Eve without God's commandment, God will kill him then."

12 Therefore did Satan work this apparition before Adam and Eve; because he sought to kill him, and to make him disappear from off the face of the earth.

13 Meanwhile the fire of sin came upon Adam, and he thought of committing sin. But he restrained himself, fearing lest if he followed this advice of Satan God would put him to death.

14 Then Adam and Eve arose, and prayed to God, while Satan and his hosts went down into the river, in presence of Adam and Eve; to let them see that they were going back to their own regions.

15 Then Adam and Eve went back to the Cave of Treasures, as they were wont, about evening time.

16 And they both arose and prayed to God that night. Adam remained standing in prayer, yet not knowing how to pray, by reason of the thoughts of his heart regarding his wedding Eve; and he continued so until morning.

17 And when light arose, Adam said unto Eve, "Arise, let us go below the mountain, where they brought us gold, and let us ask the Lord concerning this matter."

18 Then Eve said, "What is that matter, O Adam?"

19 And he answered her, "That I may request the Lord to inform me about wedding thee; for I will not do it without His order, lest He make us perish, thee and me. For those devils have set my heart on fire, with thoughts of what they showed us, in their sinful apparitions."

20 Then Eve said to Adam, "Why need we go below the mountain? Let us rather stand up and pray in our cave to God, to let us know whether this counsel is good or not."

21 Then Adam rose up in prayer and said, "O God, thou know that we transgressed against Thee, and from the moment we transgressed, we were bereft of our bright nature; and our body became brutish, requiring food and drink; and with animal desires.

C.2 Since when is it 'brutish' to need to eat and drink and since when are normal human desires relegated to 'animal' desires? Well, that clearly depends upon the person doing these things. There is the godly way and the ungodly way.

Ecclesiastes 3.22 'So I perceived that nothing *is* better than that a man should rejoice in his own works, for that *is* his heritage. For who can bring him to see what will happen after him?'

22 "Command us, O God, not to give way to them without Thy order, lest Thou bring us to nothing. For if Thou give us not the order, we shall be overpowered, and follow that advice of Satan; and Thou wilt again make us perish.

23 "If not, then take our souls from us; let us be rid of this animal lust. And if Thou give us no order respecting this thing, then sever Eve from me, and me from her; and place us each far away from the other.

24 "Yet again, O God, when Thou hast put us asunder from each other, the devils will deceive us with their apparitions, and destroy our hearts, and defile our thoughts towards each other. Yet if it is not each of us towards the other, it will, at all events, be through their appearance when they show themselves to us." Here Adam ended his prayer.

CHAPTER 73

Adam and Eve get *Married*

THEN God looked upon the words of Adam that they were true, and that he could long await His order, respecting the counsel of Satan.

2 And God approved Adam in what he had thought concerning this, and in the prayer, he had offered in His presence; and the Word of God came unto Adam and said to him, "O Adam, if only thou had had this caution at first, ere thou earnest out of the Garden of Eden into this land!"

3 After that, God sent His angel who had brought gold, and the angel who had brought incense, and the angel who had brought myrrh to Adam, that they should inform him respecting his wedding Eve.

4 Then those angels said to Adam, "Take the gold and give it to Eve as a wedding gift and betroth her; then give her some incense and myrrh as a present; and be ye, thou and she, one flesh."

C.1 God told Adam and Eve to marry from the very beginning and in fact since their creation as a man and a woman. They did not have to wait to have sex until they came out of the Garden of Eden or wait to be married with some fancy religious ceremony.

C.2 According to one of the versions of the **Lost Books of Adam and Eve**, Eve was in fact 3 months pregnant when Adam and Eve left the Garden of Eden.

C.3 Why all this rigmarole of marriage and having to fast 40 days in advance of getting married and such religious nonsense!

C.4 Somebody, and I suspect it was the Orthodox Eastern church has added their hellish ungodly doctrines to this story - what *was* an exceptionally good story concerning Adam and Eve after they left the Garden.

C.5 The Religionists are at it as usual trying to make out that sex is evil and is of Satan and should be avoided at all costs as it is carnal and but an animal lust'

C.6 This anti-sex doctrine is pure nonsense and is against nature itself in doctrine and thus anti-God and His original commandment to 'Be fruitful and fill the world with your children.

C.7 Unfortunately this false doctrine of the Devil has filled the world today where most young people under 25 in the Western nations are neither marrying nor having children and the world is killing itself off through disobedience to the 1st Commandment by God Himself to 'Be fruitful and multiply'.

C.8 There is nothing wrong with sex and marriage as God is the one who created them to be enjoyed in the right relationships.

C.9 People are not required to climb a tall tree in fasting and praying incessantly for 40 days and nights before they are worthy of getting married and enjoying animal lusts as portrayed by this originally great book which has been corrupted by too much religiosity.

C.10 The truth is that God created Adam and Eve naked as teenagers and introduced them to one another and there was no marriage ceremony or such religious nonsense. Adam took one look at Eve, her being perfectly beautiful and totally naked and he did what any normal healthy many would do. He made love with her from the moment he met her and there was absolutely nothing wrong with that.

Genesis 4.1 "And Adam knew Eve his wife; and she conceived, and bare Cain, and said, I have gotten a man from the LORD."

C.11 The religions like to put God in a box and put sex and marriage in a box and say you are not allowed any pleasure of sex unless you get married and pay a marriage fee and have a big church wedding. What a waste of money and time. When a man genuinely loves a woman and vice -versa they do not need anything but each other and God's blessing to make them fruitful in Him.

Genesis 2.24 'For this reason a man shall leave his father and his mother and be joined to his wife; and they shall become one flesh'.

---

5 Adam hearkened to the angels and took the gold and put it into Eve's bosom in her garment; and bethrothed her with his hand.

6 Then the angels commanded Adam and Eve, to arise and pray forty days and forty nights; and after that, that Adam should come into his wife; for then this would be an act pure and undefiled; and he should have children who would multiply and replenish the face of the earth.

7 Then both Adam and Eve received the words of the angels; and the angels departed from them.

8 Then Adam and Eve began to fast and to pray, until the end of the forty days; and then they came together, as the angels had told them. And from the time Adam left the garden until he wedded Eve, were two hundred and twenty-three days, that is seven months and thirteen days.

9 Thus was Satan's war with Adam defeated.

191

C.12 After the Great Flood when only 8 souls remained on the earth of 4 men and 4 women, what was God's commandment?

Genesis 9:7 "Be fruitful and multiply and fill the earth.

CHAPTER 74

The birth of Cain and Luluwa

AND they dwelt on the earth working, to continue in the well-being of their bodies; and were so until the nine months of Eve's childbearing were ended, and the time drew near when she must be delivered.

2 Then she said unto Adam, "This cave is a pure spot by reason of the signs wrought in it since we left the garden; and we shall again pray in it. It is not meet, then, that I should bring forth in it; let us rather repair to that of the sheltering rock, which Satan hurled at us, when he wished to kill us with it; but that was held up and spread as an awning over us by the command of God; and formed a cave."

3 Then Adam removed Eve to that cave; and when the time came that she should bring forth, she travailed much. So was Adam sorry, and his heart suffered for her sake; for she was nigh unto death; that the word of God to her should be fulfilled: "In suffering shalt thou bear a child, and in sorrow shalt thou bring forth thy child."

C.1 Having a baby does not mean women are 'nigh to death'. Portraying 'having a baby' as something scary and painful is a common myth of modern life of those who have not done their research.

C.2 Childbearing is totally a matter of being prepared in advance and knowing one's own body. There are exercises and things to eat that make childbearing much easier. Childbearing is more like hard work as in climbing a mountain, but not agonizingly painful. That is how my wife described it and she had a lot of children, and all of them born naturally.

C.3 The women who study natural childbirth are miles ahead of the women who do nothing to prepare for the coming of their babies. Childbearing does not have to be torturous, and is a natural process made by God that results in a big blessing: a whole new soul for the kingdom of God. I personally miss the time when we had little children, which now seems like a long time ago. I was present at the natural birth of all our babies. It was a real blessing and miracle to see the babies born. Such a beautiful experience as a couple.

4 But when Adam saw the strait in which Eve was, he arose and prayed to God, and said, "O Lord, look upon me with the eye of Thy mercy, and bring her out of her distress."

5 And God looked at His maid-servant Eve, and delivered her, and she

brought forth her first-born son, and with him a daughter.

6 Then Adam rejoiced at Eve's deliverance, and also over the children she had borne him. And Adam ministered unto Eve in the cave, until the end of eight days; when they named the son Cain, and the daughter Luluwa.

C.4 Here it is stating that Cain had a twin sister.

7 The meaning of Cain is "hater," because he hated his sister in their mother's womb; ere they came out of it. Therefore, did Adam name him Cain.

8 But Luluwa means "beautiful," because she was more beautiful than her mother.

9 Then Adam and Eve waited until Cain and his sister were forty days old, when Adam said unto Eve, "We will make an offering and offer it up on behalf of the children."

10 And Eve said, "We will make one offering for the firstborn son; and afterwards, we shall make one for the daughter."

CHAPTER 75

Birth of Abel and Aklemia

THEN Adam prepared an offering, and he and Eve offered it up for their children and brought it to the altar they had built at first.

2 And Adam offered up the offering, and besought God to accept his offering.

3 Then God accepted Adam's offering, and sent a light from heaven that shone upon the offering. And Adam and the son drew near to the offering, but Eve and the daughter did not approach unto it.

4 Then Adam came down from upon the altar, and they were joyful; and Adam and Eve waited until the daughter was eighty days old; then Adam prepared an offering and took it to Eve and to the children; and they went to the altar, where Adam offered it up, as he was wont, asking the Lord to accept his offering.

5 And the Lord accepted the offering of Adam and Eve. Then Adam, Eve, and the children, drew near together, and came down from the mountain, rejoicing.

6 But they returned not to the cave in which they were born; but came to the Cave of Treasures, in order that the children should go round it, and be blessed with the tokens brought from the garden.

7 But after they had been blessed with these tokens, they went back to the cave in which they were born.

8 However, before Eve had offered up the offering, Adam had taken her, and had gone with her to the river of water, in which they threw themselves at first; and there they washed themselves. Adam washed his body and Eve hers also clean, after the suffering and distress that had come upon them.

9 But Adam and Eve, after washing themselves in the river of water, returned every night to the Cave of Treasures, where they prayed and

were blessed; and then went back to their cave where the children were born.

10 So did Adam and Eve until the children had done sucking. Then, when they were weaned, Adam made an offering for the souls of his children; other than the three times he made an offering for them, every week.

11 When the days of nursing the children were ended, Eve again conceived, and when her days were accomplished, she brought forth another son and daughter; and they named the son Abel, and the daughter Aklia.

12 Then at the end of forty days, Adam made an offering for the son, and at the end of eighty days he made another offering for the daughter, and did by them, as he had done before by Cain and his sister Luluwa.

C.1 Why does it state 40 days for cleansing after the birth of a boy baby and 80 days for a baby girl?

Adam was sent into the Garden of Eden on the **40th day after** the creation of Eve. However, Yahweh sent Eve into the Garden of Eden on the **80th day.** The duration of **purification for the birth** of a male or female child follows the days of **purification** of Adam and Eve since the time before they enter the Garden of Eden.

C.2 The context of purification according to Jewish law for the mother is indirectly "holidays" for the mother as she is free from religious obligation to travel to worship in the sanctuary in Jerusalem and free from marital duty to fulfil the needs of her husband for the stipulated period depending on the gender of the baby. Of course the longer holidays means it is more beneficial to the mother.

Lev 12:2 Speak unto the children of Israel, saying, If a woman have conceived seed, and born a man child: then she shall be unclean seven days; according to the days of the separation for her infirmity shall she be unclean.

Lev 12:4 And she shall then continue in the blood of her purifying three and thirty days; she shall touch no hallowed thing, nor come into the sanctuary, until the days of her purifying be fulfilled.

Lev 12:5 But if she bear a maid child, then she shall be unclean two weeks, as in her separation: and she shall continue in the blood of her purifying threescore and six days.

13 He brought them to the Cave of Treasures, where they received a blessing, and then returned to the cave where they were born. After the

birth of these, Eve ceased from childbearing.

CHAPTER 76

Cain is jealous of Abel

1 AND the children began to wax stronger, and to grow in stature; but Cain was hard-hearted and ruled over his younger brother.

2 And oftentimes when his father made an offering, he would remain behind and not go with them, to offer up.

3 But, as to Abel, he had a meek heart, and was obedient to his father and mother, whom he often moved to make an offering, because he loved it; and prayed and fasted much.

4 Then came this sign to Abel. As he was coming into the Cave of Treasures, and saw the golden rods, the incense, and the myrrh, he inquired of his parents Adam and Eve concerning them, and said unto them, "How did you come by these?"

5 Then Adam told him all that had befallen them. And Abel felt deeply about what his father told him.

6 Furthermore his father Adam, told him of the works of God, and of the garden; and after that, he remained behind his father the whole of that night in the Cave of Treasures.

7 And that night, while he was praying, Satan appeared unto him under the figure of a man, who said to him, "Thou hast oftentimes moved thy father to make an offering, to fast and to pray, therefore I will kill thee, and make thee perish from this world."

8 But as for Abel, he prayed to God, and drove away Satan from him; and believed not the words of the devil. Then when it was day, an angel of God appeared unto him, who said to him, "Shorten neither fasting, prayer, nor offering up an oblation unto thy God. For, lo, the Lord has accepted thy prayer. Be not afraid of the figure which appeared unto thee in the night, and who cursed thee unto death." And the angel departed from him.

9 Then when it was day, Abel came to Adam and Eve, and told them of the vision he had seen. But when they heard it, they grieved much over it, yet said nothing to him about it; they only comforted him.

10 But as to hard-hearted Cain, Satan came to him by night, showed himself and said unto him, "Since Adam and Eve love thy brother Abel much more than they love thee, and wish to join him in marriage to thy beautiful sister, because they love him; but wish to join thee in marriage to his ill-favoured sister, because they hate thee.

11 "Now, therefore, I counsel thee, when they do that, to kill thy brother; then thy sister will be left for thee; and his sister will be cast, away."

12 And Satan departed from him. But the wicked One remained behind in the heart of Cain, who sought many a time, to kill his brother.

C.1 Cain who was of that wicked one.

I JN 3.12 Not as Cain, *who* was of that wicked one, and slew his brother. And wherefore slew he him? Because his own works were evil, and his brother›s righteous."

C.2 Cain was of that wicked one, *the serpent.* He was the child of the serpent. Adam was the Son of God, and we know that God is not wicked. That can only mean that the serpent had intercourse with Eve thus producing Cain with all the ungodly manifestations that his father (the Devil) had. (https://www.kingjamesbibleonline.org/1-John-3-12) [***See APPENDIX FOR MORE ON THIS TOPIC]

CHAPTER 77

Cain and Abel grow apart

BUT when Adam saw that the elder brother hated the younger, he endeavoured to soften their hearts, and said unto Cain, "Take, O my son, of the fruits of thy sowing, and make an offering unto God, that He may forgive thee thy wickedness and thy sin."

Ephesians 4:3 'Endeavouring to keep the unity of the Spirit in the bond of peace.

Romans 16:17 'Now I beseech you, brethren, mark them which cause divisions and offences contrary to the doctrine which ye have learned; and avoid them.

2 He said also to Abel, "Take thou of thy sowing and make an offering and bring it to God, that He may forgive thy wickedness and thy sin."

3 Then Abel hearkened unto his father's voice, and took of his sowing, and made a good offering, and said to his father, Adam, "Come with me, to show me how to offer it up."

4 And they went, Adam and Eve with him, and showed him how to offer up his gift upon the altar. Then after that, they stood up and prayed that God would accept Abel's offering.

5 Then God looked upon Abel and accepted his offering. And God was more pleased with Abel than with his offering, because of his good heart and pure body. There was no trace of guile in him.

6 Then they came down from the altar and went to the cave in which they dwelt. But Abel, by reason of his joy at having made his offering, repeated it three times a week, after the example of his father Adam.

7 But as to Cain, he took no pleasure in offering; but after much anger on his father's part, he offered up his gift once; and when he did offer up, his eye was on the offering he made, and he took the smallest of his sheep for an offering, and his eye was again on it. '

8 Therefore God did not accept his offering, because his heart was full of murderous thoughts.

9 And they all thus lived together in the cave in which Eve had brought forth, until Cain was fifteen years old, and Abel twelve years old.

CHAPTER 78

The first murder is planned

THEN Adam said to Eve, "Behold the children are grown up; we must think of finding wives for them."

2 Then Eve answered, "How can we do it?"

3 Then Adam said to her, "We will join Abel's sister in marriage to Cain, and Cain's sister to Abel."

C.1 Many people cannot understand why Adam and Eve's children had to marry their siblings. The reason is plain. There were no other humans to marry at that time.

C.2 Another important point is that humans were apparently very different in the early days before the Great Flood, and we are told by experts that humans used to have a triple helix in their DNA and not the double helix as we have in modern times. [See the **Appendix** for more about the **Triple Helix**]

C.3 The reason people are not supposed to marry close relatives in modern times is because it could lead to crazy children as the bloodline is simply too close.

C.4 In the times before the Great Flood people's DNA was more complicated and would not have had the same genetic make-up, and thus would not have the same problems.

C.5 In the times before the Flood it did not affect Cain and his sister from marrying and having kids. The kids were normal from a physical DNA point of view, but spiritually? What about Satan's seed. [See: Douglas Hamp – The corrupting of the Image:] https://youtu.be/ME-xZpd9SDk?list=PL-jDMMCskY KfpFneTdJPnHVci4a0kb94w&t=11

4 Then said Eve to Adam, "I do not like Cain because he is hard-hearted; but let them bide until we offer up unto the Lord in their behalf."

1 John 3.12 'Not as Cain, who was of that wicked one, and slew his brother. And wherefore slew he him? Because his own works were evil, and his brother's righteous.'

5 And Adam said no more.

6 Meanwhile Satan came to Cain in the figure of a man of the field, and said to him, "Behold Adam and Eve have taken counsel together

> about the marriage of you two; and they have agreed to marry Abel's sister to thee, and thy sister to him.

Proverbs 6:16-19 These six things doth the LORD hate: yea, seven are an abomination unto him: **A proud look, a lying tongue, and hands that shed innocent blood,** an heart that devises wicked imaginations, feet that be swift in running to mischief, A false witness that speaks lies, and he that soweth discord among brethren.

> 7 "But if it was not that I love thee, I would not have told thee this thing. Yet if thou wilt take my advice, and hearken to me, I will bring thee on thy wedding day beautiful robes, gold and silver in plenty, and my relations will attend thee."

Mark 4.19 'And the cares of this world, and the deceitfulness of riches, and the lusts of other things entering in, choke the word, and it becometh unfruitful.'

> 8 Then Cain said with joy, "Where are thy relations?"
>
> 9 And Satan answered, "My relations are in a garden in the north, whither I once meant to bring thy father Adam; but he would not accept my offer.
>
> 10 "But thou, if thou wilt receive my words and if thou wilt come unto me after thy wedding, thou shalt rest from the misery in which thou art; and thou shalt rest and be better off than thy father Adam."

Matthew 4.9 'All these things will I give thee if thou wilt bow down and worship me' – [Satan trying to tempt Jesus.]

> 11 At these words of Satan, Cain opened his ears and leant towards his speech.

Proverbs 17.4 'A wicked doer giveth heed to false lips; *and* a liar giveth ear to a naughty tongue.'

> 12 And he did not remain in the field, but he went to Eve, his mother, and beat her, and cursed her, and said to her, "Why are ye about taking my sister to wed her to my brother? Am I dead"'"

Exodus 21.15 'And he who strikes his father or his mother shall surely be put to death.'

Deuteronomy 27.16: 'Cursed is one who treats his father or mother contemptuously.'

And all the people shall say, 'Amen.'

> 13 His mother, however, quieted him, and sent him to the field where he had been.
>
> 14 Then when Adam came, she told him of what Cain had done.
>
> 15 But Adam grieved and held his peace and said not a word.

C.6 Why is it that Adam acts so defensively concerning an angry violent person like Cain? Please read the Appendix which explains this point very well. Adam is really in a fix, because of his and Eve's own sins in the Garden of Eden.

C.7 It is said that if another man beats one's son, depending on the circumstances and why it happened, a man might forgive the offense. However, if another man beats another man's wife, then the husband of the woman would seek revenge and deal with the violent man.

C.8 Why does Adam say nothing when Cain beats up his own mother?

C.9 There is no record of this in the Bible.

> 16 Then on the morrow Adam said unto Cain his son, "Take of thy sheep, young and good, and offer them up unto thy God; and I will speak to thy brother, to make unto his God an offering of corn."
>
> 17 They both hearkened to their father Adam, and they took their offerings, and offered them up on the mountain by the altar.
>
> 18 But Cain behaved haughtily towards his brother, and thrust him from the altar, and would not let him offer up his gift upon the altar; but he offered his own upon it, with a proud heart, full of guile, and fraud.

Proverbs 16.18 "Pride *goes* before destruction, and an haughty spirit before a fall."

> 19 But as for Abel, he set up stones that were near at hand, and upon that, he offered up his gift with a heart humble and free from guile.
>
> 20 Cain was then standing by the altar on which he had offered up his gift; and he cried unto God to accept his offering; but God did not accept it from him; neither did a divine fire come down to consume his offering.

Genesis 4.3-7 And in process of time it came to pass, that Cain brought of the fruit of the ground an offering unto the Lord. [5] But unto Cain and to his offering he had not respect. And Cain was very wroth, and his countenance fell.

[6] And the Lord said unto Cain, 'Why art thou wroth? Why is thy countenance fallen?

[7] If thou do well, shalt thou not be accepted? And if thou do not well, sin lies at the door. And unto thee shall be his desire, and thou shalt rule over him.

C.10 This Bible verse is warning Cain that if he continues with a bad attitude, then he might fall into greater sin and mischief, which is exactly what follows with the gruesome murder of his younger brother.

21 But he remained standing over against the altar, out of humour and wroth, looking towards his brother Abel, to see if God would accept his offering or not.

22 And Abel prayed unto God to accept his offering. Then a divine fire came down and consumed his offering. And God smelled the sweet savour of his offering; because Abel loved Him and rejoiced in Him.

23 And because God was well pleased with him, He sent him an angel of light in the figure of man who had partaken of his offering, because He had smelled the sweet savour of his offering, and they comforted Abel and strengthened his heart.

Genesis 4.4 And Abel, he also brought of the firstlings of his flock and of the fat thereof. And the Lord had respect unto Abel and to his offering.

24 But Cain was looking on all that took place at his brother's offering and was wroth on account of it.

25 Then he opened his mouth and blasphemed God, because He had not accepted his offering.

Leviticus 24.16 'And he that blasphemes the name of the LORD, he shall surely be put to death, *and* all the congregation shall certainly stone him: as well the stranger, as he that is born in the land, when he blasphemes the name *of the LORD*, shall be put to death.

26 But God said unto Cain, "Wherefore is thy countenance sad? Be righteous, that I may accept thy offering. Not against Me hast thou murmured, but against thyself."

1 Cor 10.10 'Neither murmur ye, as some of them also murmured, and were destroyed of the destroyer."

27 And God said this to Cain in rebuke, and because He abhorred him and his offering.

28 And Cain came down from the altar, his colour changed and of a woeful countenance, and came to his father and mother and told them all that had befallen him. And Adam grieved much because God had not accepted Cain's offering.

29 But Abel came down rejoicing, and with a gladsome heart, and told his father and mother how God had accepted his offering. And they rejoiced at it and kissed his face.

Isaiah 25:1 O Lord, thou art my God; I will exalt thee, I will praise thy name; for thou hast done wonderful.

30 And Abel said to his father, "Because Cain thrust me from the altar, and would not allow me to offer my gift upon it, I made an altar for myself and offered my gift upon it."

31 But when Adam heard this, he was very sorry, because it was the altar, he had built at first, and upon which he had offered his own gifts.

32 As to Cain, he was so sullen and so angry that he went into the field, where Satan came to him and said to him, "Since thy brother Abel has taken refuge with thy father Adam, because thou didst thrust him from the altar, they have kissed his face, and they rejoice over him, far more than over thee."

33 When Cain heard these words of Satan, he was filled with rage; and he let no one know. But he was laying wait to kill his brother, until he brought him into the cave, and then said to him:

C.11 Just look at this verse and what it reveals: When Cain heard these words of Satan, he was filled with rage.

Rage is the name of a bad and dangerous Fallen demonic spirit, which is involved in causing wars, murder, abortion, and jealousy. This spirit is also mentioned in the **Book of Enoch** by another name. Rage comes from Satan and it is also shown in his fallen angels and demons.

Enoch 69.4,7 [Talking about the Fallen angels who came down to the daughters of men in around 600 years after the Creation] And the third was Gadreel; he it is who showed the children of men all the blows of death, and led astray Eve, and showed the weapons of death to the sons of men, the shield and coat of mail, and the sword for battle, and all the weapons of death to the children of men. And from him have proceeded against who dwell on the earth from that day and for evermore.7 And the fifth was Kasdeja; this is he who showed the children of men all the wicked smitings of spirits and demons, and the smitings of the embryo in the womb, that it may pass away and the smitings of the soul. [See my book **Enoch Insights** for more details on this topic]

Ecclesiastes 7.9 'Be not hasty in thy spirit to be angry: for anger rests in the bosom of fools'.

Proverbs 22.24 'Make no friendship with an angry man; and with a furious man thou shalt not go.'

---

34 "O brother, the country is so beautiful, and there are such beautiful and pleasurable trees in it, and charming to look at! But brother, thou hast never been one day in the field to take thy pleasure therein.

35 "To-day, O, my brother, I very much wish thou would come with me into the field, to enjoy thyself and to bless our fields and our flocks, for thou art righteous, and I love thee much, O my brother! but thou hast estranged thyself from me."

Proverbs 16.29 A man of violence entices his neighbour and leads him in a way that is not good.

---

36 Then Abel consented to go with his brother Cain into the field.

Psalm 78.36 But they deceived Him with their mouth and lied to Him with their tongue.

---

37 But before going out, Cain said to Abel, "Wait for me, until I fetch a staff, because of wild beasts."

38 Then Abel stood waiting in his innocence. But Cain, the forward, fetched a staff and went out.

C.12 It would appear, that Abel, being as yet only 15 years old, was totally unaware of the grave danger that he was in.

2 Corinthians 2.11 'Lest Satan should get an advantage of us: for we are not ignorant of his devices'.

39 And they began, Cain and his brother Abel, to walk in the way; Cain talking to him, and comforting him, to make him forget everything.

C.13 Talk about 'bating a trap' for your brother! Imagine what kind of spirit Cain had as to lure his brother away from safety, by saying kind things to hypnotise Abel into a false sense of safety, when all the while he was intending to slay him. This reminds me exactly of the massive python snake Kaa in the kid's Disney movie: 'Jungle Book', when he wanted to hypnotise Mowgli, so that he could both kill him and devour him.

CHAPTER 79

Cain Is Cursed

AND so, they went on, until they came to a lonely place, where there were no sheep; then Abel said to Cain, "Behold, my brother, we are weary of walking; for we see none of the trees, nor of the fruits, nor of the verdure, nor of the sheep, nor any one of the things of which thou didst tell me. Where are those sheep of thine thou didst tell me to bless?"

C.1 This story is different from the biblical narrative. According to the Bible, Abel was a keeper of sheep and Cain a tiller of the ground.

Genesis 4.2b ". And Abel was a keeper of sheep, but Cain was a tiller of the ground."

2 Then Cain said to him, "Come on, and presently thou shalt see many beautiful things. but go before me, until I come up to thee."

3 Then went Abel forward, but Cain remained behind him.

4 And Abel was walking in his innocence, without guile; not believing his brother would kill him.

5 Then Cain, when he came up to him, comforted him with his talk, walking a little behind him; then he hastened, and smote him with the staff, blow upon blow, until he was stunned,

6 But when Abel fell down upon the ground, seeing that his brother meant to kill him, he said to Cain, "O, my brother, have pity on me. By the breasts we have sucked, smite me not! By the womb that bare us and that brought us into the world, smite me not unto death with that staff! If thou wilt kill me, take one of these large stones, and kill me outright."

7 Then Cain, the hard-hearted, and cruel murderer, took a large stone, and smote his brother with it upon the head, until his brains oozed out, and he weltered in his blood, before him.

Genesis 4.8 And Cain talked with Abel his brother: and it came to pass, when they were in the field, that Cain rose up against Abel his brother, and slew him.

And the LORD said unto Cain, 'Where *is* Abel thy brother?' And he said, I know not:

Am I my brother›s keeper?

And he said, 'What hast thou done? the voice of thy brother's blood cries unto me from the ground.'

And now *art* thou cursed from the earth, which hath opened her mouth to receive thy brother›s blood from thy hand; When thou till the ground, it shall not henceforth yield unto thee her strength; a fugitive and a vagabond shalt thou be in the earth.

---

8 And Cain repented not of what he had done.

9 But the earth, when the blood of righteous Abel fell upon it, trembled, as it drank his blood, and would have brought Cain to naught for it.

10 And the blood of Abel cried mysteriously to God, to avenge him of his murderer.

11 Then Cain began at once to dig the earth wherein to lay his brother; for he was trembling from the fear that came upon him, when he saw the earth tremble on his account.

12 He then cast his brother into the pit he made and covered him with dust. But the earth would not receive him; but it threw him up at once.

13 Again did Cain dig the earth and hid his brother in it; but again, did the earth throw him up on itself; until three times did the earth thus throw up on itself the body of Abel.

14 The muddy earth threw him up the first time, because he was not the first creation; and it threw him up the second time and would not receive him, because he was righteous and good, and was killed without a cause; and the earth threw him up the third time and would not receive him, that there might remain before his brother a witness against him.

15 And so did the earth mock Cain, until the Word of God, came to him concerning his brother.

C.1 What an incredible account of the murder of Abel by his brother Cain. First, in verse 10: '*the blood of Abel cried mysteriously to God, to avenge him of his murderer.*'

C.2 '*trembling from the fear that came upon him*' See Flavius Josephus description of Cain from the Antiquities of the Jews.

C.3 *'The earth refused three times to receive his body into the earth'* in verses 13-14 is making an incredible statement: *'Three times did the earth thus throw up on itself the body of Abel.' It threw him up the first time, because he was not the first creation; and it threw him up the second time and would not receive him, because he was righteous and good, and was killed without a cause; and the earth threw him up the third time and would not receive him'*

C.4 The above version of the murder of Abel by Cain is described in an amazing way! However, as strange as this part of the story seems, it is not the first time that I have read about the earth or Mother Earth as some would call her acting as if it were alive, believe it or not and the earth is described as female.

C.5 If you read my book '**Jasher Insights' Book II: Chapter 67.51-61,** you will also read a story about the earth acting alive.

C.6 When Pharaoh ordered all the male babies of the children of Israel to be killed, the following is what happened supernaturally by the Hand of God Himself:

Book of Jasher: 67.56 'And God had compassion over them and desired to multiply them upon the face of the land, he ordered the earth to receive them to be preserved therein till the time of their growing up, after which the earth opened its mouth and vomited them forth and they sprouted forth from the city like the herb of the earth, and the grass of the forest, and they returned each to his family and to his father's house and they remained there.'

C.7 There are also verses like that in my other book '**Ezdras Insights':**

2 ESDRAS Chapter 7.24 'And he (angel speaking to the prophet Ezra in around 500 BC) said unto me 'Not only that but ask the earth and she will tell you. Defer to her and she will declare it to you. Say to her, 'You produce gold and silver and brass and also iron and clay, but silver is more abundant than gold, and brass than silver, and iron than brass, and lead than iron, and clay than lead.'

C.8 Examples of strange and unexpected miracles in the Bible. Things are not necessarily what they seem in certain circumstances. It is as though we live in a simulation where sometimes things around us can be instantly changed if God so wills it. As they say, 'Never say never' and with God nothing is impossible.

Luke 1.37 'For with God nothing shall be impossible'.

C.9 In the Bible there are many stories of unusual and miraculous unexpected things happening. such as the talking donkey story. [See: Numbers 22.21-39]

C.10 The whale or big fish that swallowed Jonah the prophet for three days and then spewed him up on the shores of Ninevah:

Book of Jonah:1.17 'Now the Lord had prepared a great fish to swallow up Jonah. And Jonah was in the belly of the fish for 3 days and 3 nights.

Book of Jonah 2.1 'And Jonah prayed unto the Lord his God out of the fish's belly.'

211

2.10 And the Lord spoke to the fish, and it vomited up Jonah upon the dry land'.

---

16 Then was God angry, and much displeased at Abel's death; and He thundered from heaven, and lightnings went before Him, and the Word of the Lord God came from heaven to Cain, and said unto him, "Where is Abel thy brother?"

Genesis 4.9a And the Lord said unto Cain, 'Where is Abel thy brother?'

---

17 Then Cain answered with a proud heart and a gruff voice, "How, O God? am I my brother's keeper?"

Genesis 4.9b And he said, 'I know not: Am I my brother's keeper?'

---

18 Then God said unto Cain, "Cursed be the earth that has drunk the blood of Abel thy brother; and thou, be thou trembling and shaking; and this will be a sign unto thee, that whosoever finds thee, shall kill thee."

Genesis 4.10-12 And he said, 'What hast thou done?' The voice of thy brother's blood cries unto me from the ground.

[11] And now art thou cursed from the earth, which hath opened her mouth to receive thy brother's blood from thy hand; [12] When thou till the ground, it shall not henceforth yield unto thee her strength; a fugitive and a vagabond shalt thou be in the earth.

---

19 But Cain wept because God had said those words to him; and Cain said unto Him "O God, whosoever finds me shall kill me, and I shall be blotted out from the face of the earth."

Genesis 4.13-14 And Cain said unto the LORD, MY PUNISHMENT IS GREATER THAN I CAN BEAR.[14] Behold, thou hast driven me out this day from the face of the earth; and from thy face shall I be hid; and I shall be a fugitive and a vagabond in the earth; and it shall come to pass, that every one that finds me shall slay me.

---

20 Then God said unto Cain, "Whosoever shall find thee shall not kill thee;" because before this, God had been saying to Cain, "I shall forego seven punishments on him who kills Cain." For as to the word of God to Cain, "Where is thy brother?" God said it in mercy for him, to try and make him repent.

Genesis 4.15-16 And the Lord said unto him, 'Therefore whosoever slays Cain, vengeance shall be taken on him sevenfold.' And the Lord set a mark upon Cain, lest any finding him should kill him.

[16] And Cain went out from the presence of the Lord, and dwelt in the land of Nod, on the east OF EDEN.

---

21 For if Cain had repented at that time, and had said, "O God, forgive me my sin, and the murder of my brother," God would then have forgiven him his sin.

22 And as to God saying to Cain, "Cursed be the ground that has drunk the blood of thy brother" that also, was God's mercy on Cain. For God did not curse him, but He cursed the ground; although it was not the ground that had killed Abel and had committed iniquity.

23 For it was meet that the curse should fall upon the murderer; yet in mercy did God so manage His thoughts as that no one should know it and turn away from Cain.

24 And He said to him, "Where is thy brother?" To which he answered and said, "I know not." Then the Creator said to him, "Be trembling and quaking."

C.11 Here we see God curse Cain with a spirit of trembling and quaking, which would be horrific to endure, all because of one's sins and crimes. Without the Saviour we would all be lost in our sins like Cain.

---

25 Then Cain trembled and became terrified; and through this sign did God make him an example before all the creation, as the murderer of his brother. Also did God bring trembling and terror upon him, that he might see the peace in which he was at first and see also the trembling and terror he endured at the last; so that he might humble himself before God, and repent of his sin, and seek the peace he enjoyed at first.

26 And in the word of God that said, "I will forego seven punishments on whomsoever kills Cain," God was not seeking to kill Cain with the sword, but He sought to make him die of fasting, and praying and weeping by hard rule, until the time that he was delivered from his sin.

C.12 Here we see that whosoever kills Cain will be 7- fold cursed! Why is this fact so important in our story one may ask?

---

27 And the seven punishments are the seven generations during which

213

God awaited Cain for the murder of his brother.

28 But as to Cain, ever since he had killed his brother, he could find no rest in any place; but went back to Adam and Eve, trembling, terrified, and defiled with blood.

C.13 See my book **'ENOCH INSIGHTS'** chapter 64 concerning Cain.

THE LOST BOOKS OF ADAM AND EVE
BOOK 2

Cain marries Luluwa

WHEN Luluwa heard Cain's words, she wept and went to her father and mother, and told them how that Cain had killed his brother Abel.

2 Then they all cried aloud and lifted up their voices, and slapped their faces, and threw dust upon their heads, and rent asunder their garments, and went out and came to the place where Abel was killed.

3 And they found him lying on the earth, killed, and beasts around him; while they wept and cried because of this just one. From his body, by reason of its purity, went forth a smell of sweet spices.

C.1 In the above verse, it is interesting how the animals were a silent testimony that something 'out of place' had happened. There are some stories both in the Bible and apocryphal books, which talk about the behaviour of animals in strange circumstances.

C.2 In the following story from the Bible, a lion had killed the 'young prophet' but it did not eat him. God had sent the lion to kill the prophet because of his disobedience.

I Kings 13.28 And he (The Old Prophet) went and found the body (of the young prophet) lying in the road, with the donkey and the lion standing beside it. The lion had not eaten the body or mauled the donkey.

4 And Adam carried him, his tears streaming down his face; and went to the Cave of Treasures, where he laid him, and wound him up with sweet spices and myrrh.

5 And Adam and Eve continued by the burial of him in great grief a hundred and forty days. Abel was fifteen and a half years old, and Cain seventeen years and a half.

6 As for Cain, when the mourning for his brother was ended, he took his sister Luluwa and married her, without leave from his father and mother; for they could not keep him from her, by reason of their heavy heart.

7 He then went down to the bottom of the mountain, away from the

garden, near to the place where he had killed his brother.

C.3 Cain moves to the 'land of Nod' according to the Bible at the bottom of the mountain and away from the Garden of Eden.

Genesis 4.16 And Cain went out from the presence of the LORD, and dwelt in the land of Nod, on the east of Eden.

8 And in that place were many fruit trees and forest trees. His sister bare him children, who in their turn began to multiply by degrees until they filled that place.

9 But as for Adam and Eve, they came not together after Abel's funeral, for seven years. After this, however, Eve conceived; and while she was with child, Adam said to her "Come, let us take an offering and offer it up unto God, and ask Him to give us a fair child, in whom we may find comfort, and whom we may join in marriage to Abel's sister."

C.4 *'came not together after Abel's funeral, for seven years'*. Here it states that Adam and Eve stopped having sex together as a married couple, because they did not want to have children for a season of 7 years, because of their great grief at the murder of their son Abel and subsequent loss of their first-born son Cain - because of God's banishment of him.

C.5 A very severe situation indeed, with very great sorrow and personal privation.

C.6 Adam and Eve must have thought that if they had continued to 'make love' during the time of their 'great sorrow' with the loss of their righteous son Abel, that Eve would immediately get pregnant again, and they simply emotionally could not handle that possibility - at that time of very great sorrow and pain.

10 Then they prepared an offering and brought it up to the altar, and offered it before the Lord, and began to entreat Him to accept their offering, and to give them a good offspring.

11 And God heard Adam and accepted his offering. Then, they worshipped, Adam, Eve, and their daughter, and came down to the Cave of Treasures and placed a lamp in it, to burn by night and by day before the body of Abel.

C.7 At the death of Abel, Adam and Eve decided to place a lamp inside the Cave of Treasures before the body of Abel. Why did they do this one might ask? Does this also symbolise something?

217

12 Then Adam and Eve continued fasting and praying until Eve's time came that she should be delivered, when she said to Adam: "I wish to go to the cave in the rock, to bring forth in it."

13 And he said, "Go and take with thee thy daughter to wait on thee; but I will remain in this Cave of Treasures before the body of my son Abel."

C.8 Notice that by this time Adam and Eve had already had Cain and Abel, Luluwa and her sister and now Eve is expecting another child. When in time did this happen? According to the KJV of the Bible Time Chart their next child Seth was born when Adam was 130 years old. **BIBLICAL LONGEVITY TIMECHART FROM ADAM TO JOSEPH**: Patriarch Lifespans (godmadeus. com)

14 Then Eve hearkened to Adam, and went, she and her daughter. But Adam remained by himself in the Cave of Treasures.

CHAPTER 2 (81)

A 3ʳᵈ Son is born to Adam and Eve

AND Eve brought forth a son perfectly beautiful in figure and in countenance. His beauty was like that of his father Adam, yet more beautiful.

Genesis 5.3 And Adam lived 130 years and begat a son in his own likeness, after his image, and called his name Seth.

Genesis 5.4 And the days of Adam after he had begotten Seth were 800 years: and he begat sons and daughters.

Genesis 5.5 And all the days of Adam were 930 years.

2 Then Eve was comforted when she saw him and remained eight days in the cave; then she sent her daughter unto Adam to tell him to come and see the child and name him. But the daughter stayed in his place by the body of her brother, until Adam returned. So did she.

3 But when Adam came and saw the child's good looks, his beauty, and his perfect figure, he rejoiced over him, and was comforted for Abel. Then he named the child Seth, that means, "that God has heard my prayer, and has delivered me out of my affliction." But it means also "power and strength."

4 Then after Adam had named the child, he returned to the Cave of Treasures; and his daughter went back to her mother.

5 But Eve continued in her cave, until forty days were fulfilled, when she came to Adam, and brought with her the child and her daughter.

6 And they came to a river of water, where Adam and his daughter washed themselves, because of their sorrow for Abel; but Eve and the babe washed for purification.

7 Then they returned, and took an offering, and went to the mountain and offered it up, for the babe; and God accepted their offering, and sent His blessing upon them, and upon their son Seth; and they came back to the Cave of Treasures.

8 As for Adam, he knew not again his wife Eve, all the days of his life; neither was any more offspring born of them; but only those five, Cain, Luluwa, Abel, Aklia, and Seth alone.

C.1 This verse 8 is simply incorrect, as Adam and Eve continued having children throughout their long life of 930 years. According to the Book of Jubilees Adam and Eve had at least 12 sons altogether and many daughters. They had at least 24 children during their lifetime and possible a lot more.

Jubilees 4.11 And Adam knew Eve his wife and she bare him yet 9 sons.

9 But Seth waxed in stature and in strength; and began to fast and pray, fervently.

CHAPTER 3 (82)

Satan appears as a Temptress

AS for our father Adam, at the end of seven years from the day he had been severed from his wife Eve, Satan envied him, when he saw him thus separated from her; and strove to make him live with her again.

C.1 We were told in chapter 1.9 or 80.9: *'But as for Adam and Eve, they came not together after Abel's funeral or seven years.'* This was because of their great grief over the murder of their son Abel by their eldest son Cain. As a result of the murder of Abel they in fact had lost both of their first two sons.

2 Then Adam arose and went up above the Cave of Treasures; and continued to sleep there night by night. But as soon as it was light every day he came down to the cave, to pray there and to receive a blessing from it.

3 But when it was evening, he went up on the roof of the cave, where he slept by himself, fearing lest Satan should overcome him. And he continued thus apart thirty-nine days.

4 Then Satan, the hater of all good, when he saw Adam thus alone, fasting and praying, appeared unto him in the form of a beautiful woman, who came and stood before him in the night of the fortieth day, and said unto him:

5 "O Adam, from the time ye have dwelt in this cave, we have experienced great peace from you, and your prayers have reached us, and we have been comforted about you.

6 "But now, O Adam, that thou hast gone up over the roof of the cave to sleep, we have had doubts about thee, and a great sorrow has come upon us because of thy separation from Eve. Then again, when thou art on the roof of this cave, thy prayer is poured out, and thy heart wanders from side to side.

7 "But when thou was in the cave thy prayer was like fire gathered together; it came down to us, and thou didst find rest.

8 "Then I also grieved over thy children who are severed from thee; and my sorrow is great about the murder of thy son Abel; for he was righteous; and over a righteous man everyone will grieve.

9 "But I rejoiced over the birth of thy son Seth; yet after a little while I sorrowed greatly over Eve, because she is my sister. For when God sent a deep sleep over thee, and drew her out of thy side, He brought me out also with her. But He raised her by placing her with thee, while He lowered me.

10 "I rejoiced over my sister for her being with thee. But God had made me a promise before, and said, 'Grieve not; when Adam has gone up on the roof of the Cave of Treasures, and is separated from Eve his wife, I will send thee to him, thou shalt join thyself to him in marriage, and bear him five children, as Eve did bear him five.'

C.2 Notice the big lie that Satan tells whilst also masquerading as a young seductive woman, that he is claiming to be the twin sister of Eve.

C.3 Many twins were born of the gods according to legend. See the **Appendix** for more about famous and infamous twins in ancient history.

11 "And now, lo! God's promise to me is fulfilled; for it is He who has sent me to thee for the wedding; because if thou wed me, I shall bear thee finer and better children than those of Eve.

12 "Then again, thou art as yet but a youth; end not thy youth in this world in sorrow; but spend the days of thy youth in mirth and pleasure. For thy days are few and thy trial is great. Be strong; end thy days in this world in rejoicing. I shall take pleasure in thee, and thou shall rejoice with me in this wise, and without fear.

Numbers 25.1-3 While Israel remained at Shittim, the people began to play the harlot with the daughters of Moab. For they invited the people to the sacrifices of their gods, and the people ate and bowed down to their gods. So, Israel joined themselves to Baal of Peor, and the Lord was angry against Israel.

13 "Up, then, and fulfil the command of thy God," she then drew near to Adam, and embraced him.

14 But when Adam saw that he should be overcome by her, he prayed to God with a fervent heart to deliver him from her.

15 Then God sent His Word unto Adam, saying, "O Adam, that figure is the one that promised thee the Godhead, and majesty; he is not favourably disposed towards thee; but shows himself to thee at one time in the form of a woman; another moment, in the likeness of an angel; on another occasions, in the similitude of a serpent; and at another time, in the semblance of a god; but he does all that only to destroy thy soul.

C.4 This verse 15 is utterly amazing in that it reveals how Satan can show himself in many different forms including in a female form, as a woman. Sometimes Satan appears as an apparition and at other times as himself. Apparently, according to the Book of Enoch other 'fallen angels' can also be shape-shifters:

Book of Enoch:19.1 And Uriel (archangel) said to me, 'Here stand the angels who have connected themselves with women and their spirits assuming many different forms are defiling mankind and shall lead them astray into sacrificing to demons as gods. Here shall they stand until the day of the Great Judgement in the which they shall be judged until they are made an end of.'

16 "Now, therefore, O Adam, understanding thy heart, I have delivered thee many a time from his hands; in order to show thee that I am a merciful God; and that I wish thy good, and that I do not wish thy ruin."

223

CHAPTER 4 (83)

The Devil in his Real Form

1.THEN God ordered Satan to show himself to Adam plainly, in his own hideous form.

C.1 This verse 1 is likewise very interesting, because it would suggest that the spirits of the fallen angels and their sons the demons or otherwise known as the 'disembodied spirits of the giants', are able to either appear in different forms to suit a give situation according to whom they are communicating with, but more importantly, they can project an image of themselves that is not true, such as Satan being a woman when he clearly is not. That was an illusion.

C.2 Here is an example of the disembodied spirits of the Giants from before the Great Flood coming back as demons to torment mankind after the Great Flood in the book of Jubilees:

Book of Jubilees: 10.1-2 And in the third week of this Jubilee the unclean demons began to lead astray the children of the sons of Noah and to make to err and to destroy them. And the sons of Noah came to Noah their father and they told him concerning the demons which were leading astray and blinding and slaying his sons' sons.

2 But when Adam saw him, he feared, and trembled at the sight of him.

C.3 What form did Satan appear in this case? I have read about Satan being a snake or a red dragon. I have also read about him coming in the form of a man or a woman young and old. Does he sometimes show up as some sort of chimera like Pan for example as a half goat/half-man. On this occasion it is not stated in what form Satan showed himself to Adam, but obviously he was scary to look at.

3 And God said to Adam, "Look at this devil, and at his hideous look, and know that he it is who made thee fall from brightness into darkness, from peace and rest to toil and misery.

4 And look, O Adam, at him, who said of himself that he is God! Can God be black? Would God take the form of a woman? Is there any one stronger than God? And can He be overpowered?

5 "See, then, O Adam, and behold him bound in thy presence, in the air, unable to flee away! Therefore, I say unto thee, be not afraid of him; henceforth take care, and beware of him, in whatever he may do to thee."

C.4 In the Hebrew **Book of Jasher,** Satan took of different forms also. Sometimes as an old man and at another time as a young man and yet on another occasion as an inanimate object such as a deep stream of water. He came in an inanimate form to try and drown Abraham and Isaac in the desert.

JASHER 23.25 And while Abraham was proceeding with his son Isaac along the road, Satan came and appeared unto Abraham in the figure of a very aged man, humble and of contrite spirit, and he approached Abraham and said unto him, 'Art you silly or brutish, that thou go to do this thing this day to thine only son?

C.5 This story apparently happened when Abraham was called by God to go and sacrifice his only son Isaac on a mountain.

JASHER 23.29 And Satan returned and came to Isaac and he appeared unto Isaac in the figure of a young man comely and well favoured.

JASHER 23.34 And Abraham still rebuked Satan and /Satan went from him and seeing that he could not prevail against him he hid himself from them and he went and passed before them in the road; and he transformed himself into a large brook of water in the road, and Abraham and Isaac and his two young men reached that place and they saw a brook large and powerful as the mighty waters.

C.6 Both the angels of God and the Fallen angels can change a person's perception of reality upon occasion. As others have suggested this could mean that we live in a sort of very real seeming simulation or Matrix that can be altered either or in merely our perception of things.

C.7 There is a lot of evidence for this. See the Appendix about houses and places that people stayed in, whilst in a traumatic situation only the very next day or sometime later to discover that there was no such place. So, angels good and bad do influence us human beings in many ways and sometimes we do get to see amazing things that could be deemed as 'out of place' to others. I have certainly seen many things seemingly 'out of place' at times. I suppose I have had what people would call paranormal experiences both good and bad. It still is happening to me upon occasion!

C.8 I intend to write more about my paranormal experiences in my next book which will be called '**Out of the Bottomless Pit II**' I do believe in spirit helpers and angels who guard over us and help us with different ministries that we do for the Lord. In my case it is in writing. I feel compelled to write about the things that most people would avoid asking about or strange truths, because it might mean asking uncomfortable questions and seeking for answers to the paranormal.

> 6 Then God drove Satan away from before Adam, whom He strengthened, and whose heart He comforted, saying to him, "Go down to the Cave of Treasures, and separate not thyself from Eve; I will quell in you all animal lust."

C.9 Since when could normal sex of Adam with his wife Eve be classified as *'animal lust'?* That is ridiculous lie put forth by a false religious system, that likes to control people and their thinking by promoting celibacy and other ungodly practices which are not according to the Bible.

Matthew 4.11 'Then the devil left him and behold, angels came and ministered unto him.'

> 7 From that hour it left Adam and Eve, and they enjoyed rest by the commandment of God. But God did not the like to any one of Adam's seed; but only to Adam and Eve.

C.10 It looks that verse 7 is stating that no one that followed Adam and Eve of their righteous descendants suffered the most 'severe testings' that they had to endure. The loss of the Garden of Eden. Then their first born was a murderer. They then lost their beloved son Abel and Cain who was a child of Satan.

C.11 Once out of the Garden of Eden, Adam and Eve had to suffer the 'harsh terrain outside of the Garden. According to the Lost Books of Adam and Eve, they were pestered by 13 apparitions of Satan and all his dastardly tricks to try and destroy them. All of Satan's attempts to trick and kill them failed, due to God's direct intervention, by sending the 'Word of God' or his angels to rescue them time and time again from a vengeful and spiteful Satan.

> 8 Then Adam worshipped before the Lord, for having delivered him, and for having laid his passions. And he came down from above the cave and dwelt with Eve as aforetime.
>
> 9 This ended the forty days of his separation from Eve.

CHAPTER 5 (84)

Seth Tempted at 7-years-old

> AS for Seth, when he was seven years old, he knew good and evil, and was consistent in fasting and praying, and spent all his nights in entreating God for mercy and forgiveness.

C.1 This verse should say 'As for Seth when he was 7-years-old'- he knew God and the difference between good and evil. He certainly did not fast when he was 7 years old, as he needed all his sleep for growing and not fasting. The verse is far too religious.

C.2 Besides a normal child spends his energy playing and must sleep at night-time. This verse is typically deeply religious and trying to make Seth appear as a perfect little 7-year-old, and thus not human or some sort of saint that the rest of children could never attain to, so why bother trying to be like him.

> 2 He also fasted when bringing up his offering every day, more than his father did; for he was of a fair countenance, like unto an angel of God. He also had a good heart, preserved the finest qualities of his soul: and for this reason, he brought up his offering every day.
>
> 3 And God was pleased with his offering; but He was also pleased with his purity. And he continued thus in doing the will of God, and of his father and mother, until he was seven years old.
>
> 4 After that, as he was coming down from the altar, having ended his offering, Satan appeared unto him in the form of a beautiful angel, brilliant with light; with a staff of light in his hand, himself girt about with a girdle of light.

C.3 Here we see the 'folklore type' of story where some deceptive being is attempting to lure children away from their parents.

C.4 In Seth's case what protected him was his obedience to both his parents and to the Word of God.

C.5 We have all read at some time of some horror story of children suddenly 'disappearing' never to be seen or heard of again. Satan has often sent his elves and fairies and hobgoblins and other creatures to deceive children into following them throughout history only to never been seen again in many cases. What happens to these children that are led away? [See Steve Quayle's book – Little Creatures -the Gates of Hell are opening] It is an interesting book showing that Satan has many creatures working for him both big and small; some ugly and others pretty both all are lures…

C.6 Seth fortunately was one of the children who decided not to follow the 'stranger' who was offering him things that he did not have at the time. That is always the way Satan tempts people. He offers them something that at present they seemingly do not yet have. In most cases it is just a matter of being thankful for what one has and trusting the God will provide all our needs according to His riches in Christ Jesus, and not taking matters into our own hands especially if it is 'shady' or potentially dangerous in nature.

1 Corinthians 10:13 [1]There hath no temptation taken you but such as is common to man: but God is faithful, who will not suffer you to be tempted above that ye are able; but will with the temptation also make a way to escape, that ye may be able to bear it.

---

5 He greeted Seth with a beautiful smile, and began to beguile him with fair words, saying to him, "O Seth, why abide in this mountain? For it is rough, full of stones and of sand, and of trees with no good fruit on them; a wilderness without habitations and without towns; no good place to dwell in. But all is heat, weariness, and trouble."

6 He said further, "But we dwell in beautiful places, in another world than this earth. Our world is one of light and our condition is of the best; our women are handsomer than any others; and I wish thee, O Seth, to wed one of them; because I see that thou art fair to look upon, and in this land, there is not one woman good enough for thee. Besides, all those who live in this world, are only five souls.

7 "But in our world there are very many men and many maidens, all more beautiful one than another. I wish, therefore, to remove thee hence, that thou mayest see my relations and be wedded to which ever thou like.

8 "Thou shalt then abide by me and be at peace; thou shalt be filled with splendour and light, as we are.

9 "Thou shalt remain in our world. and rest from this world and the misery of it; thou shalt never again feel faint and weary; thou shalt never bring up an offering, nor sue for mercy; for thou shalt commit no more sin, nor be swayed by passions.

10 "And if thou wilt hearken to what I say, thou shalt wed one of my daughters; for with us it is no sin so to do; neither is it reckoned animal lust.

11 "For in our world we have no God; but we all are gods; we all are of the light, heavenly, powerful, strong and glorious."

C.7 Here Satan is tempting Seth in a similar way that he had tempted Eve his mother in the Garden of Eden. 'Ye shall be a gods' meaning to Seth as a 7-year-old 'You will have no one telling you what to do - like your parents - and certainly not God. 'Be like me', Satan is saying 'as I am a god and I do whatever I please and no one, I mean no one, can tell me what to do! This very temptation Satan has used throughout all history to entice and allure people away from safety to their ultimate destruction!

CHAPTER 6 (85)
Seth's Conscience Rescues Him

WHEN Seth heard these words, he was amazed, and inclined his heart to Satan's treacherous speech, and said to him, "Said thou there is another world created than this; and other creatures more beautiful than the creatures that are in this world?"

2 And Satan said, "Yes; behold thou hast heard me; but I will yet praise them and their ways, in thy hearing."

3 But Seth said to him, "Thy speech has amazed me; and thy beautiful description of it all.

4 "Yet I cannot go with thee to-day; not until I have gone to my father Adam and to my mother Eve and told them all thou hast said to me. Then if they give me leave to go with thee, I will come."

5 Again Seth said, "I am afraid of doing anything without my father's and mother's leave, lest I perish like my brother Cain, and like my father Adam, who transgressed the commandment of God. But behold, thou know this place; come, and meet me here to-morrow."

6 When Satan heard this, he said to Seth, "If thou tell thy father Adam what I have told you, he will not let thee come with me.

7 But hearken to me; do not tell thy father and mother what I have said to thee; but come with me to-day, to our world; where thou shalt see beautiful things and enjoy thyself there, and revel this day among my children, beholding them and taking thy fill of mirth; and rejoice ever more. Then I shall bring thee back to this place to-morrow; but if you would rather abide with me, so be it."

8 Then Seth answered, "The spirit of my father and of my mother, hangs on me; and if I hide from them one day, they will die, and God will hold me guilty of sinning against them.

C.1 *'The spirit of my father and my mother hangs on me'* -That is an

230

interesting expression because it would seem to imply that the spirits of Adam and Eve were very much tied to Seth emotionally and spiritually and probably because of the great sorrow that Adam and Eve had already suffered in losing their first two sons of Cain and Abel. Seth who, remember, was made in the image of his father Adam. This reminds me of Sarah of Abraham, that because she only had one child, her soul was 'all wrapped up in Isaac' as shown in the exciting Book of Jasher or in my book Jasher Insights: In this chapter Abraham was about to take Isaac up the mountain to sacrifice him as a burnt offering unto God without telling Sarah what he was intending to do...

JASHER 23.6 And Sarah said, 'Thou hast spoken well, go my Lord and do unto him as thou hast said, but remove him not at a great distance from me, neither let him remain here too long, for my soul is bound within his soul...

9 "And except that they know I am come to this place to bring up to it my offering, they would not be separated from me one hour; neither should I go to any other place, unless they let me. But they treat me most kindly because I come back to them quickly."

10 Then Satan said to him, "What will happen to thee if thou hide thyself from them one night, and return to them at break of day?"

11 But Seth, when he saw how he kept on talking, and that he would not leave him-ran, and went up to the altar, and spread his hands unto God, and sought deliverance from Him.

C.2 It is true that Satan is one big nag, but when you realise that it *is* Satan talking to you (or one of his imps), in your mind or otherwise, then rebuke him out of hand in the name of Jesus and he will stop pestering your thoughts with doubts and criticisms or hateful thoughts.

Isaiah 59.19 When the enemy shall come in like a flood, the Spirit of the LORD shall lift up a standard against him'.

12 Then God sent His Word, and cursed Satan, who fled from Him.

Philippians 2.10 That at the name of Jesus every knee should bow, of things in heaven, and things in earth, and things under the earth.

13 But as for Seth, he had gone up to the altar, saying thus in his heart. "The altar is the place of offering, and God is there; a divine fire shall consume it; so, shall Satan be unable to hurt me, and shall not take me away thence."

14 Then Seth came down from the altar and went to his father and mother, where he found in the way, longing to hear his voice; for he had tarried a while.

15 He then began to tell them what had befallen him from Satan, under the form of an angel.

16 But when Adam heard his account, he kissed his face, and warned him against that angel, telling him it was Satan who thus appeared to him. Then Adam took Seth, and they went to the Cave of Treasures, and rejoiced therein.

17 But from that day forth Adam and Eve never parted from him to whatever place he might go, whether for his offering or for anything else.

18 This sign happened to Seth, when he was nine years old.

C.3 Why does the beginning of this story state that Seth was 7 years old when he was tempted by Satan and yet now it states that 'This sign happened to Seth' when he was 9 years old. What sign is it talking about? If you find out the answer, then please let me know about this discrepancy of 2 years. Here is a far-out thing to ponder. In the case of Seth, I am certain that he was fully protected by God as he was obedient to his parents and to the Lord, but did you know that throughout history children have been led astray by strange people and beings and even Pied Piper type of persons. Some children disappeared and were never to be seen again and yet others re-appeared some years later. That will be a discussion for my next paranormal book '**OUT OF THE BOTTOMLESS PIT II**'

CHAPTER 7 (86)

Seth marries Aklia

WHEN our father Adam saw that Seth was of a perfect heart, he wished him to marry; lest the enemy should appear to him another time and overcome him.

2 So Adam said to his son Seth, "I wish, O my son, that thou wed thy sister Aklia, Abel's sister, that she may bear thee children, who shall replenish the earth, according to God's promise to us.

3 "Be not afraid, O my son; there is no disgrace in it. I wish thee to marry, from fear lest the enemy overcome thee."

4 Seth, however, did not wish to marry; but in obedience to his father and mother, he said not a word.

5 So Adam married him to Aklia. And he was fifteen years old.

6 But when he was twenty years of age, he begat a son, whom he called Enos; and then begat other children than him.

C.1 According to the KJV of the Bible, Seth had his firstborn son Enos when he was in fact 105 years old: **BIBLICAL LONGEVITY TIMECHART FROM ADAM TO JOSEPH:** Patriarch Lifespans (godmadeus.com)

Genesis 5.6 'And Seth lived an hundred and five years and begat Enos'.

C.2 Genesis 5 in fact gives the whole 'Book of Generations' from Adam to Noah and both the age of each one when they had their firstborn, as well as how old they were when they died.

7 Then Enos grew up, married, and begat Cainan.

8 Cainan also grew up, married, and begat Mahalalel.

9 Those fathers were born during Adam's lifetime and dwelt by the Cave of Treasures.

10 Then were the days of Adam nine hundred and thirty years, and those of Mahalalel one hundred. But Mahalalel, when he was grown

up, loved fasting, praying, and with hard labours, until the end of our father Adam's days drew near.

C.3 *'Mahalalel loved fasting and praying.'* Why? Does fasting help a person both physically and spiritually. Is there merit in fasting? Many would answer a resounding 'Yes' to that question.

C.4 See examples in the Bible and Apocryphal books, of people of God, like Ezra and Daniel who fasted and prayed and dedicated themselves to God's Word and who changed the fate of nations by so doing.

C.5 See my book **EZDRAS INSIGHTS** taken from **II ESDRAS** an apocryphal Book written by Ezra around 400-500 BCE.

C.6 This is the same Ezra that wrote the Book of Ezra in the Old Testament about the captivity of the Jews.

C.7 The advantage of both fasting and desperate prayer. Ezra spent 40 days fasting and praying for Israel which was in captivity. Afterwards he was assigned by the emperor of the Medio-Persian Empire to go to Israel and to rebuild the nation in around 454 BCE starting with the walls of Jerusalem that had been broken down by Nebuchadnezzar the first emperor of the Babylonian empire which preceded the Medio-Persian empire in around 589 BCE.

C.8 My book mentions both Daniel and Ezra. Daniel got the amazing dream of Daniel 7, which is talking about the 4 Beasts or World Empires yet to come after his time.

C.9 Daniel was born around 40 years before Ezra. Ezra received more information later in time about the 4th Beast: Rome which would come some 400 years after his time. Ezra described Rome in detail.

C.10 How did both Daniel and Ezra get visions and dreams of the future and even of the whole panorama of time itself? It started with fasting and praying for 21 days in Daniel's case and 40 days in the case of Ezra.

C.11 Their dedication to God literally changed the world around them.

C.12 Here is one interesting verse of many such verses from my book 'Ezdras Insights' to whet your appetite:

II Esdras 2.27 'I, Ezra, saw on Mount Zion a great multitude, which no man could number and they were praising the Lord with songs. In their midst was a young man of great stature, taller than any others, and on the head of each of them he placed a crown, but he was more exalted than they. And they were all spellbound.'

CHAPTER 8 (87)

Adam's predicts the Great Flood

WHEN our father Adam saw that his end was near, he called his son Seth, who came to him in the Cave of Treasures, and he said unto him:

2 "O Seth, my son bring me thy children and thy children's children, that I may shed my blessing on them ere I die."

3 When Seth heard these words from his father Adam, he went from him, shed a flood of tears over his face, and gathered together his children and his children's children, and brought them to his father Adam.

4 But when our father Adam saw them around him, he wept at having to be separated from them.

5 And when they saw him weeping, they all wept together, and fell upon his face saying, "How shalt thou be severed from us, O our father? And how shall the earth receive thee and hide thee from our eyes?" Thus, did they lament much, and in like words.

C.1 *"How shalt thou be severed from us, O our father?* It was as if the descendants of Adam had not experienced seeing the 'death' of a human being before, and that Adam was the first to die in the lineage of Seth. The only human being that they had heard about as having died was Adam and Eve's son Abel almost 9 centuries before. Abel was murdered in the early days after the Fall, whilst still a teenager. How tragic a start to humanity that was!

6 Then our father Adam blessed them all, and said to Seth, after he had blessed them:

7 "O Seth, my son, you know this world that it is full of sorrow, and of weariness; and thou know all that has come upon us, from our trials in it. I therefore now command thee in these words: to keep innocence, to be pure and just, and trusting in God; and lean not to the discourses of Satan, nor to the apparitions in which he will show himself to thee.

C.2 'To keep innocence' What exactly does this mean? Well, let us see what Flavius Josephus wrote in circa100 AD about Cain and his wicked children in the **'Antiquities of the Jews' Book 1 Ch 2**: *He (Cain) also introduced a* *change in that way of simplicity (innocence)– when in men lived before' and was the author of measures and weights. And whereas they lived innocently and generously whole they knew nothing of such arts, he changed the world into cunning craftiness.*

C.3 With the above description of the children of Cain is it any wonder that Seth wanted his children not to go anywhere near the children of Cain 'at the bottom of the Mountain' in this very colourful and illustrious account from the **Lost books of Adam and Eve?**

---

8 But keep the commandments that I give thee this day; then give the same to thy son Enos; and let Enos give it to his son Cainan; and Cainan to his son Mahalalel; so that this commandment abide firm among all your children.

9 "O Seth, my son, the moment I am dead take ye my body and wind it up with myrrh, aloes, and cassia, and leave me here in this Cave of Treasures in which are all these tokens which God gave us from the garden.

10 "O my son, hereafter shall a flood come and overwhelm all creatures and leave out only eight souls.

11 "But O my son, let those whom it will leave out from among your children at that time, take my body with them out of this cave; and when they have taken it with them, let the oldest among them command his children to lay my body in a ship until the flood has been assuaged, and they come out of the ship.

C.4 This last verse sounds like a prophecy that Adam was giving. Is it just possible that in the case that Adam prophesying about his body being taken on the Ark; that the prophecy never came to pass because God changed his mind about that detail as he found a better plan? Can prophecies fail or be altered? Yes, they can depending on God's highest Will.

1 Cor 13.8 Love never fails: but whether there be <u>prophecies</u>, they shall <u>fail;</u> whether there be tongues, they shall cease; whether there be knowledge, it shall vanish away.

---

12 Then they shall take my body and lay it in the middle of the earth, shortly after they have been saved from the waters of the flood.

13 "For the place where my body shall be laid, is the middle of the earth; God shall come from thence and shall save all our kindred.

---

14 "But now, O Seth, my son, place thyself at the head of thy people; tend them and watch over them in the fear of God; and lead them in the good way, Command them to fast unto God; and make them understand they ought not to hearken to Satan, lest he destroy them.

15 "Then, again, sever thy children and thy children's children from Cain's children; do not let them ever mix with those, nor come near them either in their words or in their deeds."

16 Then Adam let his blessing descend upon Seth, and upon his children, and upon all his children's children.

17 He then turned to his son Seth, and to Eve his wife, and said to them, "Preserve this gold, this incense, and this myrrh, that God has given us for a sign; for in days that are coming, a flood will overwhelm the whole creation. But those who shall go into the ark shall take with them the gold, the incense, and the myrrh, together with my body; and will lay the gold, the incense, and the myrrh, with my body in the **midst of the earth**.

C.5 This *'middle of the earth'* **in verses 14 -15** seems to be talking about an exact location in the middle of the land masses of the earth - or I should say the outer earth which is today known as Israel. Just look at a global map as Israel is right smack-dab in the Middle of the Earth. This is where eventually the descendants of Noah who originally landed on Mt Ararat which is far to the North of Israel in modern Turkey today came to, despite all the tricks of Satan to stop the Land of Israel from having ever been born. The land of Israel was obviously chosen by God Himself, and many had prophesied including Adam that the Middle of the earth would be his final burial site. Now why did he insist on that. As far we currently know from the Bible, Adam or any other of his deceased descendants were not taken on the ark of Noah.

C.6 With the blessing of having read some of the Apocryphal books we find out some remarkably interesting details which are not mentioned in the Bible. For example, it is stated that Noah took the Book of Enoch with him on the ark. (**See Appendix for more on this topic**)

C.7 If you believe, as I do, that the earth is in fact hollow, then it now starts to get interesting in understanding the Books of Jasher, Jubilees, Enoch, and 2nd Esdras which books all infer that the earth is hollow along with the Jewish book the Zohar. Let us consider the following: According to the Book of Enoch the earth used to be 6/7ths land and only 1/7 seas. Let us say for sake of argument that both inside the earth and outside the earth had one central landmass. We know that the outer earth parted into the continents at the time

237

of the Tower of Babel. What about the inner earth large central land mass?

C.7 Because of both Adam and Abraham, we have a link between the inner earth and the outer earth. The inner earth with its cave of treasures and the outer earth with its cave of Machpelah. The inner cave had the bodies of Adam and Eve and some of their descendants up until the Great Flood. After the Great Flood starting with Abraham the father of Israel another Cave was opened called Machpelah where Abraham buried his wife, Sarah. When Abraham first purchased the cave of Machpelah he discovered something strange and paranormal. He found a cave within the Cave of Machpelah according to Jewish tradition as mentioned in the book of the Zohar. When he entered the cave, he saw the bodies of Adam and Eve, which sat up and they talked to him. According to the Zohar the Garden of Eden was directly below the Cave of Machpelah where Abraham buried Sarah and eventually, he himself was also buried in that cave along with Isaac and Rebecka his wife and Jacob and his wife Leah.

C.8 There seems to be a portal in time and space between these two Caves. One contained the first man and woman in Adam and Eve and Seth and some of their descendants before the Great Flood and positioned on the inner surface of the earth. The other Cave showed the fulfilment of prophecy in the birth of the Holy land fathered by Abraham. All the righteous from Adam to Enoch to Noah all talked about the land of Shem or the land of the Semites being the descendants of Shem.

C.9 MIDDLE EARTH sticks out as an expression which has a lot more meaning than at first meets the eye. It only becomes clearer when one considers that the earth itself could indeed be hollow as suggested by Halley of Halley's Comet fame and Sir Isaac Newton and many scientists prior to the 1950's when most people used to believe that the earth is hollow and not solid. I made a video explaining why I thought that the earth is hollow and showing with a few simple experiments. Here is the link to my video on YOUTUBE: https://youtu.be/oj1i-rduA6o?t=7

---

18 "Then, after a long time, the city in which the gold, the incense, and the myrrh are found with my body, shall be plundered. But when it is spoiled, the gold the incense, and the myrrh shall be taken care of with the spoil that is kept; and naught of them shall perish, until the Word of God, made man shall come; when kings shall take them, and shall offer to Him, gold in token of His being King; incense, in token of His being God of heaven and earth; and myrrh, in token of His passion.

19 "Gold also, as a token of His overcoming Satan, and all our foes; incense as a token that He will rise from the dead and be exalted above things in heaven and things in the earth; and myrrh, in token that He will drink bitter gall; and feel the pains of hell from Satan.

C.10 See 'The 3 Kings Story who brought gold and frankincense and myrrh who came from Mesopotamia. The Bible story of the **Three Wise Men**, from the gospel of Matthew, is also known as the biblical Magi or the Three Kings. This Bible story regards a group of scholarly foreigners who travelled to visit Jesus after his birth, bearing gifts of gold, frankincense, and myrrh. After Jesus was born in Bethlehem of Judea, during the time of King Herod, Wise Men from the east came to Jerusalem and asked, 'Where is the one who has been born king of the Jews?

Matthew 2.1-2: 1 After Jesus was born in Bethlehem in Judea, during the time of King Herod, Magi from the east came to Jerusalem **2** and asked, "Where is the one who has been born king of the Jews? We saw his star when it rose and have come to worship him."

> 20 "And now, O Seth, my son, behold I have revealed unto thee hidden mysteries, which God had revealed unto me. Keep my commandment, for thyself, and for thy people,"

C.11 Another mystery is that the Cave of Machpelah where Abraham the father of Israel and his wife Sarah were buried was also near Bethlehem in Israel in Middle Earth. Could it be that the Cave of Treasures is directly below the Cave of Machpelah on the inner surface of the earth?

C.12 In answer to the question about Adam's body possibly not being taken on Noah's Ark, could the reason be why God changed His mind about this, was because just before the Great Flood conditions on the earth were totally chaotic and with much ungodliness abounding and with scary giants roaming the earth and devouring anything in sight. It would have been an extremely dangerous undertaking to transport the body of Adam around under those dangerous conditions.

C.13 Furthermore and much more importantly, Adam did not need to be moved from the located where he was buried and embalmed in the Cave of Treasures. Why? Because it turned out that later in time the Cave of Treasures became connected to the Cave of Machpelah through a Portal through the crust of the earth directly above it to the land of Bethlehem in Israel in Middle Earth. These Caves of Machpelah are known to still be there in Israel.

CHAPTER 9 (88)

The death of Adam

> WHEN Adam had ended his commandment to Seth, his limbs were loosened, his hands and feet lost all power, his mouth became dumb, and his tongue ceased altogether to speak. He closed his eyes and gave up the ghost.

C.1 This phrase *'gave up the ghost'* (or a form of it) is used 19 times in the Bible. In the Old Testament, two Hebrew words are used for the word "ghost" in this phrase: *"gava"* and *"nephesh."* In the New Testament, two Greek words are used: *"ekpneo"* and *"ekpsucho."* The literal meaning is basically "to breathe out" or "to expire." In short, to "give up the ghost" is a euphemism for dying.

As far as I know, this phrase is only used in the KJV version of the Bible.

Source: What does "gave up the ghost" mean in the Bible? - JesusAlive.cc

> 2 But when his children saw that he was dead, they threw themselves over him, men, and women, old and young, weeping.
>
> 3 The death of Adam took place at the end of nine hundred and thirty years that be lived upon the earth; on the fifteenth day of Barmudeh, after the reckoning of an epact of the sun, at the ninth hour.

C.2 Observation: I could not find a definition for the word Barmudeh. It is certainly not from Hebrew and was probably added at a later time than the manuscript which was compiled in circa 100 BCE.

C.3 Definition of *'Epact of the sun'* A word of Greek origin, applied to a number that indicates the Moon's age on the first day of the year. As the common solar year is 365 days, and the lunar year 354 days, the difference of 11 indicates that if a new moon falls on January 1st in any year, it will be 11 days old on the first day of the next year, and 22 days old on the first of the third year. Source: Epact · Astrological definition of Epact · Astrology Encyclopedia (astrologyweekly.com)

> 4 It was on a Friday, the very day on which be was created, and on which he rested; and the hour at which he died, was the same as that at which he came out of the garden.
>
> 5 Then Seth wound him up well, and embalmed him with plenty of sweet spices, from sacred trees and from the Holy Mountain; and be laid his body on the eastern side of the inside of the cave, the side of

the incense; and placed in front of him a lampstand which was kept burning.

6 Then his children stood before him weeping and wailing over him the whole night until break of day.

7 Then Seth and big son Enos, and Cainan, the son of Enos, went out and took good offerings to present unto the Lord, and they came to the altar upon which Adam offered gifts to God, when he did offer.

8 But Eve said to them "Wait until we have first asked God to accept our offering, and to keep by Him the Soul of Adam His servant, and to take it up to rest."

C.4 Why did it state in the last verse 8: *to keep by Him the Soul of Adam His servant, and to take it up to rest."*

C.5 Where did the souls of the dead go when they died in the times before the Great Flood? It would appear from the Bible that people went either down to Paradise or to Hell which was alongside it and that both of places were inside the earth.

1 Peter 4.6 For this cause was the gospel peached unto the dead.

1 Peter 3.19-20 ‹By which also he went and preached unto the spirits in prison, which sometime were disobedient, when once the longsuffering of God waited in the days of Noah, while the ark was a preparing, wherein few, that is, eight souls were saved by water›.

Ephesians 4.9-10 Now that he ascended, what is it but that he also descended first into the lower parts of the earth? He that descended is the same also that ascended up far above all heavens, that he might fulfil all things.

C.6 We know that eventually the righteous were taken up to the Heavenly City after it had been built by Jesus.

John 14:1-3 14 Let not your heart be troubled: ye believe in God, believe also in me.

2 In my Father's house are many mansions: if it were not so, I would have told you.

3 I go to prepare a place for you. That where I am there ye may be also.

C.7 It would seem that God has many different places for the souls of the dead. Look at the following verse from the Book of Enoch for this time-period before the Great Flood:

Book of Enoch 22.2 Then Raphael (the archangel) answered, one of the holy angels who was with me, and said to me, 'These hollow places have been created for this very purpose, that the spirits of the souls of the dead should assemble therein, yea that all the souls of the children of men should assemble here.

9 And they all stood up and prayed.

CHAPTER 10 (89)

Adam the 1ˢᵗ Person to Die

> AND when they had ended their prayer, the Word of God came and comforted them concerning their father Adam.
>
> 2 After this, they offered their gifts for themselves and for their father.
>
> 3 And when they had ended their offering, the Word of God came to Seth, the eldest among them, saying unto him, "O Seth, Seth, Seth, three times. As I was with thy father, so also shall I be with thee, until the fulfilment of the promise I made him-thy father saying, I will send My Word and save thee and thy seed.

C.1 Notice the way that the Lord is 'calling' Seth. Rather than the way one would speak face to face with a person. In the very last verse, it sounds more like the Lord is trying to get Seth's attention by whispering in his ear as in 'Seth, Seth, Seth'. When one normally greets a close friend, you would not say their name three times to their face. I therefore conclude that the Lord came and visited Seth but chose not to be visible on this occasion. Why? Since the beginning of time God has been trying to get His children to 'live by faith' and to believe without seeing. [See Hebrews 11]

C.2 *'As I was with thy father, so also shall I be with thee, until the fulfilment of the promise I made him-thy father saying, I will send My Word and save thee and thy seed'.*

This indeed is a wonderful promise whereby the Creator Himself or the Word of God, who is Jesus, promised repeatedly to our first ancestors that He would come in person to save people from their sins. Jesus clearly said, 'He that cometh to Me I will in no wise cast out'.

C.3 It is wonderful how the 'Lost Books of Adam and Eve' bring out very clearly that there was God the Father, God the Son and God the Holy Spirit who is also known often as Wisdom in the Old Testament of the Bible.

C.4 We see in these books how that God the Father sent His Son (Jesus) the Creator of the physical universe to Adam and Eve on many occasions to comfort and instruct them how to live in the world outside of the Garden of Eden. God has such love as to send His Word to us!

JN 6.37 All that the Father giveth me shall come to me; and him that cometh to me I will in no wise cast out.

Col. 2: 8-10 Beware lest any man spoil you through philosophy and vain deceit, after the tradition of men, after the rudiments of the world, and not after Christ. For in him dwelleth all the fulness of the Godhead bodily. And ye are complete in him, which is the head of all principality and power:

> 4 But as to thy father Adam, keep thou the commandment he gave thee; and sever thy seed from that of Cain thy brother."

C.5 Why did the Word of God tell Seth to stay away from the children of Cain? Well, what does it say in the New Testament:

1 JN 3.12,10. Not as Cain, who was of that wicked one, and slew his brother. And wherefore slew he him? Because his own works were evil, and his brother's righteous. In this the children of God are manifest, and the children of the devil: whosoever doeth not righteousness is not of God, neither he that loveth not his brother.

> 5 And God withdrew His Word from Seth.
>
> 6 Then Seth, Eve, and their children, came down from the mountain to the Cave of Treasures.
>
> 7 But Adam was the first whose soul died in the land of Eden, in the Cave of Treasures; for no one died before him, but his son Abel, who died murdered.

C.6 This is interesting, as we know from the Bible that Adam died when he was 930 years old. It is stating here that mankind lived for such a long time back then before the Great Flood that in general no one died until the year when the first man Adam died in the year 930 A.C (**A**fter **C**reation). The Great Flood happened in the year 1658. So, most people who died naturally died between the year 930 and 1658. The problem was that when wicked people lived too long then they became totally depraved and degenerated, so that lawlessness abound in the 500 years leading up to the Great Flood. Therefore, God cut man's lifespan to 120 years at the time of the Great Flood at least in the case of most people to limit wickedness. **BIBLICAL LONGEVITY TIMECHART FROM ADAM TO JOSEPH:** Patriarch Lifespans (godmadeus.com)

Gen 6.3 Then the LORD said, "My Spirit will not contend with man forever, for they are mortal; their days will be a hundred **and** twenty years."

> 8 Then all the children of Adam rose up, and wept over their father Adam, and made offerings to him, one hundred and forty days.

C.7 Why do you suppose that in the far past it states repeatedly in the Bible also that the Patriarchs would make offerings unto God when someone died or at a special Festival and all the relatives had to be there? I think the reason is that they did not have the 'written word' in the case of most people.

C.8 The wisest elder of the tribe would read 'pertinent writings' that applied to a given situation such as a birth, a death in the family, a wedding or another important occasion. He would read to all his tribe - so that they could learn to stay in tune with God's wishes. So, there were many occasions when ancient Israel and the godly before the Great Flood made offerings unto God on different occasions which would end up being a big fellowship in many cases and a call to unity and to remain righteous and in the case of these Lost Books of Adam and Eve to 'stay on the mountain' and do not go down to the children of Cain.

1 John 2:15-17 Love not the world, neither the things that are in the **world**. If any man **loves** the **world**, the **love** of the Father is **not** in him. For all that is in the **world**, the lust of the flesh, and the lust of the eyes, and the pride of life, is **not** of the Father, but is of the **world.** And the world passes away and the lust thereof but he that doeth the will of the Father will live forever.

C.9 In the time before the Great Flood it was Enoch the 7th from Adam who was accustomed to arousing the biggest fellowships of the peoples of the earth according to the Book of Jasher.

Jasher: 3.22 And the day came when Enoch went forth and they all assembled and came to him, and Enoch spoke to them the words of the Lord and he taught them wisdom and knowledge and they bowed down before him and said 'May the king live! May the king live! [See my book: **Jasher Insights]**

Seth becomes Head of Tribe

AFTER the death of Adam and of Eve, Seth severed his children, and his children's children, from Cain's children. Cain and his seed went down and dwelt westward, below the place where he had killed his brother Abel.

2 But Seth and his children dwelt northwards upon the mountain of the Cave of Treasures, in order to be near to their father Adam.

3 And Seth the elder, tall, and good, with a fine soul, and of a strong mind, stood at the head of his people; and tended them in innocence, penitence, and meekness, and did not allow one of them to go down to Cain's children.

4 But because of their own purity, they were named "Children of God," and they were with God, instead of the hosts of angels who fell; for they continued in praises to God, and in singing psalms unto Him, in their cave--the Cave of Treasures.

C.1 This verse seems out of place as the 'Children of God' cannot replace God's angels who 'fell down to the earth' in the times of Jared. Also, the timing is wrong as the Fallen angels had already fallen in the time of Jared in the 500 to 600 years after Creation. Adam died in 930 and was replaced by Seth according to this story in around 930 A.C (After Creation) **BIBLICAL LONGEVITY TIMECHART FROM ADAM TO JOSEPH:** Patriarch Lifespans (godmadeus.com)

C.2 It is difficult, I know to keep track of events, as to when exactly they happened. We must realize that 9 of the 10 generations from Adam to Noah were alive at the same time. Noah was born in the year 1056 or 126 years after the death of Adam. Enoch was translated in the year 987 or 57 years after Adam had died. Almost 1000 years is an awfully long for a person to live and a lot of events can happen in 1000 years.

C.3 Verse 4 is in my opinion is part of the false doctrine of the 'Sons of Seth' who supposedly fell and 'came into the daughters of men' and not the angels. That false doctrine came in around 300 to 400 A.D That false doctrine is easily disproved by Genesis 6 and Jasher 4, Jubilees 5.1 and many other writings such as Flavius Josephus: Antiquities of the Jews.

Gen 6.1-4 And it came to pass, when men began to multiply on the face of the earth, and daughters were born unto them, that the sons of God saw the daughters of men that they *were* fair; and they took them wives of all which they chose. And the LORD said, 'My spirit shall not always strive with man, for that he also *is* flesh: yet his days shall be an hundred and twenty years.' There were giants in the earth in those days; and also after that, when the sons of God came in unto the daughters of men, and they bare *children* to them, the same *became* mighty men which *were* of old, men of renown.

JUBILEES 5.1 And it came to pass when the children of men began to multiply on the face of the earth and daughters were born unto them, that the angels of God saw them on a certain year of this Jubilee that they were beautiful to look upon and they took themselves wives of all whom they chose and they bare unto them sons and they were giants.

---

5 Then Seth stood before the body of his father Adam, and of his mother Eve, and prayed night and day, and asked for mercy towards himself and his children; and that when he had some difficult dealing with a child, He would give him counsel.

6 But Seth and his children did not like earthly work but gave themselves to heavenly things; for they had no other thought than praises, doxologies, and psalms unto God.

Acts 6.2: Then the twelve called the multitude of the disciples unto them, and said, 'It is not reason that we should leave the word of God and serve tables.'

Ephesians 5.19 'Speaking to yourselves in psalms and hymns and spiritual songs, singing and making melody in your heart to the Lord'.

---

7 Therefore did they at all times hear the voices of angels, praising and glorifying God; from within the garden, or when they were sent by God on an errand, or when they were going up to heaven.

C.4 In putting things into proper perspective, some verses in this chapter and yet other chapters of these books seem deeply religious and a bit too much 'perfectionist'. How many people today actually find themselves 'going up to heaven' by being good? In fact, I would imagine very few. Well, I can think of Enoch, and a few others, but most of us do not get the privilege in this life of going up to heaven and back. Do not get me wrong, as I do know of a few people, who have gone to heaven in this modern life and come back to talk about it.

C.5 I think that for most of us it would be a big distraction going up to heaven when we are presently supposed to be living on the earth and learning what God wants to teach us whilst we are here. Too many heavenly experiences for us whilst still alive on the earth might hinder us from wanting to remain here, as the contrast between how things are in heaven, and how things are today on the earth is indeed very great. However, we are sent to earth by God for a reason, and we all have something important to do and discover whilst here on earth.

C.6 I find it strange that to 'talk to the dead' which by the way is 'taboo' today in most churches and religions, it was necessary for Seth to 'talk to the body of Adam'.

C.7 A typical attitude put forth by many churches is that you must be holy and perfect and never step out of line in your spiritual walk with the Lord. Their interpretation of being holy and perfect is that you have to keep coming back to the church building for Sunday service for one hour and make sure that you put money into the church building etc.

C.8 In the old days the prophets of God dedicated themselves to praying and fasting and reading God's Word which is all sorely lacking in the modern churches. As a result of their dedicated times with the Lord the prophets of God literally changed the world around them.

C.9 Religionists also give people the impression that God must be a 'sad God' and very severe and austere. Nothing could be further from the truth. God is a happy God, and He wants people to both have fun and to enjoy life. Not be overly serious and religious.

C.10 I do think that some of the original content of these Lost Books of Adam and Eve has been altered by the Orthodox church or the Catholic church in around 300-400 A.D.

C.11 From my own experience, God does not need any special location like a 'church building' or a 'grave' or tomb of the forefathers as in the 'Cave of Treasures' in the 'Lost Books of Adam and Eve', where to have to worship him, as Jesus Himself said in the Gospel of John:

Jn 4:21 Jesus saith unto her, 'Woman, believe me, the hour cometh, when ye shall neither in this mountain, nor yet at Jerusalem, worship the Father'. 23 Jesus then said to her, "But the hour cometh, and now is, when the true worshippers shall worship the Father in spirit and in truth: for the Father seeks such to worship him. 24 God is a Spirit: and they that worship him must worship him in spirit and in truth".

---

8 For Seth and his children, by reason of their own purity, heard and saw those angels. Then, again, the garden was not far above them, but only some fifteen spiritual cubits.

C.12 This description does not sound right, because not one of us can attain to heavenly places and visions by 'their own purity'. This sounds like 'religious works and this verse has probably been added 'after the fact'.

Romans 3.23: 'For all have sinned and come short of the Glory of God.'

Titus 3.5 'Not by works of righteousness which we have done but according to his mercy he Saved us, by the washing of re-generation and renewing of the Holy Ghost.'

248

Ephesians 2.8-9 'For by grace are you saved through faith, and not of yourselves. It is the gift of God. Not of works lest any man should boast'.

---

9 Now one spiritual cubit answers to three cubits of man, altogether forty-five cubits.

C.13 Why is a comparison made between a spiritual cubit and a physical cubit when we cannot even fathom spiritual measurements. Apparently, both space and time are different in the spirit world and perhaps that is what the original author was trying to portray in this story. The point here is that we are trapped in both time and space, but there exists a realm where these restrictions simply do not exist, and one cannot measure one realm with another realm's measurements.

---

10 Seth and his children dwelt on the mountain below the garden; they sowed not, neither did they reap; they wrought no food for the body. not even wheat; but only offerings. They ate of the fruit and of trees well flavoured that grew on the mountain where they dwelt.

11 Then Seth often fasted every forty days, as did also his eldest children. For the family of Seth smelled the smell of the trees in the garden when the wind blew that way.

C.14 This verse is in direct contradiction to the first book of the Lost Books of Adam and Eve chapter 1.6 *'As to the Southern side of the Garden of Eden, God did not want Adam to live there either because when the wind blew from the north, it would bring him on that Southern side, the delicious smell of the trees of the Garden.'*

---

12 They were happy, innocent, without sudden fear, there was no jealousy, no evil action, no hatred among them. There was no animal passion; from no mouth among them went forth either foul words or curse; neither evil counsel nor fraud. For the men of that time never swore, but under hard circumstances, when men must swear, they swore by the blood of Abel the just.

C.15 If you know the Lord then you do not have to be overcome by sudden fear.

Proverbs 3.25 "Be not afraid of sudden fear, neither of the desolation of the wicked, when it cometh."

I Jn 3.14 We know that we have passed from death unto life, because we love the brethren. He that loveth not *his* brother abides in death.

James 3.13 Who *is* a wise man and endued with knowledge among you? let him shew out of a good conversation his works with meekness of wisdom.

Psalm 131:2 Surely, I have composed and quieted my soul; Like a weaned child rests against his mother, My soul is like a weaned child within me.

C.16 'There was no animal passion.' What is this talking about? The problem is that some religious people teach that 'sex' is evil when in fact the scriptures do not say this. Some narrow-minded religions even teach that the 'Fall of Adam and Eve' was sex - but the normal sex between a man and a woman is certainly not evil. The first commandment by God Himself to the very first man and woman was to have lots of sex and to fill the world with their children. Nothing wrong there with sex.

C.17 However, this 'animal passion' is not talking about normal sex between a man and a woman, but about perversions and aberrations from normal sex. In the case of the children of Cain the normal male-female relationships descended into depravity, into the kinds of lusts that caused the people before the Great Flood to be destroyed, as it did with Sodom and Gomorrah after the Great Flood.

Jer.17.9 "The heart *is* deceitful above all *things*, and desperately wicked: who can know it?"

Mark 7.21-22 For from within, out of the heart of men, proceed evil thoughts, adulteries, fornications, murders, thefts, covetousness, wickedness, deceit, lasciviousness, an evil eye, blasphemy, pride, foolishness:

---

13 But they constrained their children and their women every day in the cave to fast and pray, and to worship the most High God. They blessed themselves in the body of their father Adam, and anointed themselves with it.

C.18 What does this mean that they constrained their children and their women every day in the cave to fast and pray. How could so many people live in one cave?

C.19 What does it mean that they blessed themselves in the 'body of their father Adam'?

C.20 Again this verse sounds deeply religious, restrictive, and unrealistic.

C.21 From personal experience - It is one thing to guide people in the right direction but trying to force people to be good simply does not work as God has given people the majesty of choice.

C.22 You cannot legislate righteousness – it is personal choice to do the right thing and to follow one's conscience and cannot be forced by man's religions!

C.23 The fact is that the more restrictive and severe a religion tries to be with its peoples, eventually that always backfires and most end up leaving that restrictive religion.

C.24 Historical account from before the Great Flood: In the case of the 'sons of Seth' the so-called 'good guys' the ones who were born in the first 700 years after Creation, could have mostly died from natural reasons before the time of the Great Flood.

C.25 Some of the 'Sons of Seth' died because God willed them to die before their time like Lamech the son of Methuselah who died at 777 and 5 years before the Great Flood. **BIBLICAL LONGEVITY TIMECHART FROM ADAM TO JOSEPH:** Patriarch Lifespans (godmadeus.com)

C.26 Methuselah the longest living human to have ever lived died two months before the Great Flood in 1658 according to biblical time charts.

C.27 According to the Book of Jasher, Enoch the 7th from Adam, kept the evil largely at bay in his time including the influence of the Fallen angels from around 650 after creation until his death in 987. However, by 1187 A.C in the time of his son Methuselah, the peoples of the world would no longer listen to godly counsel, and from that point on or around 200 years after the death of Enoch, the world descended into darkness and depravity from around 1187 AC until the Great Flood in 1658 AC when all, but 8 souls were all drowned. **BIBLICAL LONGEVITY TIMECHART FROM ADAM TO JOSEPH:** Patriarch Lifespans (godmadeus.com)

C.28 I find it incredibly sad to think that only 8 people were worth rescuing from the Great Flood by God Himself, but this just goes to show how horrendously wicked the world had become.

Luke 18.8b 'Nevertheless when the Son of man cometh, shall he find faith on the earth?'

C.29 Is not our world today fast descending into the same apostasy or falling away from faith in God, where hatred, violence, and deception are on every side. It is shocking that Jesus Himself warned us that 'As it was in the days of Noah, so will it be in the days that He would return the 2nd time.

Luke 17:26-30

[26] And as it was in the days of Noe, so shall it be also in the days of the Son of man.

[27] They did eat, they drank, they married wives, they were given in marriage, until the day that Noah entered into the ark, and the flood came, and destroyed them all.

[28] Likewise also as it was in the days of Lot; they did eat, they drank, they bought, they sold, they planted and they built;

[29] But the same day that Lot went out of Sodom it rained fire and brimstone from heaven and destroyed them all.

[30] Even thus shall it be in the day when the Son of man is revealed.

14 And they did so until the end of Seth drew near.

CHAPTER 12 (91)

Enos

> THEN Seth, the just, called his son Enos, and Cainan, son of Enos, and Mahalalel, son of Cainan, and said unto them:
>
> 2 "As my end is near, I wish to build a roof over the altar on which gifts are offered."

C.1 Seth wanted to 'build a roof over the altar'- presumably to beautify the altar and protect the offerings, so that the altar would both stand out, and be long-remembered.

C.2 Altars are mentioned often in the Bible. Ancient altars were raised structures that people placed sacrifices on. In the ancient world the altar was almost exclusively built as a monument to remember or commemorate a divine occurrence which took place at a certain location.

C.3 In ancient Israel, altars were significant, they symbolized communion with the Lord. They were a place of worship and a place to remember His covenant.

C.4 The "altar' was a place of "approach", a place to call upon the name of the Lord and remember His glorious promises.

C.5 The Bible describes the most sacred part of the altar, these were the four horns on the corners which symbolized God's power and might which have pointed to the four corners of the earth (**Exodus 27:2**). For the complete story about ancient altars: Ancient Altars - Background Bible Study (Bible History Online) (bible-history.com)

> 3 They hearkened to his commandment and went out, all of them, both old and young, and worked hard at it, and built a beautiful roof over the altar.
>
> 4 And Seth's thought in so doing, was that a blessing should come upon his children on the mountain; and that he should present an offering for them before his death.
>
> 5 Then when the building of the roof was completed, he commanded them to make offerings. They worked diligently at these and brought them to Seth their father who took them and offered them upon the altar; and prayed God to accept their offerings, to have mercy on the souls of his children, and to keep them from the hand of Satan.

6 And God accepted his offering and sent His blessing upon him and upon his children. And then God made a promise to Seth, saying, "At the end of the great five days and a half, concerning which I have made a promise to thee and to thy father, I will send My Word and save thee and thy seed."

7 Then Seth and his children, and his children's children, met together, and came down from the altar, and went to the Cave of Treasures, where they prayed, and blessed themselves in the body of our father Adam, and anointed themselves with it.

8 But Seth abode in the Cave of Treasures, a few days, and then suffered--sufferings unto death.

9 Then Enos, his first-born son, came to him, with Cainan, his son, and Mahalalel, Cainan's son, and Jared, the son of Mahalalel, and Enoch, Jared's son, with their wives and children to receive a blessing from Seth.

C.6 Adam's descendants through Seth until the 9th generation - Lamech - the father of Noah and their relatives all died long before the Great Flood, except for Methuselah who died two months before the Great Flood at 969 years old, and who is recorded to have been the longest living human being *ever* to have walked the planet.

C.7 All those born in the time of Noah - 600 years before the Great Flood in around 1060 AC, probably died either from the madness of men, giants, and evil overlords or at the time of the Great Flood. It was not a good time to live in those last 500 years before the Great Flood.

C.8 The last 500 years leading up to the Great Flood were the most chaotic and all the children of Seth who had gone down to the children of Cain during this period all perished in the Great Flood in the year 1658 according to biblical time charts. Remember only 8 souls survived the Great Flood. **BIBLICAL LONGEVITY TIMECHART FROM ADAM TO JOSEPH**: Patriarch Lifespans (godmadeus.com)

10 Then Seth prayed over them, and blessed them, and adjured them by the blood of Abel the just, saying, "I beg of you, my children, not to let one of you go down from this Holy and pure Mountain.

C.9 Seth got his wish as his son Enos, and his grandson Cainan, great-grandson Mahalalel, great-great-grandson Jared, and his great great-great-grandson Enoch all stayed on the mountain - that is the spiritual mountain of obedience to God and were not destroyed by either the roaming giants, crazy overlords, or the Great Flood.

11 Make no fellowship with the children of Cain the murderer and the sinner, who killed his brother; for ye know, O my children, that we flee from him, and from all his sin with all our might because he killed his brother Abel."

Ephesians 5.11: "And have no fellowship with the unfruitful works of darkness, but rather reprove *them*."

12 After having said this, Seth blessed Enos, his first-born son, and commanded him habitually to minister in purity before the body of our father Adam, all the days of his life; then, also, to go at times to the altar which he Seth had built. And he commanded him to feed his people in righteousness, in judgment and purity all the days of his life.

13 Then the limbs of Seth were loosened; his hands and feet lost all power; his mouth became dumb and unable to speak; and he gave up the ghost and died the day after his nine hundred and twelfth year; on the twenty-seventh day of the month Abib; Enoch being then twenty years old.

C.10 This is incorrect according to biblical time charts, as Enoch only lived to be 365 years old as 'God took him' or translated him, and Seth lived to be 912 years old. Enoch died before Seth in 987 AC and Seth died in 1042 AC or 55 years after Enoch. **BIBLICAL LONGEVITY TIMECHART FROM ADAM TO JOSEPH**: Patriarch Lifespans (godmadeus.com) or LONGEVITY CHART - www.outofthebottomlesspit.co.uk/450264991

14 Then they wound up carefully the body of Seth, and embalmed him with sweet spices, and laid him in the Cave of Treasures, on the right side of our father Adam›s body, and they mourned for him forty days. They offered gifts for him, as they had done for our father Adam.

15 After the death of Seth Enos rose at the head of his people, whom he fed in righteousness, and judgment, as his father had commanded him.

16 But by the time Enos was eight hundred and twenty years old, Cain had a large progeny; for they married frequently, being given to animal lusts; until the land below the mountain, was filled with them.

255

C.11 Here it is basically stating that the children of Cain multiplied like rabbits as they were given over to animal pleasures - meaning no discipline and no order when it came to sex – they had sex with all females no matter what their relationship to them and as a direct result they had many more children than the sons of Seth who stuck to godly rules when it came to sex and marriage.

C.12 It is quite easy to see why God did not want the absolute lawlessness that had existed before the great Flood to return to the earth after the Great flood, if at all possible.

C.13 As I mentioned before in my books, God put 'greater restrictions' upon Satan and the Fallen angels and what they were 'allowed to do' to lead astray mankind after the Great Flood. [**See my book JUBILEES INSIGHTS.**]

C.14 Notice that before the Great Flood there existed total anarchy in many situations, especially in the last few hundred years leading up to the Great Flood in 1658 AC.

C.15 After the Great Flood, suddenly mankind started having governments and much more controls. As someone has wisely said 'better to have some form of government then none where lawlessness just ends up running riot as in the days before the Great Flood - which was strongly influenced by both the Fallen angels and their sons the Giants.

C.16 I suppose mankind ended up not being able to rule over mankind in Pre-Flood times because the Fallen angels and their sons the Giants had become the very evil ruling class which subjugated and even devoured the people when it suited their purpose.

C.17 The centuries before the Great Flood was known as the 'golden Age' of the Fallen angels and their sons the Giants. There were apparently opposing powers ruled by the Fallen angels' sons or better known to us today as the demi-gods. There was the magnificent kingdom of Atlantis as well as another kingdom called Lemuria and another the Land of Mu. There could have been other kingdoms as well. They either ended up destroying each other or were eventually destroyed by God himself in the Great Flood.

C.18 It is interesting to discover that all around the world there are places that are radioactive from some event that happened around 4500-5000 years ago, as evidenced in both India and even here in Scotland as well as many other countries where you can find 'fused glass' on the very rocks indicating extra-ordinary high temperatures – such as a nuclear exchange would cause or laser weapons.

C.19 There is indeed a lot of evidence which one can find when reading the ancient books from India about what happened in the Pre-flood days. There were apparently gods and demi-gods with flying machines and laser or crystal technology.

C.20 I will write a lot more about this in my next book which will be called 'Out of the Bottomless Pit' II That book will be about the paranormal experiences that I personally have had in my lifetime both 'good and bad', as well as many testimonies of other people as well concerning the paranormal. Paranormal just means 'outside the normal' or in other words 'difficult to explain' in physical terms.

CHAPTER 13 (92)

The Children of Cain

> IN those days lived Lamech the blind, who was of the sons of Cain. He had a son whose name was Atun, and they two had much cattle.

C.1 Here is an interesting reference to 'Lamech the blind'. This is not Lamech - the son of Methuselah and father of Noah from Seth's lineage.

C.2 Amazingly, there was no sickness as far we know before the Great Flood - at least for the righteous as there is no mention of sickness in the Bible or the Apocryphal books in Pre-Flood times.

C.3 DEMONS: Look at the revealing following verses from the **Book of Jubilees**:

Book of Jubilees: 10:2.5 'And the sons of Noah came to Noah and told him concerning the demons which were leading astray and blinding and slaying his sons. For these are malignant and created in order to destroy.

Revelation 6:8 So I looked, and behold, a pale horse. And the name of him who sat on it was Death, and Hades followed with him. And power was given to them over a fourth of the earth, to kill with sword, with hunger, with death, and by the beasts of the earth.

C.4 Why did Lamech become blind? According to the Book of Jasher 'Lamech the blind' became cursed 7 times because he killed his great grand-father Cain.

C.5 God had put a mark upon Cain and stated that whosoever harmed Cain would be cursed 7-fold:

Genesis 4.14 So the Lord said to him, "Therefore whoever kills Cain, vengeance will be taken on him sevenfold." And the Lord appointed a sign for Cain, so that no one finding him would slay him.

C.6 Starting with Lamech, the sons of Cain started to be cursed because of their wickedness. Lamech the blind married the two daughters of Cainan from the line of Seth. Cainan was the 4th from Adam. So Lamech was born sometime around the 5th from Adam which was Mahalalel or around 395 years after Creation. **BIBLICAL LONGEVITY TIMECHART FROM ADAM TO JOSEPH**: Patriarch Lifespans (godmadeus.com)

> 2 But Lamech was in the habit of sending them to feed with a young shepherd, who tended them; and who, when coming home in the evening wept before his grandfather, and before his father Atun and his mother Hazina, and said to them, "As for me, I cannot feed those cattle alone, lest one rob me of some of them, or kill me for the sake

of them." For among the children of Cain, there was much robbery, murder, and sin.

C.7 These names Atun and Hazina cannot be the original names, but have been added much later, as they are not Hebrew names but possibly Arabic. Hebrew was the original language of Creation according to the Book of Jubilees:

Book of Jubilees.12.25-26 And the Lord God said: 'Open his mouth and ears, that he may hear and speak with his mouth, with the language which has been revealed': for it had ceased from the mouths of all the children of men from the day of the overthrow (of Babel). 'And I opened his mouth, and his ears and his lips, and I began to speak with him in Hebrew in the tongue of Creation'.

3 Then Lamech pitied him, and he said, "Truly, he when alone, might be overpowered by the men of this place."

4 So Lamech arose, took a bow he had kept ever since he was a youth, ere he became blind, and he took large arrows, and smooth stones, and a sling which he had, and went to the field with the young shepherd, and placed himself behind the cattle; while the young shepherd watched the cattle. Thus did Lamech many days.

5 Meanwhile Cain, ever since God had cast him off, and had cursed him with trembling and terror, could neither settle nor find rest in any one place; but wandered from place to place.

6 In his wanderings he came to Lamech's wives and asked them about him. They said to him, "He is in the field with the cattle."

7 Then Cain went to look for him; and as he came into the field, the young shepherd heard the noise he made, and the cattle herding together from before him.

8 Then said he to Lamech, "O my lord, is that a wild beast or a robber?"

9 And Lamech said to him, "Make me understand which way he looks, when he comes up."

10 Then Lamech bent his bow, placed an arrow on it, and fitted a stone in the sling, and when Cain came out from the open country, the shep-

herd said to Lamech, "Shoot, behold, he is coming."

11 Then Lamech shot at Cain with his arrow and hit him in his side. And Lamech struck him with a stone from his sling, that fell upon his face, and knocked out both his eyes; then Cain fell at once and died.

12 Then Lamech and the young shepherd came up to him and found him lying on the ground. And the young shepherd said to him, "It is Cain our grandfather, whom thou hast killed, O my lord!"

13 Then was Lamech sorry for it, and from the bitterness of his regret, he clapped his hands together, and struck with his flat palm the head of the youth, who fell as if dead; but Lamech thought it was a feint; so, he took up a stone and smote him, and smashed his head until he died.

C.8 Here is the same 'paraphrased' story according to the **Book of Jasher 2.26-33.** And Lamech was old and advanced in years, and his eyes were dim that he could not see, and Tubal-Cain his son was leading him and whilst he was leading him, Cain the son of Adam advanced towards them. 27 And Tubal-Cain told his father to draw his bow, and with the arrows he smote Cain who was yet afar off and slew him 29 And the Lord requited Cain's evil according to his wickedness 31 And Lamech was very much grieved at having done this and in clapping his hands together he struck his son and caused his death. 33 And the wives of Lamech (Adah and Zillah - the daughters of Cainan -grandson of Seth) hated him from that day because he slew Cain and Tubal-Cain. [See my book '**JASHER INSIGHTS' BOOK 1**]:

Genesis 4.23-24 And Lamech said unto his wives, Adah and Zillah, 'Hear my voice; ye wives of Lamech, hearken unto my speech: for I have slain a man to my wounding, and a young man to my hurt.

[24] If Cain shall be avenged sevenfold, truly Lamech seventy and sevenfold'.

CHAPTER 14 (93)

Time Passes

> WHEN Enos was nine hundred years old, all the children of Seth, and of Cainan, and his first-born, with their wives and children, gathered around him, asking for a blessing from him.

C.1 It was the year 1140 AC that Enos died or about 500 years before the Great Flood.

> 2 He then prayed over them and blessed them and adjured them by the blood of Abel the just saying to them, "Let not one of your children go down from this Holy Mountain and let them make no fellowship with the children of Cain the murderer."

C.2 Enos, like Seth his father before him on his deathbed was adjuring his sons to stay on the mountain to the sons and daughters of Cain as they were both dangerous, murderous, and licentious.

> 3 Then Enos called his son Cainan and said to him, "See, O my son, and set thy heart on thy people, and establish them in righteousness, and in innocence; and stand ministering before the body of our father Adam, all the days of thy life."
>
> 4 After this Enos entered into rest, aged nine hundred and eighty-five years; and Cainan wound him up, and laid him in the Cave of Treasures on the left of his father Adam; and made offerings for him, after the custom of his fathers.

C.3 Enos lived to be 905 years-old and he died according to the KJV of the Bible.

CHAPTER 15 (94)

Cave of Treasures becomes a Family Shrine

AFTER the death of Enos, Cainan stood at the head of his people in righteousness and innocence, as his father had commanded him; he also continued to minister before the body of Adam, inside the Cave of Treasures.

Psalm 37:6 He will bring forth your righteousness like the dawn, your justice like the noonday sun. He will make your righteous reward shine like the dawn, your vindication like the noonday sun. He will make your innocence radiate like the dawn, and the justice of your cause will shine like the noonday sun.

2 Then when he had lived nine hundred and ten years, suffering and affliction came upon him. And when he was about to enter into rest, all the fathers with their wives and children came to him, and he blessed them, and adjured them by the blood of Abel, the just, saying to them, "Let not one among you go down from this Holy Mountain; and make no fellowship with the children of Cain the murderer."

C.1 According to the Bible this is correct that Cainan lived to be 910 years old.

C.2 It would seem from these 'Lost Books of Adam and Eve' that the righteous in the times before the Great Flood were afflicted only when they got exceedingly old and were about to die.

3 Mahalalel, his first-born son, received this commandment from his father, who blessed him and died.

4 Then Mahalalel embalmed him with sweet spices, and laid him in the Cave of Treasures, with his fathers; and they made offerings for him, after the custom of their fathers.

C.3 This custom of embalming using sweet spices is quite revealing as this custom has been followed by many cultures ever since.

C.4 It was observed by Abraham in burying his wife Sarah in the Cave of Machpelah which is around 30 miles south of Bethlehem which is just South of Jerusalem.

C.5 It was observed by the Egyptians in burying their Pharaohs in pyramids and tombs. I wonder who taught the Egyptians to bury their Pharaohs in tombs or into the sides of the Pyramids that had just stood there for centuries. Strangely, it turns out that 'The pyramids' were not built by the Egyptians but were built before the Great Flood, but that is another long story for another time - and yes, it is possible to prove it.

Contention

> THEN Mahalalel stood over his people, and fed them in righteousness and innocence, and watched them to see they held no intercourse with the children of Cain.
>
> 2 He also continued in the Cave of Treasures praying and ministering before the body of our father Adam, asking God for mercy on himself and on his people; until he was eight hundred and seventy years old, when he fell sick.

C.1 According to the Biblical Time chart Mahalalel lived until he was 895 and he died in the year 1290 A.C (**A**fter **C**reation) This is indirectly telling us that all who were born at around the same time as Mahalalel did not die because of the Great Flood but they died naturally if not killed or devoured by the Giants and other creatures down in the valley. The Great Flood happened in 1658 A.C. This means that Mahalalel the 4th generation from Adam died some 368 years before the Great Flood.

C.2 I am sure you are wondering why did these descendants of Adam and Eve keep the bodies of their forefathers embalmed in the Cave of Treasures, and more importantly, why did they pray and minister before their bodies?

C.3 Was this an ancient custom? Is it still a custom today in certain cultures? Do some people who are wealthy still get buried in caves or tombs today? There are in fact many cultures who honour the dead by visiting their graves and holding prayers and victuals over their dead bodies - even in modern times.

C.4 What was the point to holding endless vigils over a dead body? They were dead after all and probably decayed and rotting and what could the dead possibly do for the living?

C.5 If this is all true, then why keep those old dead bodies around when today in modern times we would probably have told the relatives of Mahalalel that it was about time to bury those bodies in the ground and that sooner or later if they didn't watch out those old bodies would begin to stink. Didn't they know back then that it was unhygienic to keep dead bodies in a cave around the living. What did the people back there hope to gain by keeping their ancestors bodies mummified in a burial cave? Well, I suspect that it had something to do with their beliefs in the resurrection from the dead, even as it does with the mummies preserved in the pyramids in Egypt, where Pharaohs and the dead were taken to the underworld by the gods.

C.6 Most Jews and Christians believe that when they die, they either go to Paradise or Hell which lie side by side according to the parable that Jesus himself told- ['The Story of Lazarus and the Rich man - who died' - **Luke 16.19-31**]

C.7 In these Lost Books of Adam and Eve it has been stated many times over by the Lord himself that He would one day come and give His life for the souls of mankind. We today have salvation by looking to the resurrection of Christ 2000 years ago. Those in the times on Adam and Eve and their descendants looked forward to the time of the Messiah which was 4000 years in the future from the time of the creation of the world and the time of Adam and Eve.

C.8 I suspect therefore that the early patriarchs from Adam onwards were buried in a Cave like the Cave of Treasures as indeed was still the custom after the Great Flood in the times of Abraham when he buried his wife Sarah in a double cave that he bought, called Machpelah. He himself, and then Isaac and Rebecca, and then their son Jacob and his wife Leah were all buried in that cave, and if I am correct, they were also embalmed.

C.9 Notice that even in the times of Jesus, people were buried in a cave or tomb as they called it, and not interred in the ground. I think that it was because they all looked forward to the resurrection. This also happened with Jesus Christ being buried in a Cave or Tomb and embalmed. Three days later, he came back to life in his resurrection body and thus fulfilled the prayers and victuals of those from Adam to Abraham to Christ the Messiah. Christ was resurrected, and after that event, all the just and righteous ones have looked forward to also being resurrected.

1 Cor 15.19-22: RESURRECTION

20 But now is Christ risen from the dead and become the first fruits of them that slept.

21 For since by man *came* death, by man *also came* the resurrection of the dead.

22 For as in **Adam** all **die**, even so in **Christ** shall all be made alive.

C.10 CREMATIONS One thing for sure: the custom concerning burials all the way from Adam to Christ and possibly beyond his time was to bury people either in a tomb using embalming, if your family was wealthy enough, or to be buried in a common grave in the ground.

C.11 In more modern times people can choose to be buried in a coffin in the ground or to be cremated. Cremating was not considered to be a godly way of buying a person in biblical times. I guess the people were afraid that if one was cremated that all the parts of your dead body disappearing into smoke might make it difficult for them to obtain their resurrection bodies. They need not have worried about it though, as God is more than capable of finding out where all the atoms of a body are even after it has totally disintegrated. God is Creator and He can do anything including putting a human body back together and resurrecting it.

Luke 1.37 For with God nothing is impossible.

3 Then all his children gathered unto him, to see him, and to ask for his blessing on them all, ere he left this world.

4 Then Mahalalel arose and sat on his bed, his tears streaming down his face, and he called his eldest son Jared, who came to him.

5 He then kissed his face, and said to him, "O Jared, my son, I adjure thee by Him who made heaven and earth, to watch over thy people, and to feed them in righteousness and in innocence; and not to let one of them go down from this Holy Mountain to the children of Cain, lest he perish with them.

6 "Hear, O my son, hereafter there shall come a great destruction upon this earth on account of them; God will be angry with the world and will destroy them with waters.

C.12 Mahalalel prophesizes that the Great Flood would come, as did Adam before him according to these Lost Books of Adam and Eve. Enoch 7th from Adam also prophesied about the coming Great Flood.

ENOCH 83.3-4 'And thereupon a word fell into my mouth, and I lifted up my voice to cry aloud, and said, 'The earth is destroyed.' And my grandfather Mahalalel waked me as I lay near him and said unto me, 'why does thou cry so my son with such lamentation? And I recounted to him the whole vision which I had seen, and he said unto me, 'A terrible thing has thou seen my son and a grave moment is thy dream vision as the secrets of all the sin of the earth: it must sink into the abyss and be destroyed with great destruction.'

7 "But I also know that thy children will not hearken to thee, and that they will go down from this mountain and hold intercourse with the children of Cain, and that they shall perish with them.

8 "O my son! teach them, and watch over them, that no guilt attaches to thee on their account."

C.13 *'no guilt attaches to thee on their account'* This simply means that Mahalalel is instructing his son Jared to 'be faithful to warn his children' of the prophesied doom of the earth and that they should not go down the mountain and join the wicked sons of Cain. There is a similar admonition in the Book of Ezekiel:

Ezekiel 1.17-19 [17] Son of man, I have made thee a watchman unto the house of Israel: therefore, hear the word at my mouth, and give them warning from me.

¹⁸ When I say unto the wicked, you shalt surely die; and thou give him not warning, nor speak to warn the wicked from his wicked way, to save his life; the same wicked man shall die in his iniquity; but his blood will I require at thine hand.

¹⁹ Yet if thou warn the wicked, and he turn not from his wickedness, nor from his wicked way, he shall die in his iniquity; but thou hast delivered thy soul.

9 Mahalalel said, moreover, to his son Jared, "When I die, embalm my body and lay it in the Cave of Treasures, by the bodies of my fathers; then stand thou by my body and pray to God; and take care of them, and fulfil thy ministry before them, until thou enter into rest thyself."

10 Mahalalel then blessed all his children; and then lay down on his bed and entered into rest like his fathers.

11 But when Jared saw that his father Mahalalel was dead, he wept, and sorrowed, and embraced and kissed his hands and his feet; and so, did all his children.

12 And his children embalmed him carefully and laid him by the bodies of his fathers. Then they arose and mourned for him forty days.

CHAPTER 17 (96)

Jared turns martinet

C.1 What does this mean: 'Jared turns martinet'?

Martinet: (definition): someone who demands that rules and orders are always be obeyed, even when it is unnecessary or unreasonable to do so. Wow! That is a particularly good definition which leads into the big topic of the 'letter of the law' which I have covered in my last book '**Jubilees Insights'**.

C.2 Why does the title to this chapter state *sees many voluptuous sights?* There is nothing wrong with women being voluptuous, and that is often appreciated by men that women are beautiful, curvaceous, sexy and to be enjoyed in the right relationships. What is wrong with that? But of course, if it is all used as a temptation by Satan to lure people away from God and the truth then that is an entirely different matter as Jared found out – in this very chapter.

C.3 The highly religious like to denigrate normal sex and sexy women when that should not be the case. It is perversions that are the sin and not normal sex. I can tell you right now that Heaven is a very sexy place! Where your dreams are really fulfilled, if it is not perverse and does not hurt or harm anyone.

C.4 What God is against is perverseness and not the need for normal sexual relationships. After all God Himself calls us His bride and He loves us very intimately, which causes us to 'bear fruit' for Him. We are in love with Jesus and He is everything to us. Many different orders of dedicated Christian Catholic nuns have felt this way in dedicating themselves to Jesus alone as His Bride.

C.5 *'barely escaped with a clean heart'* - What is a clean heart and how does one keep a clean heart?

Psalm 51: 10-13:

[10] Create in me a clean heart, O God; and renew a right spirit within me.

[11] Cast me not away from thy presence; and take not thy holy spirit from me.

[12] Restore unto me the joy of thy salvation; and uphold me with thy free spirit.

[13] Then will I teach transgressors thy ways; and sinners shall be converted unto thee.

> THEN Jared kept his father's commandment and arose like a lion over his people. He fed them in righteousness and innocence and commanded them to do nothing without his counsel. For he was afraid concerning them, lest they should go to the children of Cain.

Job 3.26 'For the thing I greatly feared has come upon me, and what I dreaded has happened to me'.

C.6 *'Jared arose like a lion over his people'* That to us in modern days does not sound like a good thing, as it sounds like Jared became a 'dictator' giving out dictums which had to be obeyed irrespective of the situation. It sounds like he got under the 'letter of the law' about righteousness.

C.7 The only lion that I would trust to lead mankind would be the Lion of Judah -Jesus Christ himself as in the Millennium.

C.8 Obedience is not something one can force, as it must come from the heart and be willingly given.

> 2 Wherefore did he give them orders repeatedly; and continued to do so until the end of the four hundred and eighty-fifth year of his life.

C.9 According to the Biblical Timeline in the KJV of the Bible Jared lived to be 962 years of age or the 2nd longest lived person in history!

> 3 At the end of these said years, there came unto him this sign. As Jared was standing like a lion before the bodies of his fathers, praying and warning his people, Satan envied him, and wrought a beautiful apparition, because Jared would not let his children do aught (anything) without his counsel.

C.10 'Satan envied him' Why did Satan envy Jared and many other right-eous people throughout time itself? Satan envies the fact that other people are much closer to God than he is, and by inference are also destined to be greater than he is - though he be the god of Evil and the 'father of lies' and evil beings. So, if he finds a person who is very dedicated to God - he will then seek to destroy them in his rage and fury of jealousy as to their 'rela-tionship with God'. This has been the case all through history – look at all the martyrs and how they died. Satan is jealous of the truly righteous as he has apparently 'missed the boat' to heaven and the only boat he is going to catch is the one right back down to Hell, the Bottomless Pit and eventually the 'Lake of fire'.

C.11 In the case of Jared, it looks like Satan was jealous of him for perhaps a different reason. What does Satan want more than anything? To be worshipped like the most High. In his twisted mind he thinks that to get that he needs to totally 'control' mankind as he will seemingly largely 'win' in the future 'Mark of the Beast' that most people will readily take.

C.12 Is it just possible that Satan envied Jared because of his ability to 'control' people? Jared was able to command thousands of people or even hundreds of thousands of people- to 'stay on the spiritual mountain of God's will – but it was by force.

C.13 The fact it stated Jared was a Lion. The problem with total control is that people become too dependent on the leader instead of getting their own instructions from God Himself, which is what is really needed.

C.14 Too much dependence on one leader can be a big hinderance to progress if the individual people are not allowed to make helpful changes to get even God's work done. Life is full of changes.

C.15 Well, Jared held the children of Seth together for a season but then they backslide in droves or wave after wave until only a handful remained. Forced obedience is no obedience at all. It must come willingly and from the heart.

C.16 With a future like Satan's, no wonder he is jealous of the righteous, as he refuses to repent, he simply tries to destroy all the good people and in fact all of God's Creation in revenge.

C.17 Notice how Satan has appeared as an apparition to different descendants of Adam throughout these stories of the 'Lost Books of Adam and Eve', as he also did with Adam and Eve. Satan often disguises himself to this victims and tricks them into believing that the things they are seeing around them at that moment are real when they are in fact not. All of Satan's tricks are ultimately for the purpose of destroying his victims by cunning.

---

4 Satan then appeared to him with thirty men of his hosts, in the form of handsome men; Satan himself being the elder and tallest among them, with a fine beard.

5 They stood at the mouth of the cave, and called out Jared, from within it.

6 He came out to them, and found them looking like fine men, full of light, and of great beauty. He wondered at their beauty and at their looks; and thought within himself whether they might not be of the children of Cain.

7 He said also in his heart, "As the children of Cain cannot come up to the height of this mountain, and none of them is so handsome as these appear to be; and among these men there is not one of my kindred-- they must be strangers."

C.18 Today people are deceived in the very same way. Aliens/gods/Fallen Angels who come to people in the world today acting superior and trying to 'educate' the peoples of the earth. My advice is to 'Stay close to Jesus' every day, so as not to be deceived by these entities or (fallen angels masquerading as aliens). Deception is very much Satan's Game even today in modern times.

C.19 *'As the children of Cain cannot come up to the height of this mountain, and none of them is so handsome as these appear to be*

'they must be strangers'. The Fallen angels co-habited with the daughters of Cain for a season in order to get into this dimension as they saw the women as 'fit extensions'[Septuagint] to bring their sons, the Giants into this plane of existence. The 'Fallen angels' normally prefer each other rather than women apparently. Thus, we see what happened in the story of Sodom and Gomorrah.

C.20 Even today people would say there are entities or aliens or 'strangers' that we cannot quite explain as they are from another dimension. There are UFOs, that the Fallen angels use as their inter-dimensional vehicles, to travel around the universe and beyond.

---

8 Then Jared and they exchanged a greeting and he said to the elder among them, "O my father, explain to me the wonder that is in thee, and tell me who these are, with thee; for they look to me like strange men."

9 Then the elder began to weep, and the rest wept with him; and he said to Jared: "I am Adam whom God made first; and this is Abel my son, who was killed by his brother Cain, into whose heart Satan put to murder him.

10 "Then this is my son Seth, whom I asked of the Lord, who gave him to me, to comfort me instead of Abel.

11 "Then this one is my son Enos, son of Seth, and that other one is Cainan, son of Enos, and that other one is Mahalalel, son of Cainan, thy father."

C.21 Here is Satan putting on a 'poor me' show. He loves to get people to feel sorry for him and think that God has mistreated him when it is all the other way around.

---

12 But Jared remained wondering at their appearance, and at the speech of the elder to him.

13 Then the elder said to him, "Marvel not, O my son; we live in the land north of the garden, which God created before the world. He would not let us live there, but placed us inside the garden, **below** which ye are now dwelling.

C.22 Satan is talking as if he had been Adam. 'Created before the world'. How could Satan and his band live in the *'land to the north of the garden'* and *'which God created before the world'*? What was in existence before the creation of the world? Only the spirit world and beautiful lands like the Garden of Eden in heavenly realms. So, this fake elder was describing another realm or dimension from before Time itself began for the physical realm.

C.23 Jared did not catch on that Satan was getting all twisted up in his own lies as he got some of the facts all wrong. Lying is a dangerous game, because you can get all mixed up as to exactly what really happened and end up being confused which is what seems to have happened here.

C.24 Satan gets his facts all wrong. Unfortunately, Jared does not even notice. According to the beginning of these Lost Books of Adam and Eve the Garden of Eden was to the North of the Cave of Treasures and further up the mountain. It was separated from this dimension by a portal and guarded by a Cherubim. Satan stated above that where he lived was below the Garden of Eden when being an imposter and claiming that he was Adam the great-great-great grandfather of Jared. Of course, it is true that Satan's real abode more and more is down in the earth and certainly below the mountain whether speaking physically as in this story or spiritually.

---

14 "But after that I transgressed, He made me come out of it, and I was left to dwell in this cave; great and sore troubles came upon me; and when my death drew near, I commanded my son Seth to tend his people well; and this my commandment is to be handed from one to another, unto the end of the generations to come.

15 "But, O Jared, my son, we live in beautiful regions, while you live here in misery, as this thy father Mahalalel informed me; telling me that a great flood will come and overwhelm the whole earth.

16 "Therefore, O my son, fearing for your sakes, I rose and took my children with me, and came hither for us to visit thee and thy children; but I found thee standing in this cave weeping, and thy children scattered about this mountain, in the heat and in misery.

C.25 The Choice to Live A 'Simpler' Life. It never ceases to amaze me how those who are 'worldly' - Definition: meaning they 'believe in this world' and take 'no thought of death' and 'life after death' and 'no thought for the consequences of their actions', - they think that there is 'no Judgement to come'.

C.26 We are exhorted in the scriptures to:

I Jn 2: 15-17 'Love not the world, neither the things that are in the world. If any man love the world, the love of the Father is not in him.

[16] For all that is in the world, the lust of the flesh, and the lust of the eyes, and the pride of life, is not of the Father, but is of the world.

[17] And the world passes away, and the lust thereof: but he that doeth the will of God abides for ever.

C.27 Worldly people often cannot understand those who wish to live a different style of life than themselves.

C.28 Those 'given over to wantonness, drunkenness and excess' and in the case of the powerful to wasting nations, in their constant seeking after money, success and power, don't get the point that there is a 'much higher goal' to life than all of those temporal things which don't satisfy in the long run.

Galatians 5: 19-21 Now the deeds of the flesh are evident, which are: immorality, impurity, sensuality, idolatry, sorcery, enmities, strife, jealousy, outbursts of anger, disputes, dissensions, factions, envying, drunkenness, carousing, and things like these, of which I forewarn you, just as I have forewarned you, that those who practice such things will not inherit the kingdom of God. <Source: https://bible.knowing-jesus.com/topics/Licentiousness>

C.29 Of course there are demonic powers which are always trying to minimize the 'truth of salvation' and of the importance of 'eternal life' in the minds of the people.

Ephesians 6.12 'For we wrestle not against flesh and blood, but against principalities, against powers, against the rulers of the darkness of this world, against spiritual wickedness in high places'.

C.30 The demonic powers teach people through the devilish doctrine and LIE of Evolution that man is just an accident that happened and that he will soon 'die like a dog' and that that is the end - no spirit and no eternal future. Well, that could not be further from the truth!

C.31 God's true followers are normally not rich people, and not well-known as they prefer to dedicate themselves to worshipping God rather than to run to the riots of excesses of drinking and all kinds of lusts that are taking over the world today.

Ephesians 5.18 'And be not drunk with wine, wherein is excess; but be filled with the Spirit.

Ephesians 4.17-19 So this I say, and affirm together with the Lord, that you walk no longer just as the Gentiles also walk, in the futility of their mind, being darkened in their understanding, excluded from the life of God because of the ignorance that is in them, because of the hardness of their heart; and they, having become callous, have given themselves over to sensuality for the practice of every kind of impurity with greediness.

Source: https://bible.knowing-jesus.com/topics/Licentiousness

C.32 Many cannot understand that one can get 'much more satisfaction' by simply knowing God in a very personal way by having a direct communication with him in all that they do and living naturally according to his laws.

C.33 I am stating by personal experience that it is much more fun to include

God in one's life and that it is much more rewarding that merely running to the excesses of life in the hope of them satisfying our soul - which they simply can't do, as God Himself has made an 'emptiness' inside each person that can only be filled with Him and His eternal Love in order to make one both happy and fulfilled and saved through His son Jesus Christ.

II Cor. 5.17 Therefore if any man be in Christ, he is a new creature: old things are passed away; behold, all things are become new. [See 'how to get saved' – See **Salvation** on my website: SALVATION - www.outofthebottomlesspit. co.uk/418605189]

C.34 Having an intimate relationship with the Lord. This is largely done through quietness and meditation in the Word of God.

C.35 It *is* also possible to hear from God and get His answers to everything in our lives. That is rewarding, satisfying, and fulfilling daily and is essential to our spiritual and physical well-being.

C.36 The truth be told - It is quite simple to 'get saved' and 'escape the fires of Hell', and does not depend on man's religions, churches or traditions and ceremonies. One must be as a little child:

Matthew 18.3 "And said, Verily I say unto you, 'Except ye be converted, and become as little children, ye shall not enter into the kingdom of heaven.'"

2 Corinthians 11:3 "But I fear, lest by any means, as the serpent beguiled Eve through his subtilty, so your minds should be corrupted from the simplicity that is in Christ."

---

17 "But, O my son, as we missed our way, and came as far as this, we found other men below this mountain; who inhabit a beautiful country, full of trees and of fruits, and of all manner of verdure; it is like a garden; so that when we found them we thought they were you; until thy father Mahalalel told me they were no such thing.

18 "Now, therefore, O my son, hearken to my counsel, and go down to them, thou and thy children. Ye will rest from all this suffering in which ye are. But if thou wilt not go down to them, then, arise, take thy children, and come with us to our garden; ye shall live in our beautiful land, and ye shall rest from all this trouble, which thou and thy children are now bearing."

C.37 Spiritual fight on the mountain against Satan. Satan tempted Jesus with the kingdoms of this world.

Matthew 4.1,8-9: Then was Jesus led up of the Spirit into the wilderness to be tempted of the devil. "Again, the devil taketh him up into an exceeding high mountain, and showed him all the kingdoms of the world, and the glory of them and saith unto him,

'All these things will I give thee, if thou wilt fall down and worship me'.

> 19 But Jared when he heard this discourse from the elder, wondered; and went hither and thither, but at that moment he found not one of his children.

C.38 He could not at that moment find any of his children. They are hidden from his sight temporarily by Satan.

> 20 Then he answered and said to the elder, "Why have you hidden yourselves until this day?"
>
> 21 And the elder replied, "If thy father had not told us, we should not have known it."
>
> 22 Then Jared believed his words were true.

C.39 Do not listen to Satan not even for a moment. Slam the door in his face even if it cuts his nose off. Give no place to the Devil.

1 Peter 5:8-9 Be sober, **be vigilant**; because your adversary the devil, as a roaring lion, walketh about, seeking whom he may devour: 9 Whom resist steadfast in the faith, knowing that the same afflictions are accomplished in your brethren that are in the world.

> 23 So that 'elder' (Satan in disguise) said to Jared, "Wherefore didst thou turn about, so and so?" And he said, "I was seeking one of my children, to tell him about my going with you, and about their coming down to those about whom thou hast spoken to me."

C.40 Here it appears that Jared cannot find any of his children when normally they are right there along with his wife. He is puzzled as to why he cannot see or find any of them. It is as though Satan has put Jared in some sort of trance where he can only see the vision or apparitions that Satan has placed all around him.

C.41 I can personally testify that when something like this happens and one encounters something supernatural or paranormal and it can be good or bad - that those around you do not seem to notice what is going on around you. In other words, others do not see the same thing. It has happened to me upon several occasions which I will write more about in my next book **'OUT OF THE BOTTOMLESS PIT II'**

> 24 When the elder heard Jared's intention, he said to him, "Let alone that purpose at present, and come with us; thou shalt see our country; if the land in which we dwell pleases thee, we and thou shall return hither

and take thy family with us. But if our country does not please thee, thou shalt come back to thine own place."

C.42 Satan (elder) is deliberately trying to minimize the importance of Jared seeking counsel of one of his relatives to confirm that it would be alright for him to go with this stranger and his 'men.' And continues to entice Jared away from his purpose down the mountain to the sons of Cain in the valley.

25 And the elder urged Jared, to go before one of his children came to counsel him otherwise.

26 Jared, then, came out of the cave and went with them, and among them. And they comforted him, until they came to the top of the mountain of the sons of Cain.

C.43 Jared is lured away from the Cave of Treasures by the Devil and brought to the top of the mountain where he can see down into the valley below where live the sons of Cain.

27 Then said the elder to one of his companions, "We have forgotten something by the mouth of the cave, and that is the chosen garment we had brought to clothe Jared withal."

28 He then said to one of them, "Go back, thou, someone; and we will wait for thee here, until thou come back. Then will we clothe Jared and he shall be like us, good, handsome, and fit to come with us into our country."

29 Then that one went back.

30 But when he was a short distance off, the elder called to him and said to him, "Tarry thou, until I come up and speak to thee."

31 Then he stood still, and the elder went up to him and said to him, "One thing we forgot at the cave, it is this--to put out the lamp that burns inside it, above the bodies that are therein. Then come back to us, quick."

C.44 More tricks and ruses of Satan. He promises to get a beautiful garment for Jared to make him appear wonderful like the other 'men who are with Satan. All these handsome men are in fact the Fallen angels.

C.45 Whilst Jared is distracted standing at the top of the mountain looking into the valley far below his enemy has now got him totally off-guard and he sends ones of his fallen angels to go and 'put out the Lamp' in the cave which I suppose symbolizes the 'Presence of God' like the Shekinah Glory that was to be in the Jewish Temple many 1000's of years later.

C.46 Jared's job was to stay close to God and to protect his tribe from the attacks of their enemies and from the attacks of Satan. He was also supposed to 'Stay on Guard' against all the attacks of Satan and his job was to guard the 'Flame of Truth' of the Words of God and His presence mong men. As they say when the cat's away the mice will play. So, it was, and Satan (disguised as the elder) managed to put 'the Lamp' out in the Cave of Treasures where all the bodies of Jared's ancestors were. That was Adam, Seth, Enos, Cainan, and Mahalalel

---

32 That one went, and the elder came back to his fellows and to Jared. And they came down from the mountain, and Jared with them; and they stayed by a fountain of water, near the houses of the children of Cain, and waited for their companion until he brought the garment for Jared.

33 He, then, who went, back to the cave, put out the lamp, and came to them and brought a phantom with him and showed it them. And when Jared saw it, he wondered at the beauty and grace thereof and rejoiced in his heart believing it was all true.

C.47 This is indeed odd at first: *'and brought a phantom with him'* 'and when Jared saw it he *'wondered at the beauty and grace thereof'*, and *'rejoiced in his heart believing it was all true'* Whatever the phantom or apparition was, it was something that reassured Jared that everything was all right and that it was OK to go with this elder who said that he was Adam Jared's great-great-great-grandfather. Could this 'phantom' or apparition have been an imitation of the spirit of the Lord, or the 'Shekinah Glory' as mentioned in the Old Testament?

C.48 Great Signs and Wonders in the Last Days: Satan has his imitations of everything that God has created. In the End-time according to the Bible, Satan will have his son the Anti-Christ ruling the whole world in great power, and he will have his false prophet working for his son the Anti-Christ. The false prophet also acts as a sort of false 'Holy Spirit'. These three make what is called the 'Satanic Trinity': Satan, the Anti-Christ, and the False prophet. Just as Satan has put on a big show of many apparitions in these ancient 'Lost Books of Adam and Eve', so will he also put on a big show in the Last Days which will soon be upon us.

Revelations 13.13-14 And he doeth great wonders, so that he makes fire come down from heaven on the earth in the sight of men, 14 And deceives them that dwell on the earth by *the means of* those miracles which he had power to do in the sight of the

Beast.

> 34 But while they were staying there, three of them went into houses of the sons of Cain, and said to them, "Bring us to-day some food by the fountain of water, for us and our companions to eat."
>
> 35 But when the sons of Cain saw them, they wondered at them and thought: "These are beautiful to look at, and such as we never saw before." So, they rose and came with them to the fountain of water, to see their companions.

C.49 Look at the reaction of the children of Cain when they saw these 'beautiful' men. They treated them as if they were gods.

> 36 They found them so very handsome, that they cried aloud about their places for others to gather together and come and look at these beautiful beings. Then they gathered around them both men and women.

C.50 Notice how the people willingly brought all their woman and made them available for these god's pleasure.

> 37 Then the elder said to them, "We are strangers in your land, bring us some good food and drink you and your women, to refresh ourselves with you."
>
> 38 When those men heard these words of the elder, every one of Cain's sons brought his wife, and another brought his daughter, and so, many women came to them; everyone addressing Jared either for himself or for his wife; all alike.
>
> 39 But when Jared saw what they did, his very soul wrenched itself from them; neither would he taste of their food or of their drink.
>
> 40 The elder saw him as he wrenched himself from them, and said to him, "Be not sad; I am the great elder, as thou shalt see me do, do thyself in like manner."
>
> 41 Then he spread his hands and took one of the women, and five of his companions did the same before Jared, that he should do as they did.

C.51 Where have we heard of this before? Local peoples willingly giving their woman whether it be their wives or their daughters to total strangers who happened to desire and want them. We have heard many times before of ancient cultures who when they met the 'gods' who came from the sky in flying chariots and who sometimes were giants or the sons of the fallen angels that the native peoples would willingly give their women to these gods and demi-gods. We see this also in both Greek and other mythologies. Maybe there is indeed some truth in ancient mythology?

C.52 Here the Devil in the form of the 'Elder' is taking one of the women and so did 5 of his companions grab hold of 5 other beautiful women with the intent to use and abuse them. After Jared had been clothed in fine raiment, they advised him to do likewise, but he was horrified and rightly so and drew back totally aghast!

C.53 The 'elder' had tricked Jared by telling him that he and his companions were in fact Adam, Seth, Enos, Cainan and Mahalalel which would account for 5 of the 'men with the 'elder' grabbing the women in the same way that Satan (the elder) did.

---

42 But when Jared saw them working infamy he wept, and said in his mind, 'My fathers never did the like.'

43 He then spread his hands and prayed with a fervent heart, and with much weeping, and entreated God to deliver him from their hands.

44 No sooner did Jared begin to pray than the elder fled with his companions; for they could not abide in a place of prayer.

C.54 Satan flees when he sees the weakest saint upon his knees.

James 4.7 Submit yourselves therefore to God. Resist the devil, and he will flee from you.

---

45 Then Jared turned round but could not see them but found himself standing in the midst of the children of Cain.

C.55 After praying desperately the whole apparition of the elder and all his handsome men disappeared like a mist which suddenly dissipates.

---

46 He then wept and said, "O God, destroy me not with this race, concerning which my fathers have warned me; for now, O my Lord God, I was thinking that those who appeared unto me were my fathers; but I have found them out to be devils, who allured me by this beautiful apparition, until I believed them.

47 "But now I ask Thee, O God, to deliver me from this race, among

---

whom I am now staying, as Thou didst deliver me from those devils. Send Thy angel to draw me out of the midst of them; for I have not myself power to escape from among them."

48 When Jared had ended his prayer, God sent His angel in the midst of them, who took Jared and set him upon the mountain, and showed him the way, gave him counsel, and then departed from him.

C.56 Fortunately for Jared as he had been tricked by an apparition and did not give in to any devilish temptations Satan had no more power over him and God's angel was able to carry him back up the mountain as normally once those on the mountain had willingly gone down the mountain, they were not able to return to the mountain.

CHAPTER 18 (97)

Jared's Children Fall

THE children of Jared were in the habit of visiting him hour after hour, to receive his blessing and to ask his advice for everything they did; and when he had a work to do, they did it for him.

2 But this time when they went into the cave they found not Jared, but they found the lamp put out, and the bodies of the fathers thrown about, and voices came from them by the power of God, that said, "Satan in an apparition has deceived our son, wishing to destroy him, as he destroyed our son Cain."

C.1 Here can clearly see that Satan was the one who deceived Cain and ended up destroying his soul and making him totally evil.

C.2 It is also interesting that it stated in this verse that Satan first appeared to his potential 'victims' as an apparition or in a disguised visual form. Satan can apparently disguise himself in many forms. In modern times Satan has been increasingly restricted by God Himself in making such appearances before mankind. We do hear of Satan showing up in person upon occasion in certain testimonies told by others but not like the above description or am I perhaps wrong about this assessment, and that Satan does appear unto some people but that now it is much more in directly wicked situations like those of witch-craft and idol-worshipping, where Satan shows up to 'bless' his followers.

C.3 But for the righteous like Jared in this story, I only know of one person who confessed that he had seen Satan and that was John Todd the Christian writer. Sadly, he eventually died as a martyr! He was once at the very head of witchcraft covens and was on the top counsel of 13 witches in the USA. Miraculously he got saved due to the persistent prayers of a concerned pastor. It was during the battle for his Salvation that Satan showed up in person apparently dressed in a deep purple long robe. So, I suppose such an apparition could still happen today. **[See the movie: The Devil's Advocate for more on Satan's apparitions]**

3 They said also, "Lord God of heaven and earth, deliver our son from the hand of Satan, who wrought a great and false apparition before him," They also spake of other matters, by the power of God.

4 But when the children of Jared heard these voices they feared and stood weeping for their father; for they knew not what had befallen him.

5 And they wept for him that day until the setting of the sun.

6 Then came Jared with a woeful countenance, wretched in mind and body, and sorrowful at having been separated from the bodies of his fathers.

C.4 This situation reminds me of the parallel in the spiritual realm. 'Neglect not to fellowship with one another as the manner of some is:

Hebrews: 10.25 "Not forsaking the assembling of ourselves together, as the manner of some *is*; but exhorting *one another*: and so much the more, as ye see the day approaching."

C.5 The difference in Jared's case is that he was upon occasion able to communicate with the dead or let us say the spirit of Adam came and talked with him. Does the Bible tell us that the dead can come and be spirit helpers and guides to the living? There are countless examples in the Bible:

Hebrews 12.1 Wherefore seeing that we also are compassed about with so great a cloud of witnesses…

7 But as he was drawing near to the cave, his children saw him, and hastened to the cave, and hung upon his neck, crying, and saying to him, "O father, where hast thou been, and why hast thou left us, as thou wast not wont to do?" And again, "O father, when thou didst disappear, the lamp over the bodies of our fathers went out, the bodies were thrown about, and voices came from them."

8 When Jared heard this he was sorry, and went into the cave; and there found the bodies thrown about, the lamp put out, and the fathers themselves praying for his deliverance from the hand of Satan.

C.6 Why the need to keep the Cave of Treasures always lit up? Do the tombs of the dead need protecting? Well, from the above verse the light of the LAMP keeps evil spirits away from the tombs of Jared's ancestors. We have all heard that sometimes graves are desecrated in modern times, and there has been some poltergeist activity where the graves have been disrupted and the graveyard seemingly shaken about and moved somewhat. Where do those Halloween type stories come from - concerning the 'disturbed grave-yards'? Supposedly, by bad spirits. The above story is similar.

9 Then Jared fell upon the bodies and embraced them, and said, "O my fathers, through your intercession, let God deliver me from the hand of Satan! And I beg you will ask God to keep me and to bide me from him unto the day of my death."

C.7 Here is an interesting verse from the book of Enoch about the dead and to this story - those in the 'Garden of Life':

Enoch 61.10 And all who sleep not above in heaven shall bless him. All the holy ones who are in heaven shall bless Him, and all the elect who dwell in the 'Garden of Life', and every spirit of light who is able to bless, and glorify and extol, and hallow thy name, and all flesh shall beyond measure glorify and bless thy name forever and ever. [Editor: This verse is also talking about Jesus as are the preceding verses in Enoch Ch 61. See my book Enoch Insights]

---

10 Then all the voices ceased save the voice of our father Adam, who spake to Jared by the power of God, just as one would speak to his fellow, saying, "O Jared, my son, offer gifts to God for having delivered thee from the hand of Satan; and when thou bring those offerings, so be it that thou offer them on the altar on which I did offer. Then also, beware of Satan; for he deluded me many a time with his apparitions, wishing to destroy me, but God delivered me out of his hand.

11 "Command thy people that they be on their guard against him; and never cease to offer up gifts to God."

12 Then the voice of Adam also became silent; and Jared and his children wondered at this. Then they laid the bodies as they were it first; and Jared and his children stood praying the whole of that night, until break of day.

13 Then Jared made an offering and offered it up on the altar, as Adam had commanded him. And as he went up to the altar, he prayed to God for mercy and for forgiveness of his sin, concerning the lamp going out.

14 Then God appeared unto Jared on the altar and blessed him and his children and accepted their offerings; and commanded Jared to take of the sacred fire from the altar, and with it to light the lamp that shed light on the body of Adam.

CHAPTER 19 (98)

Backsliding

THEN God revealed to him again the promise He had made to Adam; He explained to him the 5500 years and revealed unto him the mystery of His coming upon the earth.

2 And God said to Jared, "As to that fire which thou hast taken from the altar to light the lamp withal, let it abide with you to give light to the bodies; and let it not come out of the cave, until the body of Adam comes out of it.

3 But, O Jared, take care of the fire, that it burn bright in the lamp; neither go thou again out of the cave, until thou receive an order through a vision, and not in an apparition, when seen by thee.

C.1 Sometimes this story is like a simple illustration as to how we should enter the presence of the Highest with praises and thanksgivings. The Lamp is symbolic of the Light of God's presence. A lamp that we should never let go out or be put out by others.

Ps 91.1 He that dwelleth in the secret place of the Most High shall abide under the shadow of the Almighty, I will say of the Lord He is my refuge and my fortress my God; in him will I trust.

Ps 119.105 Thy Word is a Lamp until my feet and a light unto my path.

4 "Then command again thy people not to hold intercourse with the children of Cain, and not to learn their ways; for I am God who loves not hatred and works of iniquity."

5 God also gave many other commandments to Jared and blessed him. And then withdrew His Word from him.

6 Then Jared drew near with his children, took some fire, and came down to the cave, and lighted the lamp before the body of Adam; and he gave his people commandments as God had told him to do.

7 This sign happened to Jared at the end of his four hundred and fiftieth year; as did also many other wonders, we do not record. But we

record only this one for shortness's sake, and in order not to lengthen our narrative.

C.2 Notice in this last verse how it is stating 'we' do not record... This is showing that there was more than one writer involved in the putting together these lost Books of Adam and Eve. What it sounds like to me is that there was one main writer of the stories, but that he had to counsel with other initiated writers to confirm that the re-assembled story was exactly the same as the older version that was falling apart at the time of re-writing the Lost Books of Adam and Eve in circa 100 BC.

Proverbs 15.22 Without counsel purposes are disappointed: but in the multitude of counsellors, they are established.

C.3 If my assumption is correct, then it would also show that the lost Books of Adam and Eve were held in great esteem in 100 BC.

C.4 If one considers that it took 70 learned Jewish scholars to help assemble the Septuagint version of the Old Testament in 300 BC and 70 scholars to assemble the entire King James version of the Bible in 1601, then for the Lost Books of Adam and Eve to get the attention of several writers or more at the time of compiling in 100 BC, shows without a doubt that the Lost Books of Adam and Eve were very important books and highly esteemed by the writers of that time.

C.5 According to the Bible, Jared lived to be 962 years of age. Here it is stating that in the year when Jared was 450 years old that this part of the story of the 'Lost books of Adam and Eve' happened.

C.6 According to the KJV of the Bible that would put the date at 910 A.C According to the Bible Adam died at 930 A.C, and Enoch died at 976 A.C According to the Book of Jasher the whole world departed from the 'ways of Enoch' within 200 years of his death or no later than 1176. The world descended into absolute Chaos from around 1200 to the year of the Great Flood in 1658. **[See Jasher Insights Book I]**

8 And Jared continued to teach his children eighty years; but after that they began to transgress the commandments, he had given them, and to do many things without his counsel. They began to go down from the Holy Mountain one after another, and to mix with the children of Cain, in foul fellowships.

C.7 The sons of Seth started to backslide from the ways of righteousness and went down the spiritual mountain to get there from God's Mountain down into the cesspool of the valley villains.

C.8 It would appear in this story that the sons of Seth also had to come down from a physical mountain as well to get down to the valley.

C.9 To Live on The Mountain or In the Valley? Mountains have always signified God's territory & the godly places where there are always few people. The valleys always signify where the masses are, and valleys are generally man's territory - full of peoples and noise and things that distract from the beautiful sights and visions that one can have on the mountain. On the mountain you feel closer to God. The streams that cascade down the mountain have pure waters for those on the mountain to drink. On the mountain the air is purer than down in the stinking valley with all its pollution especially in modern times.

9 Now the reason for which the children of Jared went down the Holy Mountain, is this, that we will now reveal unto you.

CHAPTER 20 (99)

The Revolt

> 1 AFTER Cain had gone down to the land of dark soil, and his children had multiplied therein, there was one of them, whose name was Genun, son of Lamech the blind who slew Cain.

C.1 It is also mentioned in the Book of Jasher that it was indeed this Lamech the blind who slew his great-great grandfather Cain by accident with a bow - thinking that Cain whom he vaguely could see in the distance, was a wild animal coming towards him, whilst he was with his youngest son Tubal Cain.

C.2 See my book **'Jasher Insights' Book 1** to read the amazing details of this sad story where 'Lamech the Blind' not only accidently killed his great-great grandfather Cain but in his semi-blindness accidently smote his youngest son on the head so hard that he also died. Lamech's two wives Adullah and Zilah forsook him for a season because of this. This is also mentioned in the Bible:

C.3 This 'Lamech the blind' was not the same Lamech as Lamech the son of Methuselah who was born some 3 generations later or in 874 years After Creation according to K.J. Bible Time charts.

C.4 Genun is also known as Jubal.

> 2 But as to this Genun, Satan came into him in his childhood; and he made sundry trumpets and horns, and string instruments, cymbals and psalteries, and lyres and harps, and flutes; and he played on them at all times and at every hour.

C.5 'Came into him childhood' It sounds here that Satan had possessed Jubal/Genun since he was child.

C.6 This description is later mirrored in the description of Pan the satyr or half-goat and half man creature always playing a flute and enticing people through his music.

C.7 This is not surprising as his father was Lamech the blind who slew Cain his great great-grandfather and was cursed 7 times worse than Cain because of it.

Genesis 4.15: And the LORD said unto him, 'Therefore whosoever slays Cain, vengeance shall be taken on him sevenfold. And the LORD set a mark upon Cain, lest any finding him should kill him.'

C.8 It was indeed in the time of the 'sons of Lamech the blind' that great debauchery began on the face of the earth in the early days or around 450 years after Creation and 1200 years before the Great Flood. This is an interesting extra detail from those early times.

C.9 The evil that began by the sons of Cain in around 450 AC and the even greater evil of the Fallen angels coming into the daughters of Cain in the 'days of Jared' or around 650 AC was somewhat 'held back' for around 243 years during the time of Enoch from 743 until his translation in 987 A.C, as he had a lot of power over the kings of the earth according to the apocryphal book of Jasher.

C.10 The kings of the earth were afraid of Enoch as he had power over 'Fallen angels' and according to the Book of Enoch itself he rebuked the fallen angels to their faces for their crimes. He was made 'King of Kings' by 120 kings of the earth according to the Book of Jasher.

C.11 After having finished his testimony Enoch was 'translated' or 'taken up to heaven' by God himself in the year 987 AC. His son Methuselah continued for another 200 years instructing the kings of the earth not to go astray as many of the children of Cain had done.

C.12 Finally, everyone rejected Methuselah's witness from God in around **1187** and from point on most of the children of Seth came down the spiritual mountain and joined the sons of Seth and the world descended into chaos and lawlessness. [See my books 'Enoch Insights' and 'Jasher Insights' for the complete story]

C.13 I knew from the Bible that Jubal was the maker of instruments, but I did not realize that in his case the instruments were made under the inspiration of Satan himself using music to hypnotize people into some sort of trance. Of course, this is not to say that musical instruments are evil in themselves, but it is how they are used and with what spirit either good or bad that really matters.

Gen. 4:21 And his brothers name was Jabal. He was the father of all who play stringed instruments (lyres) and pipes.

C.14 It is mentioned in the Bible that Satan was created with musical instruments embedded in his body:

Ezekiel 28.13 Thou hast been in Eden the garden of God; every precious stone was thy covering, the sardius, topaz, and the diamond, the beryl, the onyx, and the jasper, the sapphire, the emerald, and the carbuncle, and gold: the workmanship of thy tabrets and of thy pipes was prepared in thee in the day that thou was created.

3 And when he played on them, Satan came into them, so that from among them were heard beautiful and sweet sounds, that ravished the heart.

4 Then he gathered companies upon companies to play on them; and when they played, it pleased well the children of Cain, who inflamed themselves with sin among themselves, and burnt as with fire; while Satan inflamed their hearts, one with another, and increased lust among them.

> 5 Satan also taught Genun to bring strong drink out of com; and this Genun used to bring together companies upon companies in drink-houses; and brought into their hands all manner of fruits and flowers; and they drank together.

C.15 It sounds like another powerful evil spirit or demon was introduced to mankind: Bacchus. The demon god of drinking and more importantly - Addictions.

> 6 Thus did this Genun multiply sin exceedingly; he also acted with pride and taught the children of Cain to commit all manner of the grossest wickedness, which they knew not; and put them up to manifold doings which they knew not before.
>
> 7 Then Satan, when he saw that they yielded to Genun and hearkened to him in everything he told them, rejoiced greatly, increased Genun's understanding, until he took iron and with it made weapons of war.

C.16 As far as the Bible says it was not Jabal who invented the weapons of war but his brother Tubal Cain.

Gen.4.22 And Zillah, she also bare Tubal-cain, the forger of every cutting instrument of brass and iron: and the sister of Tubal-cain was Naamah.

C.17 Tubal Cain is mentioned as being the first blacksmith. He was a descendant of Cain and son of 'Lamech the blind' and Zillah

C.18 Here we have a situation which shows the serious dangers of compromising with evil. It proved to be a bad idea for the sons of Seth to intermarry with the children of 'Cain the murderer' and eventually led to their subsequent complete downfall in the centuries to come except for Methuselah, Lamech (the good one) and Noah.

C.19 The righteous sons of Seth? There were very few good sons of Seth! Most of their descendants died in the Great Flood wherein according to the Bible only 8 souls were saved – Noah, his three sons and their three wives. All the rest had compromised and blatantly become very evil. Noah and his sons warned the world for 120 years whilst they were building the ark of God. This happened starting 1538 years **A**fter **C**reation and the Great Flood eventually came in 1658 A.C

Book of Jasher 2.17 And Lamech, the son of Methuselah, became related to Cainan by marriage, and he took his two daughters for wives. and Adah conceived and bare a son to Lamech and called his name Jabal. And she conceived again and bare a son to Lamech, and she called his name Jabal.

C.20 Cainan was the son of Enos, who was the son of Seth, who was the son of Adam. Cainan was born 325 years after Creation according to the KJV version of the biblical time-charts.

> 8 Then when they were drunk, hatred and murder increased among them; one man used violence against another to teach him evil taking his children and defiling them before him.

C.21 How sick and depraved the world became in early days after Creation or from the 3rd century AC and started by the sons of Cain.

> 9 And when men saw they were overcome, and saw others that were not overpowered, those who were beaten came to Genun, took refuge with him, and he made them his confederates.
>
> 10 Then sin increased among them greatly; until a man married his own sister, or daughter, or mother, and others; or the daughter of his father's sister, so that there was no more distinction of relationship, and they no longer knew what iniquity is; but did wickedly, and the earth was defiled with sin, and they angered God the Judge, who had created them.
>
> 11 But Genun gathered together companies upon companies, that played on horns and on all the other instruments we have already mentioned, at the foot of the Holy Mountain; and they did so in order that the children of Seth who were on the Holy Mountain should hear it.

C.22 Satan had total control in the above situation with the sons of Cain and now he wanted to use them to entice the righteous sons of Seth to come down from their mountainous abode far above them using musical instruments to seduce them into coming down from their 'righteous' mountain.

> 12 But when the children of Seth heard the noise, they wondered, and came by companies, and stood on the top of the mountain to look at those below; and they did thus a whole year.
>
> 13 When, at the end of that year, Genun saw that they were being won over to him little by little, Satan entered into him, and taught him to make dyeing-stuffs for garments of divers patterns and made him understand how to dye crimson and purple and what not.

C.23 We see that sometime later in the generation of Jared that Fallen angels came to the earth to pollute the earth and its wicked ways even more.

14 And the sons of Cain who wrought all this, and shone in beauty and gorgeous apparel, gathered together at the foot of the mountain in splendour, with horns and gorgeous dresses, and horse races, committing all manner of abominations.

15 Meanwhile the children of Seth, who were on the Holy Mountain, prayed and praised God, in the place of the 'hosts of angels' who had fallen; wherefore God had called them "angels," because He rejoiced over them greatly.

C.24 God would certainly not call his children 'angels' as it says in the scriptures that God puts 'no trust' in his angels. Why? Probably because a 'third' of them betrayed Him. See the next chapter concerning the false doctrine of the 'The unrighteous' 'Children of Seth' being the ones who came down to the licentious daughters of Cain and not Fallen angels. A doctrine created by the Catholic church around the 3rd– 4th century A.D

Job 4.18 'Behold, He puts no trust in his servants and charged his angels with folly'

Revelation 12:9 And the great dragon was cast out, that old serpent, called the Devil, and Satan, which deceives the whole world: he was cast out into the earth, and his angels were cast out with him.

16 But after this, they no longer kept His commandment, nor held by the promise He had made to their fathers; but they relaxed from their fasting and praying, and from the counsel of Jared their father. And they kept on gathering together on the top of the mountain, to look upon the children of Cain, from morning until evening, and upon what they did, upon their beautiful dresses and ornaments.

17 Then the children of Cain looked up from below, and saw the children of Seth, standing in troops on the top of the mountain; and they called to them to come down to them.

18 But the children of Seth said to them from above, "We don't know the way." Then Genun, the son of Lamech, heard them say they did not know the way, and he bethought himself how he might bring them down.

19 Then Satan appeared to him by night, saying, "There is no way for them to come down from the mountain on which they dwell; but when they come to-morrow, say to them, 'Come ye to the western side of the

mountain; there you will find the way of a stream of water, that comes down to the foot of the mountain, between two hills; come down that way to us.'"

20 Then when it was day, Genun blew the horns and beat the drums below the mountain, as he was wont. The children of Seth heard it and came as they used to do.

21 Then Genun said to them from down below, "Go to the western side of the mountain, there you will find the way to come down."

22 But when the children of Seth heard these words from him, they went back into the cave to Jared, to tell him all they had heard.

23 Then when Jared heard it, he was grieved; for he knew that they would transgress his counsel.

24 After this, a hundred men of the children of Seth gathered together and said among themselves, "Come, let us go down to the children of Cain, and see what they do, and enjoy ourselves with them."

25 But when Jared heard this of the hundred men, his very soul was moved, and his heart was grieved. He then arose with great fervour, and stood in the midst of them, and adjured them by the blood of Abel the just, "Let not one of you go down from this holy and pure mountain, in which our fathers have ordered us to dwell."

26 But when Jared saw that they did not receive his words, he said unto them, "O my good and innocent and holy children, know that when once you go down from this holy mountain, God will not allow you to return again to it."

27 He again adjured them, saying, "I adjure by the death of our father Adam, and by the blood of Abel, of Seth, of Enos, of Cainan, and of Mahalalel, to hearken to me, and not to go down from this holy mountain; for the moment you leave it, you will bereft of life and of mercy; and you shall no longer be called 'children of God,' but 'children of the devil.'"

28 But they would not hearken to his words.

29 Enoch at that time was already grown up, and in his zeal for God, he arose and said, "Hear me, O ye sons of Seth, small and great--when ye transgress the commandment of our fathers, and go down from this holy mountain--ye shall not come up hither again for ever."

30 But they rose up against Enoch, and would not hearken to his words, but went down from the Holy Mountain.

31 And when they looked at the daughters of Cain, at their beautiful figures, and at their hands and feet dyed with colour, and tattooed in ornaments on their faces, the fire of sin was kindled in them.

32 Then Satan made them look most beautiful before the sons of Seth, as he also made the sons of Seth appear of the fairest in the eyes of the daughters of Cain, so that the daughters of Cain lusted after the sons of Seth like ravenous beasts, and the sons of Seth after the daughters of Cain, until they committed abomination with them.

33 But after they had thus fallen into this defilement, they returned by the way they had come, and tried to ascend the Holy Mountain. But they could not, because the stones of that holy mountain were of fire flashing before them, by reason of which they could not go up again.

34 And God was angry with them and repented of them because they had come down from glory and had thereby lost or forsaken their own purity or innocence and were fallen into the defilement of sin.

35 Then God sent His Word to Jared, saying, "These thy children, whom thou didst call 'My children, behold they have transgressed My commandment, and have gone down to the abode of perdition, and of sin. Send a messenger to those that are left, that they may not go down, and be lost."

36 Then Jared wept before the Lord and asked of Him mercy and forgiveness. But he wished that his soul might depart from his body, rather than hear these words from God about the going down of his

children from the Holy Mountain.

37 But he followed God's order and preached unto them not to go down from that holy mountain, and not to hold intercourse with the children of Cain.

38 But they heeded not his message and would not obey his counsel.

CHAPTER 21 (100)

Jared predicts the Flood

> AFTER this another company gathered together, and they went to look after their brethren; but they perished as well as they. And so it was, company after company, until only a few of them were left.

C.1 This is such a tragic story how most of the righteous fell away from their 'steadfastness' and didn't follow the ways of the Lord anymore but descended from the mountain to the children of Cain and became just like them - 'wicked'.

C.2 They were all destroyed at the time of the Great Flood some 236 years later. Imagine the great sorrow that God felt when He could only save 8 souls from the entire planet out of perhaps billions of people.

C.3 Our world today is fast moving in the same direction as before the Great Flood. Of course it is true that many righteous people died before the Great Flood including Methuselah the son of Enoch who was the oldest man to have lived on the earth at 969 years old and he died 2 months before the Great Flood as did Lamech his son at 777 years old die 5 years before the Great Flood and there were many more righteous people whom God willed to die before the Great Flood came upon all the wicked of the earth.

C.4 One can easily see that Lamech died naturally before his time at only 777 years old. He did not live to be over 900 years old as his ancestors had done. God simply 'willed' some of the righteous to 'pass on' rather than 'face the Great Flood'.

> 2 Then Jared sickened from grief, and his sickness was such that the day of his death drew near.

C.5 Jared was in fact the 2nd oldest person to have ever lived. According to biblical times charts he lived to be 962 years old and died circa 430 years after his son Enoch in the year 1422 AC or around 236 years before the Great Flood which occurred in 1656 according to the KJV of the Bible.

C.6 More on the life of Jared 6th from Adam. It is true that Jared saw a lot of sorrow in this lifetime spanning from 460AC to 1422AC [AC =After Creation], as he witnessed the effects of the Fallen angels coming down to earth, living with the daughters of men, and defiling them resulting in Giants being created. Then he gradually saw through his lifetime the total fall away from faith of all the children of Seth except for Methuselah, Lamech (the good one), and Noah. He also had to witness the total depravity of the Giants and their fathers the Fallen angels who ended up descending into total madness and depravity. These gods and demi-gods were very violent and 'lorded it' over much of mankind. Sometimes, the Giants wantonly devoured the people. Many strange hybrid creatures and resultant monsters were created in that time period of the 500 years leading up to the Great Flood. They were finally all destroyed in the judgment of the Great Flood by God Himself. [See **Genesis 6**, and the **Books** of **Enoch**, **Jasher**, and **Jubilees**, as well as **The Antiquities of the Jews** by **Josephus** the ancient Jewish historian.]

3 Then he called Enoch his eldest son, and Methuselah Enoch's son, and Lamech the son of Methuselah, and Noah the son of Lamech.

4 And when they were come to him, he prayed over them and blessed them, and said to them, "Ye are righteous, innocent sons; go ye not down from this holy mountain; for behold, your children and your children's children have gone down from this holy mountain, and have estranged themselves from this holy mountain, through their abominable lust and transgression of God's commandment.

5 "But I know, through the power of God, that He will not leave you on this holy mountain, because your children have transgressed His commandment and that of our fathers, which we had received from them.

6 "But O my sons, God will take you to a strange land, and ye never shall again return to behold with your eyes this garden and this holy mountain.

C.7 'God will take you to a 'strange land' This could be referring to mankind who probably lived inside the earth until the Great Flood coming out to the outer surface of the earth on the waters of the Great Flood and seeing the outer surface of the earth where we live today for the very first time. A place where people age much faster. According to ancient books such as the Zohar written in Hebrew - the Garden of Eden is inside the earth inside the Hollow Earth.

7 "Therefore, O my sons, set your hearts on your own selves, and keep the commandment of God which is with you. And when you go from this holy mountain, into a strange land which ye know not, take with you the body of our father Adam, and with it these three precious, gifts and offerings, namely, the gold, the incense, and the myrrh; and let them be in the place where the body of our father Adam shall lay.

C.8 Prophecy concerning Noah and the coming Great Flood.

C.9 'set your hearts on your own selves' What does that mean?

C.10 I try to always check the KJV of the Bible as well as the Septuagint at times concerning different things that I read in apocryphal books and other Jewish and Hebrew books. Amazingly there nearly always agree in most things.

---

8 "And unto him of you who shall be left, O my sons, shall the Word of God come, and when he goes out of this land he shall take with him the body of our father Adam, and shall lay it in the middle of the earth the place in which salvation shall be wrought."

9 Then Noah said unto him, "Who is he of us that shall be left?"

10 And Jared answered, "Thou art he that shall be left. And thou shalt take the body of our father Adam from the cave and place it with thee in the ark when the flood comes.

11 "And thy son Shem, who shall come out of thy loins, he it is who shall lay the body of our father Adam in the middle of the earth, in the place whence salvation shall come."

12 Then Jared turned to his son Enoch, and said unto him, "Thou, my son, abide in this cave, and minister diligently before the body of our father Adam all the days of thy life; and feed thy people in righteousness and innocence."

13 And Jared said no more. His hands were loosened, his eyes closed, and he entered into rest like his fathers. His death took place in the three hundred and sixtieth year of Noah, and in the nine hundred and eighty-ninth year of his own life; on the twelfth of Takhsas on a Friday.

14 But as Jared died, tears streamed down his face by reason of his great sorrow, for the children of Seth, who had fallen in his days.

C.11 The old false doctrine from the Catholic church in around 300+ AD of it being the 'Fallen Sons of Seth' and not 'Fallen Angels' that came down from the mountain and had intercourse with the licentious daughters of Cain is what happened in Genesis 6. That old doctrine could have been taken from this very book as far as I can see – The Lost Books of Adam and Eve Book 2. It could have been used and misinterpreted to create a false doctrine in the 3rd to 4th century A.D.

C.12 The time sequence is wrong according to the KJV biblical time-chart. The time when the sons of Seth came down from the mountain to the daughters of Cain was in the time of Cainan 4th from Adam.

C.13 Lamech the blind married two of the daughters of Cainan 4th from Adam and their sons were Jubal and Jabal and that was in and around 400 A.C that he begat children including daughters. The Fallen angels however came down in the time of Jared and his son Enoch who confronted them to their faces. See the book of Enoch. The Fallen angels fell at least 100 or more years after the children of Seth started to come down the mountain to the daughters of Cain.

C.14 Adah and Zilla compromised their convictions of living according to the 'children of Seth which they were and ended up, marrying one of the sons of Cain the 'Lamech the blind' by 'going down the mountain'. A seeming little disobedience to the laws of Seth, led to total disaster as regarding the Sons of Seth.

ENOCH 2.16 And these are the names of the children of Cainan; the name of the first-born Mahalalel, the second Enan, and the third Mered, and their sisters were Adah and Zillah; these are the five children of Cainan that were born to him.

ENOCH 2.17 And Lamech, (7th from Adam through the 'Sons of Cain' lineage) who the son of Methusael, became related to Cainan (4th from Adam through Seth) by marriage, and he took his two daughters for his wives (circa 400- 450 A.C), and Adah conceived and bare a son to Lamech, and she called his name Jabal.

C.15 Time chart comparison Jared 7th from Adam through Seth was born in 460 AC. 'Lamech the blind' was also 7th from Adam through Cain.

C.16 Cain started having children at least 50 years before the birth of Seth the son of Adam. So, the 7th generation of Cain's children happened much sooner that the 7th generation through Seth. Seth was Adam's third son born in 130 AC. As mentioned earlier in this 'Lost books of Adam and Eve book 2': 'But by the time Enos was eight hundred and twenty years old, Cain had a large progeny; for they married frequently, being given to animal lusts; until the land below the mountain, was filled with them'.

C.17 There is obviously nothing wrong with sex between male and female of adult age, which is better protected by marriage according to God himself. What happened in the case of the sons of Cain? Well, they did produce a lot more children than Seth's lineage because they were like the Fallen angels: excessively lustful, sensual and they abused the woman all the time - who in turn kept getting pregnant. It was in fact the licentious daughters of Cain that enticed the Sons of Seth to come down from the mountain to join their wild orgies.

Jude: 1.7-8,19: Even as Sodom and Gomorrah, and the cities about them in like manner, giving themselves over to fornication, and going after strange flesh, are set forth for an example, suffering the vengeance of eternal fire. [8] Likewise also these filthy dreamers defile the flesh, despise dominion, and speak evil of dignities. [19] These be they who separate themselves, sensual, having not the Spirit.

C.18 Adam's first-born Cain was the father of Enoch who was the father of Irad, who was the father or Mechuyael who was the father of Methusael who the father of was 'Lamech the blind'.

ENOCH 2.18-20 And she conceived again and called his name Jubal and Zilah her sister was barren in those days and had no offspring.

19 For in those days the sons of men began to trespass against God and to transgress the commandments which he had commanded to Adam, to be fruitful and to multiply in the earth.

20 And some of sons of men caused their wives to drink a draught that would render them barren in order that they might retain their figures and whereby their beautiful appearance might not fade; and Zillah drank with them.

C.19 Now in modern times it is quite easy to disprove the above-mentioned doctrine of the 'Sons of Seth' being the 'Fallen angels' of Genesis 6 who came down from heaven and were seduced by the daughters of Cain.

C.20 Here is a quote also mentioned in my book 'Enoch Insights' 'Aside from the Book of Jude, Peter, and Paul's affirmations of the angelic/hybrid interpretation of the Book of Enoch. The Catholic church's Origen known as the father of theology - affirmed the Book of Enoch and the fact that angels could and did cohabitate with the daughters of men. He even warned against possible angelic and or Nephilim infiltration of the church itself. Oddly, whilst thousands of his writings are still considered by them as 'sacred' this very issue got him labelled as a heretic when the faulty 'Sons of Seth' doctrine was conceived during his time!

C.21 What does Satan fear most: Is it not exposure! Those running the organized Catholic church were obviously already going seriously astray in the 3rd to 4th century in them being afraid of labelling the angels of Satan as 'Fallen angels' and inherently evil and they were the ones who originally corrupted the daughters of men accorded to Genesis 6 – so they persecuted Origen - the father of Theology!

Gen 6.2 That the sons of God saw the daughters of men that they were fair; and they took them wives of all which they chose. There were giants in the earth in those days.

Jubilees 5.1 And it came to pass when the children of men began to multiply on the face of the earth and daughters were born unto them, that the angels of God saw them on a certain year of this Jubilee that they were beautiful to look upon; and they took themselves wives of all whom they chose, and they bare unto them sons and they were giants.

---

15 Then Enoch, Methuselah, Lamech and Noah, these four, wept over him; embalmed him carefully, and then laid him in the Cave of Treasures. Then they rose and mourned for him forty days.

---

16 And when these days of mourning were ended, Enoch, Methuselah, Lamech and Noah remained in sorrow of heart, because their father had departed from them, and they saw him no more.

C.22 According to the Bible Enoch died 430 years before his father Jared at the young age of only 365 years old in the year 987 A.C, but Jared was one of the oldest persons to have ever lived and died at the ripe old age of 962 in the year 1422 A.C. Only his grandson Methuselah the son of Enoch lived even longer to 969 years of age.

CHAPTER 22 (101)

Only 3 Righteous Men are Left

> BUT Enoch kept the commandment of Jared his father and continued to minister in the cave.

C.1 So what is this Cave of Treasures as it would appear to be more spiritual than physical at this point. It states in the verse that Enoch kept the commandment of his father Jared and continued to minister in the cave. What exactly did that mean?

C.2 This book is based on a mountain that is a physical mountain but at the same time it is talking about being on a spiritual mountain.

C.3 No wonder that it states that Jared was very sorrowful at the enormous number of backslidings of his people from the mountain. Jared more than any other person saw for literally 9 centuries of depravity and debauchery and the descent into total madness of the whole world in Pre-flood times under the guidance of both Satan and his Fallen angels.

> 2 It is this Enoch to whom many wonders happened, and who also wrote a celebrated book; but those wonders may not be told in this place.

C.4 Here is a clear mention of the Book of Enoch. Look at the following two verses, one from the Book of Enoch and the other from the book of Jude in the Bible which mirror each other showing that the New Testament Christians as well as the Jews believed in the Book of Enoch, as is also mentioned in these 'Lost books of Adam and Eve'.

Book of Enoch 1.6 And behold! He cometh with ten thousands of His holy ones to execute judgement upon all and to destroy all the ungodly and to convict all flesh of all the works of their ungodliness which they have ungodly committed, and of the hard things which ungodly sinners have spoken against Him

Jude 1.14-15 And Enoch also, the seventh from Adam, prophesied of these, saying, 'Behold, the Lord cometh with ten thousand times ten thousands of his Saints.' 'To execute judgment upon all, and to convince all that are ungodly among them of all their ungodly deeds which they have ungodly committed, and of all their hard speeches which ungodly sinners have spoken against him.'

C.5 The fact that here in these Lost Books of Adam and Eve it mentions the Book of Enoch is very important. It shows that the Book of Enoch was already a famous book at the time these books were written in circa 100 BC.

C.6 The important thing is that the Book of Enoch was assembled in around 300 BC from a much older book. It was originally written in Pre-Flood times and given by Enoch to Noah to take on the Ark according to the Book of Noah which has a few chapters inserted into the Book of Enoch. I believe that the same is true of these Lost Books of Adam and Eve that they were re-assembled in around 100 BC, but it is likely that they were taken from much older writings from the Pre-Flood times.

C.7 See my book 'Enoch Insights' for much more info about Enoch and his celebrated book. The life of Enoch is mentioned in detail in my other book 'Jasher Insights' Book I, and in 'Jubilees Insights'

---

3 Then after this, the children of Seth went astray and fell, they, their children, and their wives. And when Enoch, Methuselah, Lamech and Noah saw them, their hearts suffered by reason of their fall into doubt full of unbelief; and they wept and sought of God mercy, to preserve them, and to bring them out of that wicked generation.

C.8 This was a very frustrating time to live in, when many of your own relatives did not walk in the path of righteousness, and eventually you saw your own relatives perish, as did Noah see his relatives perish, at the time of the Great Flood.

---

4 Enoch continued in his ministry before the Lord three hundred and eighty-five years, and at the end of that time he became aware through the grace of God, that God intended to remove him from the earth.

C.9 It is stating here that Enoch lived to be 385 years which is off by 20 years according to the Bible which states that Enoch was translated when he was 365 years old. Just a detail.

---

5 He then said to his son, "O my son, I know that God intends to bring the waters of the Flood upon the earth, and to destroy our creation.

6 "And ye are the last rulers over this people on this mountain; for I know that not one will be left you to beget children on this holy mountain; neither shall any one of you rule over the children of his people; neither shall any great company be left of you, on this mountain."

7 Enoch said also to them, "Watch over your souls, and hold fast by your fear of God and by your service of Him, and worship Him in upright faith, and serve Him in righteousness, innocence and judgment, in repentance and also in purity."

8 When Enoch had ended his commandments to them, God transported him from that mountain to the land of life, to the mansions of

> the righteous and of the chosen, the abode of Paradise of joy, in light that reaches up to heaven; light that is outside the light of this world; for it is the light of God, that fills the whole world, but which no place can contain.

C.10 According to the Book of Jasher, Enoch did instruct many hundreds of thousands of people including over 100 kings for 243 years before he was taken up to heaven. After he was translated it was hardly 200 years later in the time of his son Methuselah that nearly everyone refused to obey God's commandments any longer.

C.11 The 'great fall' of most people into darkness happened around 1187 A.C. This explains why Noah and his sons had no converts even after warning people for 120 years in the days before the Great Flood.

C.12 The Great Flood according to the Bible happened in 1658. This would mean that most of the planet descended into anarchy and chaos for almost 500 years leading up to the Great Flood.

> 9 Thus, because Enoch was in the light of God, he found himself out of the reach of death; until God would have him die.
>
> 10 Altogether, not one of our fathers or of their children, remained on that holy mountain, except those three, Methuselah, Lamech, and Noah. For all the rest went down from the mountain and fell into sin with the children of Cain. Therefore, were they forbidden that mountain, and none remained on it but those three men.

C.13 I think that it is important for Bible students to have an excellent grasp of the **LONGIVITY CHART** from Adam to Joseph with the correct time sequencing as shown in the KJV of the Bible. Get a copy of the Time-Chart and put it on your wall or your office when you are studying the Bible and books like this one. I have explained why the Septuagint version of the time sequence is incorrect and why it was corrupted, which is a shame because in general the Septuagint is an excellent copy of the Old Testament. It was originally translated into the Greek language in around 300 BCE. I will attempt to explain why the numbers do make sense in the Bible.

C.14 If we look at the KJV of the Bible we can plot a Time-chart the lineage of Adam and then Seth, Enos, Cainan, Mahalalel, Jared, Enoch, Methuselah, Lamech, Noah for the first ten generations leading up to the Great Flood. These ten generations covered a period of 1658 years.

C.15 Adam had Seth when he was 130 years old, but also remember that Cain and Abel had also been born long before this time. From reading the book of Jubilees it would appear than Adam and Eve had already had 2 sons and 3 daughters by the time Seth was born when Adam was 130 years old.

It would also appear that his first children had been born within the first 50 years of his life. So why did he stop having any more children until he was 130 years old?

C.16 We are told that just like Jared in this story of Adam and Eve that because Adam and Eve were so sorrowful over what happened to their dear beloved son Abel when Cain had murdered him according to the Book of Jubilees, that they stopped having children for a season. Why am I mentioning this in particular? Well, let us now examine when Noah had his first child. Why did he wait until he was 502 years old before having children? We are told that he did not want to have children because the world was too wicked! God specifically told him to marry and have children as He would protect them from all the evil and from his impending judgements of the coming Great Flood.

C.17 The following is a chart of the first 10 generations from Adam to Noah showing the age at which they started having children apart from Adam who already had 4 other children by this time.

Adam 130, Seth 105, Enos 90, Cainan 70, Mahalalel 65, Jared 162, Enoch 65, Methuselah 187, Lamech 182, Noah 502

C.18 We know from the Book of Jubilees concerning the Story of Adam and Eve that Adam had children before 50 years old, and from the Lost Books of Adam and Eve in this story above that Jared was full of sorrow in his time because so many of the children of Seth 'left the mountain' or spiritually speaking they fell away from their faith and followed the 'Devils crowd' instead down in the Valley of this story from the Lost books of Adam and Eve. We also can see that Jared waited until he was 162 before having any children as did Methuselah until he was 187 and Lamech until 182 as well as Noah who waited until he was 502 years old. I think the reason they all delayed having children was probably because they were abhorred by the depraved conditions of mankind and how that it was continually deteriorating and getting much worse in every way -so they delayed in having children hoping for better times until in Noah's case God specifically told him to both marry and have children as God had a plan to save both him and his wife and children through the Ark.

C.19 Enoch by contrast, the son of Jared, had his first child when he was 65, but he was specifically called by God for a special ministry and although he only lived to be 365 years old - notice that his son Methuselah was the oldest person to have ever lived at 969 years old. He died just months before the Great Flood. Methuselah carried on the ministry of Enoch his father for hundreds of years according to the book of Jasher, until his godly witness was totally rejected by everyone except two men: his son Lamech, and Noah. Lamech died 5 years before the Great Flood at 777 years old. Only Noah and his wife alone survived with their 3 sons and their wives to go through the judgement of the Great Flood.

C.20 Again, if we examine the numbers above the father of Jared was Mahalalel who had his firstborn when he was 65. Mahalalel was born before the Sons of Seth started 'falling from faith' and coming down from the mountain. The sons of Seth started falling approximately 450 years after Creation onwards. Jared was born 460 years after Creation.

C.21 So Jared experienced early on the descent of the sons of Seth down the spiritual mountain to join the sons of Cain in the valley increasingly so throughout all his life.

C.22 It is also stated that in the days of Jared the 'Angels of God came down on mount Hermon and had intercourse with the daughters of men. This event happened around the time of the birth of Enoch or just before being 622 years after Creation.

C.23 As is said 'do not give the Devil an inch or he will take a mile'. Because of Satan's protegee in Jubal, the sons of Cain started doing depraved things that they had never thought of until his time. Then they went to entice the sons of Seth to be disobedient and to come down from their spiritual mountain of obedience to God. Having let down their guard Satan must have been laughing his head off as he instructed the Fallen angels to go down to the women on the earth and procreate with them to try and destroy the DNA of mankind so that the promised Messiah would never be able to be born. Fortunately, God managed to hinder the Devils plan but at a very great price. Only Noah and a total of 8 souls survived the Great Flood.

C.24 Is it generally true that before the Great Flood no-one was sick or harmed by plagues and sicknesses and afflictions. If generally true 'Lamech the blind' was an exception but then he had been cursed 7-fold. Cain when he was cursed did receive a 'mark' on his head also, which I suppose could be deemed an affliction.

C.25 See the influence of sicknesses in the Book of Jubilees. There was much less oxygen in the atmosphere after the Great Flood. Today oxygen levels are getting too low, especially in the big cities. On average the oxygen levels around the planet are around 20%. In the cities it is often 19% or less and 19% is what is called a critical threshold of oxygen. With insufficient oxygen in the atmosphere, it causes all kinds of maladies such as lung problems and skins irritations and mental illnesses – according to experts like Dr Philip B James who founded the Hyperbaric Oxygen Treatment centres in the UK back in the early eighties.

C.26 DINOSAURS, OXYGEN & CO2: Higher Oxygen levels are known to kill things like cancer and all kinds of maladies. The world before the Great Flood was indeed designed by God himself like a massive external and internal hyperbaric oxygen chamber. The amount of oxygen would have been much greater and so was the atmospheric pressure. Having been a patient using hyperbaric oxygen - the benefits are amazing. Greater oxygen content on the earth would mean that bigger creatures could have roamed the earth like pterodactyls which modern scientists tell us should not have been able to fly as their lungs were too small. With a much higher oxygen content in the atmosphere under greater pressure it would have been possible for dinosaurs to both breath and live well upon the earth in Pre-Flood conditions. Scientists are baffled as to how dinosaurs in general could have lived in many cases having such massive bodies – they relegate such things to millions of years ago in their minds - but it did not have to be that way if the actual planet were much more protected in the times before the Great Flood with a canopy of water high up in the atmosphere both inside and outside the planet. This acted to keep out all dangerous UV light and cosmic rays and as a result mankind lived to a very great age before the Great Flood and in fact according to the Bible up to almost 1000 years old. Another interesting fact is that greater CO_2 levels causes the vegetation and trees to grow much bigger and higher. The Global Warming consensus which blames CO_2 as being dangerous must be totally wrong!

C.27 Assuming that the earth is indeed hollow:

The Inner earth due to its original design by God allowed for a lot more vegetation and much bigger trees. The bigger vegetation produced much more oxygen. This helped everyone to be much healthier. Read about the Book of Remedies in my book 'Jubilees Insights' and why it was given to Noah by the angels according to the ancient Book of Jubilees which was written in Hebrew? For some reason by the testimony of others, Inner Earth even to this day has different characteristics than the outer earth. There is evidence according to the highly decorated Admiral Byrd (who allegedly flew his plane inside the earth back in 1926 and in 1947), that the dinosaurs are still alive inside the earth. We have also heard different stories that people who descended into the inner earth lived longer than we who live on the outer surface. Due to the barbaric conditions on the earth, I think that it is highly likely that bigger creatures have with time fled to inner earth through the Northern and Southern Apertures for sanctuary.

C.28 After reading this book, I would suggest that the next book to read in chronological order of time would be the Book of Enoch which is fully contained in my book 'Enoch Insights' and my books 'Jasher Insights' Book 1 and 'Jubilees insights' as all talk about this time of the fallen angels and the descent into chaos of mankind starting in the days of Jared and his son Enoch.

C.29 In summary: Satan managed to first get into Cain the first son of Adam and Eve, and thus Cain's children became very evil. They were then used by Satan to entice the righteous away from true godliness and they forsook the mountain of spiritual strength, light, reason, love, and kindness. Because mankind in general 'let the Devil in' that it was not but a century later that the first '200 Fallen angels' fell to the earth upon Satan's instructions no doubt, enticed by the licentious daughters of Cain.

C.30 Evil Came to The Earth in the 1st '500 Years' After the Creation

The 6th from Adam was Jared who was born in 460 A.M.

A key event that happened in the life of Jared was that the Fallen Angels came down to the earth and corrupted the daughters of men.

In the Lost Book of Adam and Eve Book 2 it states that the righteous stay on the mountain until the 6th generation and then they were seduced to come down the mountain to the temptations of the licentious daughters of Cain.

If we look at the 1st 500 years of our world's history we see the very beginning of the 1st 500 years where Evil entered into human life in the form of Satan himself as the fallen angel in the Garden of Eden tempting Eve, then great Evil is sown through Cain: murder and raping and pillaging, and hundreds of years later came the first 200 Fallen angels down to the earth to land on Mt Hermon circa 500 to 600 After Creation – **[See Flavius Josephus: The Antiquities of the Jews]**

APPENDIX I

C.1) Origin of THE LOST BOOKS OF ADAM AND EVE? Leonhard Rost writes: "There can be no doubt that the lost original can be ascribed to a Jewish author who probably lived in Palestine—possibly toward the end of the first century B.C. The year A.D. 70 is the *terminus ante quem* since the Temple—of Herod? —is still standing. The author may have had affinities with Essene circles, as the ascetic features (especially the Apocalypse's description of the physical separation of the sexes, even for animals) suggest." (*Judaism Outside the Hebrew Canon*, p. 154) Life of Adam and Eve (earlyjewishwritings.com)

BACKGROUND TO THE LOST BOOKS OF ADAM AND EVE: The Forgotten Books of Eden: The First Book of Adam and Eve: The First Book of Adam and Eve (sacred-texts.com)

C.2) There can be no doubt that there existed at an early date, perhaps even before the destruction of the Second Temple in 70 AD of a collection of legends of Adam and Eve which have been partially preserved, not in their original language, but somewhat changed.

It is possible to prove that the Apocryphas, Apocalypsis Mosis— as Tischendorf, following a copyist's erroneous inscription, called the book— and Vita Adæ et Evæ, and to a certain degree even their Slavonic, Syriac, Ethiopic, and Arabic offshoots, are of identical Jewish origin. ADAM, BOOK OF - JewishEncyclopedia.com

Adam, the handiwork of the Lord (Ab. R. N. i., end), lived with Eve in the Garden of Eden, which was situated in the East (Book of Enoch, xxxii.; B. B. 84a). Their food, which they also distributed to the lower animals (Gen. R. xix. 5), consisted of the fruit of the trees in the garden, the only nourishment then allowed to living beings (Sanh. 59b). For their protection two angels were set apart (Ḥag. 16a), known (Ber. 60b) as מכובדים or the partakers of the majesty (כבוד) (*kabod*), called in Latin *virtutes*, from *virtus*, corresponding to *kabod*. But one day when the guarding angels had ascended to heaven to sing their hymn (שירה) to the Lord (Ḥul. 91b), Satan thought the time opportune to carry out his evil designs against Adam. Satan hated Adam, for he regarded him as the cause of his fall. After God had created man, He ordered all the angels to prostrate themselves before Adam, but Satan rebelled against God's command, despite the direct bidding of Michael "to worship the image of YHW" (יהו) and answered proudly: "If God be angry against me, I will exalt my throne above the stars of God" (compare Isa. xiv. 13). Whereupon God "cast him out from heaven with all his host of rebellious angels" (Slavonic Book of Enoch, xxxi. 18, and Mek., Shirah, § 2). And Satan the Adversary (Suk. 52a) selected the serpent for his tool, as it was not only the most subtle of all animals, but also remarkably like man, for it had been endowed with hands and legs like him (Gen. R. xix. 1). ADAM, BOOK OF - JewishEncyclopedia.com

C.3 Check out this above link as it has some amazing original information concerning the **LOST BOOKS OF ADAM AND EVE** which can be traced far back in time. The books were of Jewish origin but were tampered with in the different translations.

APPENDIX II

C.1 What really happened in that Garden of Eden and did Eve do more than just eat the 'Forbidden Fruit' from the 'Tree of Knowledge'?

C.2 Did Eve in fact have sex with the Devil and then become pregnant by Satan and thus was the mother of the first murderer Cain? An incredibly sad story, if true, for the beginning of humanity!

I Jn 3.12 Not as Cain, who was of that wicked one, and slew his brother. And wherefore slew he him? Because his own works were evil, and his brother's righteous.

Jn.8.44 Ye are of *your* father the devil, and the lusts of your father ye will do. He was a murderer from the beginning, and abode not in the truth, because there is no truth in him. When he speaks a lie, he speaks of his own: for he is a liar, and the father of it.

C.3 And Satan spoke to the serpent: "Be my instrument, and through thy mouth will I utter a word which shall enable thee to seduce man" (Pirķe R. El. xiii.). After some pleading the serpent succeeded in persuading Eve to eat of the forbidden fruit of the tree of knowledge—a fig-tree (Gen. R. xv. 7)—which the serpent had shaken for her (Ab. R. N. i. 4, ed. Schechter). But the serpent had infused lust into the fruit, and when Eve had eaten of it the sexual desire awoke in her.), and at the same moment she became aware that she had been undone and "had lost the garment of righteousness in which she had been clothed" (Gen. R. xix. 6, Pirķe R. El. xiv.). Adam, too, after he had eaten of the forbidden fruit, experienced a sense of loss and cried out: "What hast thou done? Thou hast removed me from the glory of the Lord" (Ab. R. N. i. 6, ed. Schechter).

(Slavonic Book of Baruch, xcvii.; Apoc. Abraham, xxiii., and Pirķe R. El. xxi.), ADAM, BOOK OF - JewishEncyclopedia.com

C.4 Eve being 3 months pregnant, when she had just come out of the Garden of Eden is mentioned in VITA ADAE ET EVAE which is Latin for 'The Life of Adam and Eve': Chapter XVIII 'And there to weep bitterly and groan aloud. And she made there a booth, while she had in her womb offspring of three months old' (Cain)- from the Apocrypha and Pseudepigrapha of the Old Testament -R.H.Charles - Oxford: Clarendon Press 1913

C.5 *"And when Cain had travelled over many countries, he, with his wife, built a city which he called Enoch after the name of his firstborn son, in the land of Nod, and there he settled his abode where also he had children. However, he did not accept his punishment in order to amend, but to increase his wickedness; for he only aimed to procure everything that was for his own bodily pleasure, though it obliged him to be injurious to his neighbours.*

He augmented his household substance with much wealth, by raping and violence; he excited his acquaintance to procure pleasures and spoils by robbery and became a great leader of men into wicked courses. He also introduced a change in that way of simplicity wherein men lived before; and was the author of measures and weights. And whereas they lived innocently and generously while they knew nothing of such arts, he changed the world into cunning craftiness. He, first of all set boundaries about lands: he built a city, and fortified it with walls, and he compelled his family to come together to it; and called that city Enoch, after the name of his eldest son Enoch. [After many generations there arose a man, whose name was Lamech]; who had seventy-seven children by two wives, Silla, and Ada. Of those children by Ada, one was Jabal: he erected tents, and loved the life of a shepherd. But Jubal, who was born of the same mother with him, exercised himself in music; and invented the psaltery and the harp. But Tubal, one of his children by the other wife, exceeded all men in strength, and was very expert and famous in martial performances. He procured what tended to the pleasures of the body by that method; and first of all invented the art of making brass. Lamech was also the father of a daughter, whose name was Naamah. And because he was so skilful in matters of divine revelation, that he knew he was to be punished for Cain's murder of his brother, he made that known to his wives. Nay, even while Adam was alive, it came to pass that the posterity of Cain became exceeding wicked, everyone successively dying, one after another, more wicked than the former. They were intolerable in war, and vehement in robberies; and if anyone were slow to murder people, yet was he bold in his profligate behaviour, in acting unjustly, and doing injuries for gain."- FLAVIUS JOSEPHUS – THE ANTIQUITIES OF THE JEWS BOOK 1 CHAPTER 2. *[Translated by William Whitson]* SOURCE: genesis 4, josephus on cain (alittleperspective.com)

C.6 Looking at these above verses from Josephus in around 100 AD about the character of Cain, it is so obvious that Cain was born or fathered by Satan. Somehow Satan persuaded Eve to have sex with him which resulted in the birth of Cain and was probably the real reason why Adam and Eve got kicked out of the Garden of Eden as it was devil worship!

'He also introduced a change in that way of simplicity wherein men lived before and was the author of measures and weights. And whereas they lived innocently and generously while they knew nothing of such arts, he changed the world into cunning craftiness.'

C.7 It would also seem that Cain was the father of the merchants who get rich by cunning craftiness.

Hosea 12.7 'He is a merchant, the <u>balances of deceit</u> are in his hand: he loveth to <u>oppress</u>'.

James 5.1-4 'Go to now, ye rich men, weep and howl for your miseries that shall come upon you. 2 Your riches are corrupted, and your garments are motheaten. 3 Your gold and silver is cankered; and the rust of them shall be a witness against you and shall eat your flesh as it were fire'. 4 Behold, the hire of the labourers who have reaped down your fields, which is of you kept back by **fraud**, cries: and the cries of them which have reaped are entered into the ears of the Lord of sabaoth.

APPENDIX III: From Chapter 1 verse 3: 'Dark':

C.1 Destroying the wicked and Evil spirits is what the Lake of Fire is for. If we consider the following verses, we find a paradox. Is this what eventually happens, in order to bring about Universal Conciliation for all humans?

Revelations 21.8 'But the fearful, and unbelieving, and the abominable, and murderers, and whoremongers, and sorcerers, and idolaters, and all liars, shall have their part in the lake which burns with fire and brimstone: which is the second death.

C.2 This verse above from Revelations 21.8 is describing all the worse types of people as being thrown into the Lake of Fire.

Revelations 22.15 Outside are the dogs, those who practice magic arts, the sexually immoral, the murderers, the idolaters and everyone who loves and practices falsehood.

C.3 This verse of **Revelations 22.15** appears to be describing the same type of people who had previously been thrown into the Lake of Fire, and that now have been forcibly purged from their diabolical iniquities of rebellion, and have been recreated as new people, and who have now come to live outside of the Heavenly City, where they can also be healed of their sicknesses and sins from the leaves from the Tree of life, which those of the Heavenly City will minister unto them. Those described here, are the same as those described as **not** being in the **Book of Life** in **Revelations 20**.

Revelation 20:13-15 'And the sea gave up the dead which were in it; and death and hell delivered up the dead which were in them: and they were judged every man according to their works. [14]And death and hell were cast into the lake of fire. This is the second death. [15]And whosoever was not found written in the book of life was cast into the lake of fire'.

C.4 I believe it likely that it is talking about the humans being forcible changed, who went into the Lake of Fire, and not the Devil and his angels who are totally destroyed, so that Evil itself cannot come back again.

[10]And the Devil that deceived them was cast into the lake of fire and brimstone, where the beast and the false prophet are, and shall be tormented day and night for ever and ever.

[11]And I saw a great white throne, and him that sat on it, from whose face the earth and the heaven fled away; and there was found no place for them.

[12]And I saw the dead, small and great, stand before God; and the books were opened: and another book was opened, which is the book of life: and the dead were judged out of those things which were written in the books, according to their works.

C.5 It is important that the evil spirits that have been in rebellion against

God for thousands of years, are **not allowed** to come back again, after the Great White Throne Judgment and the New Heaven and New Earth appears, wherein will dwell only righteousness.

C.6 Eventually Satan and his fallen angels will be totally destroyed, unless they repent before the time of the Great white Throne Judgment. One of the first things that God made, was the Judgement and Lake of Fire, as a warning to Satan and the Fallen angels, as to what would eventually happen to them if they did not turn from their diabolical rebellion against God.

Jude 1.6,13-15 And the angels, which kept not their first estate, but left their own habitation, he hath reserved in everlasting chains under darkness unto the judgment of the great day.

13 Raging waves of the sea, foaming out their own shame; wandering stars, to whom is reserved the blackness of darkness forever.

14 And Enoch also, the seventh from Adam, prophesied about these, saying, 'Behold, the Lord cometh with ten thousands of his saints,

15 To execute judgment upon all, and to convince all that are ungodly among them of all their ungodly deeds which they have ungodly committed, and of all their ungodly deeds which they have committed, and of all their hard speeches which ungodly sinners have spoken against him.

Enoch 1.6 And behold! He cometh with ten thousands of His holy ones to execute judgement upon all and to destroy all the ungodly and to convict all flesh of all the works of their ungodliness which they have ungodly committed, and of the hard sayings which ungodly sinners have spoken against Him

C.7 Universal Reconciliation: The reason I think that the '**dark**' nature will be forcibly purged from the humans, but not Satan and the Fallen angels, who are all cast into the Lake of Fire after the Great White Throne Judgment circa 1000 year from now, or at the end of the Golden Age of the Millennium, is because humans have only lived one life upon the earth and cannot easily see God. It takes faith for humans to believe in God. On the other hand, Satan and the Fallen angels have known about God for thousands of years and yet they are in direct rebellion and defiance of God Himself. Satan fell in the spirit world long before the Creation of the physical realm because he refused to acknowledge Jesus as the Son of God and the heir of God as he thought that that title should have gone to him. Satan fell because of pride.

APPENDIX IV

TWINS

1) Why does the **LOST BOOK OF ADAM AND EVE** state that Abel had a twin sister, and that Cain had a twin sister? This is certainly not a biblical account.

What do we know from history about notable TWINS?

2) The Bible tells us that Rebecca and Isaac had twins and that they were 'fighting each other' even in the womb! Jacob and Esau. Esau ended up trying to kill his twin brother Jacob according to the Book of Jasher. **[See my books JASHER INSIGHTS BOOK I AND II]**

3) Jacob's two wives were twin sisters: Rachel and Leah and were his cousins.

4) In mythology we hear that Rome was founded by a set of twin brothers called Romulus and Remus who were brought up by a she-wolf after they had been abandoned by their parents (gods). Romulus killed Remus to start Rome.

5) We hear about Atlantis being founded by 5 sets of twin brothers who father was a god, Poseidon.

6) In ancient times some cultures were afraid of twins as they thought that they were fathered by the gods or the demi-gods.

7) Of course, most of us in modern times probably know someone who had twins and they are great people. I have sons-in-law who are identical twins. Nothing strange.

8) I hope to investigate this topic more in my next book which will be called 'Out of the Bottomless Pit II about the paranormal. I will look at Atlantis and other mysteries such as the ancient books from India that are fascinating and talk about ancient empires that ruled with flying machines and had lasers and crystal power. Apparently, several conflicting empires fought against each other and probably wiped each other out in the times before the Great Flood. Were they descended from the gods?

9) As I have mentioned Cain killed his brother Abel and I have even heard some say that they were twins. I do not think that they themselves were twins, but I do think that Cain was fathered by a god - Satan.

10) Is it possible that twins are mentioned in the Lost Books of Adam and Eve because these books were originally written a long time before the 5 books of the Torah of Moses time?

11) What if the original Lost Books of Adam and Eve were written long before the Great Flood or around 600-900 years after Creation by the descendants of Adam and Eve

12) If this is correct, then it means that the Lost Books of Adam and Eve were written 1800 to 2000 years before the Torah was even written. There is a lot more to investigate about this topic, but the writers of the Lost Books of Adam and Eve were not afraid to mention twins.

For a comprehensive list of twins and the gods: **Twins in mythology - Wikipedia**

APPENDIX V - TRIPLE HELIX

C.1 I think it likely that although people still had the 'triple helix' in their bodies until the Great Flood, starting with Adam and Eve who 'lost their lumines-cence', or 'bright nature' mankind became increasingly limited in the use of 'extra abilities' until mankind became truly as the description 'mud-bound' man - no longer able to float or fly or go on spirit trips at will and enjoy the amazing joys of the Garden of Eden. At present about the closest any of us could get to the 'Garden of Eden' would be in a vivid dream whilst on a 'dream channel'.

C.2 I suggest you get a copy of Douglas Hamp's 'Corrupting the Image' Book 1, as it alludes to some amazing abilities of Adam and Eve, as to life as it truly was before the Great Flood.

C.3 Someone just sent me the following link to yet another interesting book which talks about Adam and Eve and their original Triple Helix 'bright nature':

SOURCE: A Beautiful Delusion | William F Kinney

C.4 How was it genetically even possible for Noah's wife to have three differ-ent children with the same father Noah?

If there used to be a Triple Helix originally in mankind's DNA in Pre-Flood times, then this could easily answer the age-old question as to 'How was Noah's wife able to have three different sons. One white, one brown and one black.

C.5 If it is true that the DNA of humans was altered by God Himself at or around the time of the Great Flood, then the following is a distinct possibility.

C.6 Double Helix: When we only have a double helix in our DNA, then the possibilities for our children are limited to 2 strands of DNA from the mother and 2 from the father, which would give the child its appearance. In other words, you have just **2 x 2 = 4** possibilities.

C.7 Triple Helix: However, if humans used to have 3 DNA strands each, then the possibilities in the children would be **3 x 3 = 9** possibilities.

C.8 Noah, the biological father of **3 different sons**? If Noah did indeed have a Triple Helix in his DNA chromosome make-up, then this could mean that even if Noah was the biological father of all three sons, which is indisputable, then the DNA of both Noah and his wife, (being some of the very last born before the Great Flood) had to be very different.

C.9 Possibly, Noah and his wife's DNA was influenced by the DNA of his father Lamech and grandfather or even great grandfather, as well as all the ancestors of his wife.

C.10 We don't have enough details as to who Lamech married or what race she was, and same goes for the grandfather and great grandfather of Noah and of course the ancestors of his wife.

C.11 I think it likely that with the Triple Helix, Noah's wife inherited some traits from her ancestors as well as Noah's ancestors which became evident in Noah's wife having Ham, Shem, and Japheth. One black child, one brown and one white.

C.12 Those who know about the Triple Helix are divided as to when mankind lost the Triple helix. Some say at the time Adam and Eve were kicked out of the Garden of Eden and Lost their 'Bright nature' according to these lost Books of Adam and Eve, others think it more likely that the Triple helix was taken away by God Himself at the time of the Great Flood.

C.13 The fact that Noah's wife gave birth to three very different sons, which is a thing that 'genetically speaking' could not happen today.

C.14 This clearly shows that it was indeed at the time of the Great Flood that God took away from mankind the blessing of the Triple Helix and its many abilities.

C.14 The **Great Flood Judgment** and the **Wrath of God Judgment**. Everything got changed including the DNA of mankind at the time of the Great Flood. The Triple Helix is brought back in time for the Millennials, just after the Wrath of God.

C.15 God will have to reverse the curse that was imposed on mankind at the time of the Great Flood, sometime after the Wrath of God. Those fortunate souls who get to survive and live into the Golden age of the millennium will find their bodies changed back into the type of bodies that those people from Pre-Flood times had or a Triple Helix.

C.16 Triple Helix imitators. The wicked merchants are seeking to immortalize themselves by trying to bring back the Triple Helix ahead of the time ordained by God.

C.17 God will cause the whole world to go back to the conditions in the atmosphere as was afforded before the Great Flood. The protective canopy of water around the earth will be brought back. That canopy protects mankind from dangerous UV radiation as well as cosmic radiation, and will allow man to live a much longer life, such as those before the Great Flood

C.18 Today it is called **Transhumanism**. Why would they be wanting to bring the Pre-Flood conditions back to the earth? The Elite, and more importantly the devils and demons that control them, want to get back to the 'Golden Age' that existed in the 500 years leading up to the Great Flood when apparently both Fallen angels and demi-gods ran the world by force in such Pre-Flood empires such as Atlantis, Lemuria, and Mu and yet others.

APPENDIX VI - 5500 YEARS OR 5 AND A HALF DAYS

C.1 – LOST BOOK OF ADAM AND EVE BOOK 1 - Pg. 14: A Possible meaning of the '5500 years' or '5 and a half days'?

According to the Bible, by counting back to Adam in the biblical chronologies we find that the earth is around 6000 years old plus or minus a few hundred years on either side. The Jewish calendar says that this current year of 2021 is the year 5781. When the Lord told Adam and Eve that there would yet be another 5500 years until they could get back into the Garden of Eden, exactly what did He mean? Was this number of 5 and half days the original number

315

given by God, or has it been altered by man, as we have apparently already passed the 5500-year mark and we are much closer to 6000 years since the Creation than any other number, as far as we can understand? Another possibility concerning the 5500 number is it just possible that the 5500 was altered from the original number of say 6000 years because the story was not written until around 500 years after Creation. The apocryphal book of Jasher states that it was Cainan or the 4th descendant from Adam that was the first person to write things down. Other books state that it was Enoch the 7th from Adam who was the first to write things down. I was looking at my biblical time chart, and it is true that 500 years after Creation was a very pivotal time in history.

C.2 ALL EVIL SEEDS SOWN IN THE FIRST 500 YEARS

This sowing of Evil took an evil uglier turn when in around 500 years after Creation the Fallen angels fell and assisted the licentious daughters of Cain to tempt the righteous on the mountain to come down according to these Lost Books of Adam and Eve. If we see that God had stated that he would send His Word to die for all of mankind and all the sins of the world - then it was indeed in the first 500 years that all evil had been sown. Could this be the reason the number given by God as 5500 was counted by Him as he could see the future and knew that He would have to redeem mankind for all the evil as originally sown in the first 500 years of mankind's beginnings?

C.3 When I first saw this strange number of 5500, I had the impression that I had seen this number before, but where? How could 6000 years of history have almost completely passed according to the Bible itself until the present date of 2021 and yet God had apparently told Adam and Eve a specific 5500 years until the birth of the Messiah or should have been His 2nd Coming? It is true that Christ died for all sinners 2000 years ago – but mankind has not returned to the Garden of Eden yet. That can only happen with the 2nd Coming of the Messiah - Jesus Christ when He ushers in the golden Age of the Millennium.

C.4 Then I remembered a Biblical 7000 Year history chart. This chart pointed out that every 500 years or so some major Event happened on the earth that was out of the ordinary.

C.5 Personally, I have never thought that exact date setting is really that important as the scripture tells us:

1 Cor 13.8 'Though there be prophecies, yet shall they fail, whether there be knowledge it shall vanish away'.

C.6 So many people have given out prophecies about the Last Days & The End of The World, but exact date setting is something that I am very wary of – as most date-setting never turns out right. Why is that do you think? I think that God saying that He wants us to trust Him as to when He returns in the 2nd coming of Christ and to wait patiently until that day is finally realized.

C.7 Exact dates are often not needed and can be confusing. On the other hand: Are there any exact dates, times, or events that we can count on without being too dogmatic with the exact year month and minute of the 2nd coming of Christ and the subsequent End of the world?

C.8 Using the Bible as the ultimate authority on such matters, if we look at the books of Daniel and Revelation, they both talk about the Last 7 Years of history. We are told that the Tribulation will last exactly 1260 days of three and a half years on at least 3 different occasions. These 1260 days are the days of what is known as a prophetic year of 360 days.

C.9 When it comes to exact date setting let us stick with what we know from the Bible and not what man says as he is nearly always wrong. God Himself largely shields the exact day dates from our eyes until the day that it is to be fulfilled as we are all supposed to live by faith and not by sight.

C.10 The whole reason for our existence on earth is to learn to trust God completely about everything including the exact day and date that He will return to take us all up to heaven. Prophecies are clouded in mystery, and it is done deliberately. Jesus Himself talked in parables as did Enoch in the Book of Enoch.

APPENDIX VII: 7000 YEAR TIME-TABLE

The following timetable is counted in **years after Creation**

Approx Year	Good Event	Actual Date	Bad Event
0	Creation		
8			Fall of man. Satan the snake
500	Jared f. of Enoch	460	Fallen angels fell from heaven.
1000	Noah	1000	500 years of chaos until the Great Flood
1500	Noah saved	1658	The Great Flood
2000	Abraham	1952	The tower of Babel
2500	Moses	2500	The 10 Plagues on Egypt
3000	King David	2970	Philistines and Israel's enemies subdued.
3500	Ezra -Temple Rebuilt	3540	Babylon Empire Fell
4000	Messiah is born	4BC	70 AD Israel is destroyed by the Romans
4500	Constantine	500 AD	The Roman Empire Fell
5000	Roman Catholics	1000 AD	The Dark Ages/Inquisition
5500	Martin Luther/ Nostradamus	1500	Fall of Roman Catholic Empire (Renaissance of Learning)

6000	Return of Jesus Christ - Millennium	2000	Fall of Satan & the 7th World Empire
7000	The Great White Throne Judgment	3000 Satan thrown into the Lake of Fire	
7000	THE NEW HEAVEN & THE NEW EARTH -THE ETERNAL AGE		

C.5 As one can clearly see there is indeed some great importance to the number 500 years as something of major historical importance that happens around that time. This would seem to be by 'divine design' to keep things changing on the earth in 'man's world'. For the first 500 years after Christ there was lots evangelizing the world. When the Roman empire was taken over in 500 AD, most of Christianity itself became compromised as Christianity became the official religion. By the year 1000 the world was very dark spiritually. Finally, the year 1500 brought the renaissance of learning as the world finally started coming out of the Dark ages of the years 1000-1500. Year 2000 mankind descending into Darkness as one can clearly see now in 2021 the whole world is descending into Satanic insanity and yet the light is still here.

APPENDIX VIII: BIBLICAL NUMEROLOGY

C.1 The number 6 is the number of a man. It was in the 6th Generation that the Fallen angels fell. Jared the 6th from Adam was sorrowful and died in sorrow because of the Fall of the righteous with only Methuselah and Lamech and Noah left of the righteous and still on the mountain according to the Lost Books of Adam and Eve. We are told that God formed the earth in 6 days and on the 7th He rested. We are also told that man shall rule for 6000 years, and the 7th Millennium will be the Golden age of Love & Peace with Christ ruling and the saints reigning together with Him. The end of the 6000 years of man's awful reign on earth is marred even more with the coming of the 666 -meaning the Trinity of Satan, his son the Antichrist and man. When God originally told Adam and Eve how long it would be until they could regain Paradise and enter back into the Garden of Eden in the Lost books of Adam and Eve -giving the number 6000 was not a positive number to give – considering all I have mentioned about the number 6 above. What about the number 5500? This number is apparently an exceptionally good number 5 equals Grace. Double 55 means double amount of Grace. This number of 55 was also attributed to the great man of faith - Abraham as he died at 175 years old = 7 x 5 x 5 meaning God's number and double Grace.

C.2 The biblical number of 5500: The Meaning of Numbers: The Number 5

The number 5 symbolizes God's grace, goodness and favour toward humans and is mentioned 318 times in Scripture. Five is the number of Grace, and multiplied by itself, which is 25, is 'grace upon grace'.

John 1:16 "And of his fulness have all we received, and grace for grace."

The Ten Commandments contains two sets of 5 commandments. The first five commandments are related to our treatment and relationship with God, and the last five concern our relationship with other humans.

C.3 In summary: We can see the 55 as double Grace both in the case of the Saviour as the Word of God and 55 in the 10 Commandments given to Moses on the mountain and 55 to the father of Israel Abraham.

C.4 In conclusion perhaps God did not want to use the number 6000 as the number had a bad connotation in general.

John 2.25 'And he needed not that any man should testify of man for he knew what was in man' – implying not much good.

C.5 The number 6 is the number of a man, and 666 Satanic wickedness comes just before Jesus' 2nd Coming. Not to mention the coming Wrath of God from Revelations chapter 16.

C.6 Perhaps the Lord wanted Adam and Eve to get their eyes upwards on somethings more positive to think on - the good things to counteract all the negative happenings in the world and thus he gave them the mysterious number of 5 and a half days out of 7 or 5500 years as this number is much more in line with the number 7000 - the 7000 years of the Golden Age of Love and Peace –The number 5500 would seem much more in character with returning to the Garden of Eden for Adam and Eve.

APPENDIX IX: 4000 or '5500' years from Creation to the time of Christ?

Currently the two dominant dates for Creation that exist using the Biblical model are about 5500 BC and about 4000 BC. These are calculated from the genealogies in two versions of the Bible, with most of the difference arising from two versions of Genesis. The older dates of the Church Fathers in the Byzantine Era and in its precursor, the Alexandrian Era, are based on the Greek Septuagint. The later dates of Archbishop James Ussher and the Hebrew Calendar are based on the Hebrew Masoretic text.

The earliest extant Christian writings on the age of the world according to the Biblical chronology are by St. Theophilus of Antioch (AD 115-181), the sixth bishop of Antioch from the Apostles, in his apologetic work *To Autolycus*, and by Julius Africanus (AD 200-245) in his *Five Books of Chronology*. Both early Christian writers, following the Septuagint version of the Old Testament, determined the age of the world to have been about 5,530 years at the birth of Christ... This system presents in a masterful way the mystical coincidence of the three main dates of the world's history: the beginning of Creation, the Incarnation, and the Resurrection of Christ. All these events happened, according to the Alexandrian chronology, on the 25th of March; furthermore, the first two events were separated by the period of exactly 5500 years **St. Hippolytus.**

St. Hippolytus of Rome (ca.170-235) maintained on Scriptural grounds that the Lord's birth took place in 5500 AM.

SOURCE: Byzantine Creation Era Calendar / OrthoChristian.Com

APPENDIX X: EXTREME LONGEVITY

WHY DID ADAM AND EVE LIVE SO LONG, OR 930 YEARS TO BE EXACT?

In writing initially about Adam and Eve, I came to realize that this is not just a story of what it was like to have been created as a teenage couple that stayed together for life; and life was an exceedingly long time back then, before the Great Flood, as Adam lived to be 930 years old. So, Eve was probably also around the same age when she died just after Adam died.

A couple could learn a lot in 930 years!

There are unbelievably beautiful things to bring out about old age and the sticking together of an older couple through thick and thin all throughout their lives. It shows wisdom, in fact deep wisdom. There were certain types of joys and trials and tests when they were noticeably young. Different types of trials when they got older and even different trials and experiences when they were incredibly old. 'All things work together for good to those who love God' Ro.8.28

Ref: Sarah of Abraham when 90 years old had a baby to her delight. Sarah with Isaac. Abraham lived longer and fathered 6 more children after the death of Sarah. Severe tests indeed. All of God's great men and women suffered terrible trials and afflictions one way or the other, and they were not given everything on a plate most of the time. Those who truly follow God, or the Lord Jesus, very often do not have easy lives, but that is by choice to 'live by faith' and to trust God for everything.

Psalm 34.19: 'Many are the afflictions of the righteous, but the Lord delivers them out of them all'. God has to test His own children, as he has very great things in store for them if they just continue to hold on in faith through all the fiery trials and tests. (See Hebrews chapter 11)

Why afflictions, pains, sorrows, privations, heartbreaks, disappointments, loneliness, and oppressions of depression? What is it all for? Can't we just get rid of the bad and live in some self-imposed paradise, by making loads of money and working exceptionally hard, where everything is exactly the way we want it to be? What is the catch? It is particularly important to trust God that He knows better than us as to what we need at any given moment in time either good or seeming bad. 'Oh no' you might say.

Luke 1.37: 'For with God nothing shall be impossible'.

Proverbs 5: 'Commit thy way unto the Lord, trust also in Him and He shall bring it to pass'.

The Bride of Christ was created by the Lord, with God himself using opposing forces in our lives such as Himself and Satan to mould us into what we need to be for His ultimate glory. See the story of JOB to see an extreme case. Even 'getting old' is not meant to be a curse either - we are one step closer to heaven or the ultimate paradise where all our dreams really will come completely true. God will either take care of us or take us home one or the other. Either way we have got it made!

John 14 'behold I go to build a place for you that where I am there you may be also – forever, Jesus.

APPENDIX XI FALLEN ANGELS - NEPHILIM

*Fallen angels** are known today as **devils,** and their sons the **Giants** before the Great Flood are known as **demons,** as they were born of Fallen angels and the beautiful women on the earth according to **GEN 6** in the Bible. When the **Giants** died before the Great Flood, they then came back as **demons** after the Great Flood to harm the humans on the earth. [See: **Jubilees Insights**]

Why afflictions, pains, sorrows, privations, heartbreaks, disappointments, loneliness, and oppressions of depression II? Well, choice is the answer to the above question. From reading extensively and praying about this important question as to why God allowed 'Evil' to enter the Garden of Eden, apparently it started in the spirit world long before the actual physical universe was created by God. At one time the heavenly spirit world was only filled with wonderful people and angels and creatures of God and there was no evil. However, God had created Choice. Why? I asked the Lord that question one time and He told me it was because He wanted all His Creation to love and worship Him as God, but of their own free will and not by force as in some oppressive religions.

You all know the story how that God's most powerful archangel Lucifer fell and took one third of God's angels with Him. As related so well in Ezekiel Chapter 28 in the Bible as well as Isaiah Chapter 14 and Revelations 12:6. After Lucifer God's top archangel fell and went his own way with this whole host of Fallen angels, God realized that if he couldn't even trust His angels then who could be trusted? What about all the people and spirits and beings in Heaven? Could they really be trusted, if tempted or given a choice to do good or evil? It was then that God decided to create the physical universe and to separate it from the spiritual dimensions in such a way that humans would no longer be able to directly see God and His angels and indeed the inhabitants of heaven.

Of course, God knew that Adam and Eve would fall from grace and be led astray by Satan, but He also knew that in their suffering and making mistakes and asking for forgiveness that they would end up much closer to the heart of God, than if everything had stayed perfect and heavenly. The original Books of Adam and Eve are remarkably interesting and mention many points, some of which are mentioned in the Bible and some in the apocryphal books and yet with also many new details to those of us who have never read these books before. These books bring out the emotions of Adam and Eve just after getting kicked out of the Garden of Eden so well.

Having studied these and many other books like them, I conclude that the Garden of Eden was a sort of 'in between' dimension which was perhaps more heavenly than earthly. Is there a connection with the dream world of when people are sleeping at night in the 'Rest Zone'? What happens to us when we are sleeping. We are told by scientists that if we did not dream then we would die physically, but why? It was as it were God's infant cradle of civilization which would in fact prepare God's first man and women for the much more difficult physical life which they were soon about to enter. According to the Books of Adam and Eve, when they first were kicked out of the Garden of Eden they were in very great sorrow and confused as how to even walk or eat or take care of themselves. Whilst in the garden they had apparently been fully taken care of by the angels and ministering spirits by their own testimony in these deeply enlightening books. Once out of the garden of Eden Adam and Eve did not have a clue what to do and how to do it and therefore, they had to get very desperate in prayer before God and of course God answered his first human children and took good care of them. They did also have a lot of trouble initially with the attacks of Satan against them with his cunning disguises and temptations. Satan was constantly trying to destroy Adam and Eve from the Garden of Eden onwards as he was jealous of them believe it or not...You want to know why? Well, according Book 1 of Adam and Eve it was because, they unlike himself could find forgiveness by God and thus be brought into closer fellowship with God. Satan could not do that because as the Bible very succinctly puts it 'Satan is the father of all the children of Pride' – The book of Job. Only by humbling ourselves can we find forgiveness.

There is an incredible statement in these books where Satan states that he hates Adam and Eve and all mankind. Why does he hate mankind? Because those of mankind that become righteous and truly follow God and are eventually saved by the Word of God will replace the Fallen angels.

I have never actually heard that said before although in the Bible, the Psalms do state 'Thou has created us a little lower than the angels and crowned us with glory and honour'. Another verse in the New Testament affirms 'What know ye not that we shall judge angels?'

So, one way or the other Satan and his fallen angels hate mankind with a vengeance and want to destroy all of God's original physical creation. Fortunately for us God is the boss and is in perfect control of His creation and there is nothing that Satan can do without permission. Satan is limited according to the choices of mankind.

In the 2nd book of Adam and Eve, we see how that the righteous remained living on the mountain, not far from the Garden of Eden which was higher up the mountain both physically and spiritually as stated in these books and (guarded by an angel with a flaming sword) who was not allowed to allow Adam and Eve back into the garden of Eden according to both the Bible and this Book of Adam and Eve Book 1. The children of Cain lived at the bottom of the mountain. Those at the bottom of the mountain could not go up the mountain and those who had decided to join in the orgies and parties of the licentious daughters of Cain were not permitted to return to the mountain.

God had created some sort of 'spiritual gulf' between those on the mountain – i.e., the righteous and those on the bottom of the mountain – the wicked. In the Bible Jesus Himself told the story of Lazarus and the Rich man and how that there was a 'spiritual gulf' between them. Lazarus in Paradise in the centre of the earth, and the wicked rich man who had oppressed Lazarus during his lifetime in Hell. These two places, one good and other bad were side by side with a dimensional gap between them, although they could speak to each other across the dimensional barrier. That certainly sounds familiar does not it. No man has seen God at any time and lived - John 1.18. & Exodus 33.20: However, we can still talk to God as communicating from one dimension to yet a higher dimension. This brings up the topic of portals.

APPENDIX XII: WHEN WAS THE HEAVENLY CITY BUILT?

We have always assumed, as Christians, that Jesus started to build the Heavenly City right after His Resurrection.

Is that correct, however? Or do the Apocryphal books of Adam and Eve suggest that perhaps the Heavenly City was always 'a work in progress', as having happened much earlier in time and even possibly as far back as at the beginning of the Creation of the earth?

Throughout the scriptures - including the Apocryphal books - the New Heaven and New Earth are mentioned, both in the book of Ezekiel chapters 40, and also mentioned in detail in Revelations 21-22. [See similarities between the stories of the Heavenly City: ezekiels-temple-johns-city-compared-2.pdf (kingdomline.com)]

God used Jesus as His Word together with His Holy Spirit to create all the physical universe including the earth the moon and the stars and constellations according to the Bible.

Jesus as Creator was in creating Adam and Eve was also making a Bride for Himself through all the righteous souls that would eventually be born on earth starting with Adam and Eve. It took many thousands of years to create the fulness of the Bride as stated clearly in Hebrews 11.40:

Hebrews 11.40: 'God having provided some better thing for us, that they without us

323

should not be made perfect.

What exactly does Hebrews 11.40 mean?

Answer: [That **they without us should not be made perfect** - Believers before the flood, after the flood, under the law, and since the law, make but one Church. The Gospel dispensation is the last, and the Church **cannot** be considered as complete till the believers under all dispensations are gathered at the time of Christ's 2nd coming] **Source:** biblehub.com/niv/hebrews/11-40. htm

Does it not stand to reason that God the Creator would have started to build His Heavenly City earlier in time, but that it was not yet filled with millions of mansions but was always a work in progress from the Creation of the Earth onwards until the last righteous soul went up to heaven.

THE HEAVENLY CITY – AN ON-GOING PROJECT?

Why I believe that the Heavenly City or New Jerusalem was started as an on-going project by the Lord Creator (Jesus) around about the same time as the physical creation, but that it grew with time as the Bride herself came into being as being all the righteous souls that were yet destined to live on the earth who would make the right decisions to obey and follow God and His Commandments. Consider the following points as part of this argument:

1) The argument is put forth that Jesus went to build the Heavenly city after His Resurrection and not before - all because of John 14.30 'Behold I go to prepare a place for you that where I am there shall you be also'.

2) The Book of Revelation in chapters 21 – 22, in mentioning the incredible and pleasurable Heavenly City and describes her: 'As a Bride adorned for her husband' Sounds very intimate, doesn't it? We the saved are married to Jesus and will become His Bride and all of us will live with Jesus in the Heavenly City, which is a place of Heavenly love and intimacy and resultant creativity.

3) Consider the following: Scripture tells that after Jesus' resurrection that he went down and visited the souls in Hell and took the 'Keys of Death and Hell away from Satan' –

Revelation 1:18 "I am he that live, and was dead and behold, I am alive for evermore, Amen; and **have the keys of hell and of death.**

After His Resurrection, Jesus opened the doors of hell and paradise and many people who had perished at the time of the Great Flood heard Jesus' witness and many millions received Him. Jesus took them out of Hell and took them where? Is it not logical that He would have to already had a place built to hold all of them in advance of doing this.

Of course, the problem is that many churches teach that you either get saved or go to Hell, and that once in Hell or the Lake of Fire then is no hope for you. The protestant churches make no distinction between Hell and the Lake of Fire. However, according to scripture there is a big between Hell and the

Lake of Fire. The difference is that Hell is like a prison where you serve a time sentence for your crimes whilst on earth and the Lake of Fire is for the incalcitrant rebels like Satan and His Fallen angels - who always refuse to repent and change and obey God. In the Lake of Fire there will no longer be any choice about repenting. Its inmates are forcible altered and cleansed of their diabolical iniquities by spiritual fire. Their diabolical crimes are literally eating them alive. 'Their worm never dies, and their fire is not quenched. These beings created the evil and in the Lake of Fire it will literally eat them alive until they are made an end of at least as regarding the EVIL natures and all that is left is their original basic being which is eternal - before it was corrupted by Evil. The good news is that eventually all of God's Creation will be restored to perfection and there will be no more Evil or evil people and at last all will have learned to love and obey God because he really loves each of us very much and is trying to teach us about real love is loving God and following Him and concern and caring for others.

We find that the same people as mentioned in Revelation 21 as being thrown into the Lake of Fire are later mentioned in revelation 22 as living outside of the Heavenly city. They have all been turned back to how they used to be before sin entered both spiritual and physical existence. Then finally God's entire creation will have been returned to perfection an all will finally obey God and do His bidding and not their own. Of God always knows what is best for us His children and constantly has our interests at heart if He knows that they will be good for us and edifying. God is not some old 'fuddy-duddy' goody - goody church restrictive religionist who wants His children to be denied every pleasure that He has created. That is all Satan's idea and binds the 'religionists' by his 'letter of the law' bondage of the Old Testament and sadly many churches do not have the 'freedom of spirit' as even mentioned in the New Testament. Religions are in general 'claptraps of self-righteous' 'letter of the law' control systems that do not allow for the 'freedom of God's Spirit or any new radical ideas in other words - and that is why so many modern churches are all but spiritually dead as mentioned in the Book of Revelations chapter 3. So many churches today are just like described as the church of Sardis and Laodicea:

Rev.3:1-2 And unto the angel of the church in Sardis write, These things saith he that hath the seven Spirits of God, and the seven stars; I know thy works, that thou hast a name that thou live, and art **dead**. Be watchful, and strengthen the things which remain, that are ready to die: for I have not found thy works perfect before God.

Rev.14-20 And unto the angel of the Laodiceans write: 'I know your works, that you are neither cold nor hot; I would that you be either cold or hot. So then, because you are lukewarm, and are neither cold nor hot, I will spew you out of My mouth'.

Heaven is an extension, an amplification of all the beautiful things that we currently enjoy on earth. Heaven is the absolute best of what we already can enjoy on earth minus all the heartaches and sorrows and loneliness that so many suffer not to mention no more pains and death.

2 Pe 3: 18-20 'For Christ also suffered once for sins, the righteous for the unrighteous, to bring you to God. He was put to death in the body but made alive in the Spirit. … he went and made proclamation to the imprisoned spirits - to those who were disobedient long ago in the days of Noah while the ark was being built'.

4) If the Heavenly City had not already been built at the time of Christ, then what Jesus said in Jn 14.2-3 would feasibly not have been possible. Of course, that is using the premise that God took those new souls to the Heavenly City.

Jn 14.2-3 In my Father's house are many mansions: if *it were* not *so*, I would have told you. I go to prepare a place for you. And if I go and prepare a place for you, I will come again, and receive you unto myself; that where I am, *there* ye may be also.

5) There is more evidence to show that the Heavenly city was probably in existence and was being built gradually from the days of the first human beings on the planet – Adam and Eve.

6) It is stated that many of the ancient patriarchs and those born before the time of Jesus had to wait until the Resurrection and Jesus' personal visit down to Hell and to Paradise before they could be taken to the Heavenly City. All the righteous before the time of Jesus when they died apparently went to live in paradise which is in the heart of the earth and alongside hell.

7) Jesus, after His Resurrection travelled down to both Paradise and Hell and he took all the saved of all generations from Adam to all the souls who died in faith until His resurrection and took them all up to the Heavenly City.

8) When Jesus sated in Jn 14.30 'Behold I go to prepare a place for you that where I am there Ye might be also, He was probably talking about the mansions in heaven and not about the massive overall structure of the Heavenly city described so well by John in Revelations Chapters 21-22.

9) The heavenly City could have itself have already been built, as well as the mansions prepared for the 'righteous' long in advance of the inhabitants having been taken to these heavenly abodes.

10) Paradise is also a beautiful place inside the heart of the earth as described by Jesus Himself in the amazing and informative story of Lazarus and the rich man. One went to Paradise and the other to the flames and torture of Hell itself. These domains were 'side by side', but a great gulf was fixed between them.

11) This is where we are headed! The Heavenly City, which is the hope of all ages: That now unseen eternal world where we shall dwell with Him forever! – The Heavenly City described in the grand finale of the Bible, Relation 21 and 22, the thunderous climax of the symphony of God, a place of such resplendent beauty that it lifts you into the heavenlies, beyond the imagination of man! The Heavenly City of our eternal future happiness, our Eternal Home in Paradise!

12) Bible verses about the **Heavenly City**:

Revelation 21.1-5 'Then I saw "a new heaven and a new earth," for the first heaven and the first earth had passed away, and there was no longer any sea. ²I saw the Holy City, the new Jerusalem, coming down out of heaven from God, prepared as a bride beautifully dressed for her husband. ³And I heard a loud voice from the throne saying, "Look! God's dwelling place is now among the people, and he will dwell with them. They will be his people, and God himself will be with them and be their God. ⁴"He will wipe every tear from their eyes. There will be no more death' or mourning or crying or pain, for the old order of things has passed away." ⁵He who was seated on the throne said, "I am making everything new!" Then he said, "Write this down, for these words are trustworthy and true."

Revelation 21.22 did not see a temple in the city, because the LORD God Almighty and the Lamb are its temple.

Hebrews 13.14 'For here we have no continuing city, but we seek one to come'

Isaiah 65.17 See, I will create new heavens and a new earth. The former things will not be remembered, nor will they come to mind.

Isaiah 66.22-24 As the new heavens and the new earth that I make will endure before me," declares the LORD, "so will your name and descendants endure. ²³From one New Moon to another and from one Sabbath to another, all mankind will come and bow down before me," says the LORD. ²⁴"And they will go out and look on the dead bodies of those who rebelled against me; the worms that eat them will not die, the fire that burns them will not be quenched, and they will be loathsome to all mankind.

2 Peter 3.10-13: "But the day of the Lord will come as a thief in the night, in which the heavens will pass away with a great noise, and the elements will melt with fervent heat; both the earth and the works that are in it will be burned up. Therefore, since all these things will be dissolved, what manner of persons ought you to be in holy conduct and godliness, looking for and hastening the coming of the day of God, because of which the heavens will be dissolved, being on fire, and the elements will melt with fervent heat? Nevertheless we, according to His promise, look for new heavens and a new earth in which righteousness dwells."

Psalm 72:11 "Yea, all kings shall fall down before Him; all nations shall serve Him."

Isaiah 9:7
"Of the increase of His government and peace there will be no end, upon the throne of David and over His kingdom, to order it and establish it with judgment and justice from that time forward, even forever. The zeal of the Lord of hosts will perform this."

Isaiah 60:21
"Also your people shall all be righteous; they shall inherit the land forever, the branch of My planting, the work of My hands, that I may be glorified."

Zechariah 9:10
"I will cut off the chariot from Ephraim and the horse from Jerusalem; the battle bow shall be cut off. He shall speak peace to the nations; His dominion shall be 'from sea

to sea, and from the river to the ends of the earth.' "

Luke 1:32–33
"He will be great and will be called the Son of the Highest; and the Lord God will give Him the throne of His father David. And He will reign over the house of Jacob forever, and of His kingdom there will be no end."

Psalm 72:7
"In His days the righteous shall flourish, and abundance of peace, until the moon is no more."

Isaiah 11:6–9
"The wolf also shall dwell with the lamb, the leopard shall lie down with the young goat, the calf and the young lion and the fatling together; and a little child shall lead them. The cow and the bear shall graze; their young ones shall lie down together; and the lion shall eat straw like the ox. The nursing child shall play by the cobra's hole, and the weaned child shall put his hand in the viper's den. They shall not hurt nor destroy in all My holy mountain, for the earth shall be full of the knowledge of the Lord as the waters cover the sea."

Isaiah 66:22
'For as the new heavens and the new earth which I will make shall remain before Me,' says the Lord, 'So shall your descendants and your name remain.' "

Psalm 87.1-3,5-7 'His foundation is in the holy mountains. 2 The Lord loveth the gates of Zion more than all the dwellings of Jacob. 3 Glorious things are spoken of thee, O city of God.[5] And of Zion it shall be said, This and that man was born in her: and the highest himself shall establish her.[6] The Lord shall count, when he writes up the people, that this man was born there. Selah.[7] As well the singers as the players on instruments shall be there: all my springs are in thee.

APPENDIX XIII: Critique of the 'LOST BOOKS OF ADAM AND EVE' by this author: S.N.Strutt

C.1 Sadly, in my opinion the **1st** Book of Adam and Eve has been influenced by teachings of self-suffering or self-flagellation* (*Definition: 'The action of flogging oneself, especially as a form of religious discipline' or excessive criticism of oneself.)

C.2 In the case of the 1st Book of Adam and Eve - it is manifested in the times that Adam and Eve attempt suicide on several occasions and the Devil burns and scars them and almost kills them in another part of the story. Why weren't God's angels more on the job of protecting Adam and Eve in the Lost Books of Adam and Eve one might ask?

C.3 In the 2nd Book of Adam and Eve the verse talking about the 'gold and the myrrh and frankincense' seems like it has been added in in the centuries after the birth of Christ. From what I can gather it was the Orthodox Eastern church which had something to do with these Lost Books of Adam and Eve.

It is very possible that the original book was itself altered to include Orthodox theology.

C.4 We can see an example of Orthodox church influence in the Lost Books of Adam and Eve as their Bibles also state that it would be 5500 years from Creation until the Messiah which is taken right out of the Septuagint which was a Greek translation of the Torah or Old Testament in circa 300 BCE. The other Western churches have the time from creation to the birth of Christ as 4000 years including the Catholic church. This is also the same difference in the time sequence between the KJV of the Bible giving 4000 years from Creation until the birth of Christ and the Septuagint giving 5500 years.

C.5 I suspect that this part of the original story or Genesis chapters 1, 2 and 3 all about Adam and Eve and the 'Tree of the Knowledge of Good and Evil' were deliberately omitted from this book or better said 'deliberately taken out of the original Lost Books of Adam and Eve'.

C.6 I will tell you why. I think that the Orthodox church who influenced this Book of the 'Lost Books of Adam and Eve' in around 350-500 AD decided that they did not like the constant referral to Satan as influencing the lives of Adam and Eve. Why would that be you may well ask? Apparently, something happened in the Garden of Eden that most people are unaware of - something that must have been akin to 'idol worship', that religious authorities simply did not want known for one reason or the other. Many people don't know that for the exact same reasons, the Book of Enoch was banned by the Catholic church for 1000 years as it exposed both Satan and the fallen angels. It is only during the past 200 years that we have had the privilege of reading this book. See my book Enoch Insights.

C.7 What do I think it was? Well, I have written a lot about this topic in my other books of 'Jubilees Insights' and 'Jasher insights' about the fact that Eve did not just eat a forbidden fruit in the Garden. Why would just eating a fruit cause Adam and Eve to be judged very severely and kicked out of the Garden of Eden?

C.8 What was Satan offering them – 'to be as gods' – what did they do to fall to Satan's temptations in the Garden of Eden? What really went wrong in the Garden of Eden that resulted in severe judgement. I will give you a clue.

C.9 One of the versions of these Lost Books of Adam and Eve stated that Eve was pregnant when she left the Garden of Eden. Her first born son Cain ended up being the first murderer?!

C.10 Eve being 3 months pregnant, when she had just come out of the Garden of Eden is mentioned in VITA ADAE ET EVAE which is Latin for 'THE LIFE OF ADAM AND EVE': Chapter XVIII 'And there to weep bitterly and groan aloud. And she made there a booth, while she had in her womb offspring of three months old' (Cain)- from the Apocrypha and Pseudepigrapha of the Old Testament -R.H.Charles - Oxford: Clarendon Press 1913.

1 John 3.12 Not as Cain who was 'of the wicked one' and murdered his brother. And why did he murder him? Because his works were **evil** and his brother's righteous.

APPENDIX XIV: ACCOUNTABILITY: God could not judge Adam and Eve unless they were fully accountable.

Genesis 2.21 And the LORD God caused a deep sleep to fall upon Adam, and he slept: and he took one of his ribs, and closed up the flesh instead thereof;

22 And the rib, which the LORD God had taken from man, made he a woman, and brought her unto the man.

23 And Adam said, 'This *is* now bone of my bones, and flesh of my flesh: she shall be called Woman, because she was taken out of Man'.

24 Therefore shall a man leave his father and his mother and shall cleave unto his wife: and they shall be one flesh.

25 And they were both naked, the man and his wife, and were not ashamed.

C.1 Analysing these 5 verses, let us consider the following:

1) Adam himself was created outside the Garden out of dust and was then placed inside the Garden of Eden-

Genesis 2.88 And the LORD God planted a garden eastward in Eden; and there he put the man whom he had formed.

2) Eve was brought to Adam whilst he was in the Garden of Eden

3) The introduction of the institution of marriage is proclaimed, but it does not say that Adam 'married' Eve on the spot, immediately after Eve was created and brought to Adam naked, contrary to what some say.

4) If we are to take the Lost Books of Adam and Eve seriously then it looks like whilst Adam and Eve were in the Garden of Eden, they had almost adult physical bodies, but they had only just been created and they needed time to learn some of the things that we all learn in the first 18 years of our lives, howbeit much quicker in only 7 years rather than 18.

5) It is true that the Bible states that God asked Adam to name all the animals which indeed would have required a high I.Q, but he did have God helping him directly whilst in the Garden of Eden.

Genesis 2.19-20 '19 And out of the ground the LORD God formed every beast of the field, and every fowl of the air; and brought them unto Adam to see what he would call them: and whatsoever Adam called every living creature, that *was* the name thereof. 20 And Adam gave names to all cattle, and to the fowl of the air, and to every beast of the field.

C.2 By Adam and Eve's own confession in the Lost books of Adam and Eve they were shocked when Satan 'tempted them with getting married! Why was that? Before reading the Lost Books of Adam and Eve, I always thought that they were married from the moment Adam met Eve, but the Bible does not exactly say that and there could be some time delay between Genesis 2.23 and 2.24, as it is not clear enough in the Bible to state they immediately got married.

C.3 Let us face it, it takes time to know each other and to be friends before one normally gets married. So why the seeming difference with Adam and Eve?

C.4 The Bible is the greatest book for the basics in knowing God and His plans for mankind.   ,

C.5 I think it likely that many details have in the process of time and for convenience or other reasons have been omitted from the Bible by man. Think how many times the Bible was destroyed by one World Empire or the other and had to be re-written as with Moses 3500 years ago then Ezra 1000 years later and around 100 AD after the destruction of the Temple and Israel in 70 AD by the Romans and in1611 by King James of England.

C.6 Miraculously despite bestial man and his hellish anti-God governments, God has made sure that we still at least have the basics by giving us the Bible.

C.7 Unfortunately, 15 apocryphal books were taken out of the KJV of the Bible in 1885 apparently to save money, which was a noticeably big mistake as the apocryphal books show many of the details left out of the Bible such as in the Book of Jubilees.

C.8 How could Adam and Eve be held accountable by God for giving into Satan's temptations unless they were 'of age'? According to the book of Jubilees Adam and Eve were in the Garden for a full 7 years before the slimy snake tempted Eve to do evil and eat the fruit of the Tree of the knowledge of Good and Evil, which supposedly caused the Fall.

C.9 I remember reading that the Lord Creator in the 'Lost books of Adam and Eve' had stated that Adam and Eve only 'lasted one day' and then they fell. Does this statement conflict with the Book of Jubilees or is there more to the story than we are told in the truly short narrative of Adam and Eve in the Bible?

C.10 I know many Bible scholars will argue that the Bible states that God created Adam full grown and naked and that when Adam met Eve, he 'knew her' right away saying she is now bone of my bone and flesh of my flesh and she shall be called woman as she was taken out of man.

C.11 However, what if the short account in the Bible is accurate and yet there are some time delays between verses as one can find in the writings of the prophets where one verse, they are talking about one topic and suddenly the next verse leaps to the far future or even the past. If we consider the Book of Jubilees or 'Little Genesis' as it is called.

C.12 What if it is true that Adam and Eve were 7 years in the Garden of Eden before Evil was allowed to enter the Garden in the form of Satan possessing a snake and both speaking to and tempting Eve.

C.13 My question is what were Adam and Eve doing for those 7 years in the Garden of Eden other than enjoying the Garden and the presence of the Lord and His angels? Life is always full of progress and normally we learn as we grow. Most of the things we learn we learn in the first 5 years of life.

C.14 What if when God created Adam and Eve there were created as probably 18 years old and a 16-year-old in their flesh. However, their minds and spirits were lacking in training. For this reason, God put them in the Garden of Eden for another purpose than just to till the Garden. They were in the Garden of Eden to learn from God and the angels all the things that a baby and a little child and then a teenager would learn and then as young adults. This process was done quicker than normal from a child's mind to a young adult in only 7 years.

C.15 Even if Adam and eve were created as already 18 and 16 years old physically there was obviously much knowledge that Adam and Eve had not yet acquired as they had just been created. It takes time and experience to learn anything. They did not have the advantage of being born through the 'womb of a woman', because God had not yet created another woman before Adam and Eve came along.

C.16 How would Adam and Eve learn all the things that one learns as a baby and then a toddler and a small child and older child and then as a young teen and as an older teen and then a young adult and then and adult and mature adult. So many things to learn. Also consider that we learn a lot whilst we are sleeping so it was necessary to seclude Adam and Eve for a season in the Garden of Eden in a completely protected environment until they had learned all the basics that each one of us has learned in a much longer period.

C.17 The Garden of Eden acted as a 'womb' for Adam and Eve whilst they learned all the basics of life. I do not think they were created automatically as 'know-it-all' as portrayed by some biblical teachers.

C.18 I think that if the Lost Books of Adam and Eve have got the narrative right then Adam and Eve got married right after being kicked out of the Garden of Eden or 7 years after they first met as they had a lot of training to do and so much to learn.

C.19 By the time the snake tempted Eve, she had to be at an age of accountability or around 16 years old.

C.20 It is interesting that in the Lost Book of Adam and Eve Book 1-chapter LXXII **(72)** they did not get married right away and in fact in chapter 72 Adam and Eve thought it an abhorrent to get married without counselling with the Lord. Here is the quote from LXXII (72) v.19 And he answered her, "That I may request the Lord inform me about marrying you; for I will not do it without his permission or else He will make us perish you and me. For those devils have set my heart on fire, with thoughts of what they showed us, in their sinful apparitions.

C.21 The Lord did however confirm that they were to marry. Their initial reluctance to marry at first could have been a teenage reaction.

C.22 In the Bible it just states that God created Eve out of a rib in Adam's side and brought the woman naked to Adam and talks about 'what marriage is' but gives no exact details.

Genesis2.23-24 And Adam said, 'This *is* now bone of my bones, and flesh of my flesh: she shall be called Woman, because she was taken out of Man'. 24 Therefore shall a man leave his father and his mother and shall cleave unto his wife: and they shall be one flesh.

C.23 OBS. Comments 23-27 are more by frequent reading, and not something that I can fully prove:

'I think that women might find it offensive that Eve had to show up naked and meet the first naked man Adam, as she did not 'know him from Adam'- literally.

What if instead, she was wearing a 'robe of light' and had a 'bright nature', as brought out in these Lost Books of Adam and Eve as she met Adam in the Garden of Eden, where she was fully protected.

C.24 God never intended that woman should feel immediately threatened by having to have sex with someone they did not know, just because the Bible perhaps missed out the fact that Adam and Eve were not entirely naked.

C.25 Women also do not like to be seen as merely a sex object or a baby factory to have an incessant number of kids with or be forced upon by men.

C.26 Look at this quote from Flavius Josephus from The Antiquities of the JEWS Book 1 Chapter 1: 'Adam had no female companion, no society, for there was no such created, and that he wondered at the other animals which were male and female, he laid him asleep, and God took away one of his ribs, and out of it formed the woman; whereupon Adam knew her when she was brought to him, and acknowledged that she was made out of himself. The name of this woman was Eve, which signifies the mother of all living.'

C.27 All the ancient texts give the impression that Adam 'jumped' Eve as soon as he saw her, but is that the real story? That is simply not true to human nature, as it takes time to get to 'know' someone. Firstly, to understand each other, then take it one step at a time. Well, that is how most serious male/female relationships begin - slowly.

C.28 Sadly, once Adam and Eve were of age, despite all they learned, they still failed the very first temptation by Satan. I think it likely that Eve had talked with the snake upon various occasions and was familiar with the snake, but it was only when the snake became possessed by Satan for a moment, (as shown in 'The Lost books of Adam and Eve') that she was tempted to disobey God and she ate from the fruit of the Tree of the knowledge of Good and Evil.

C.29 Warning to Stay on The Wall and to Watch: These Lost Books of Adam and Eve have given us a clear warning as to why mankind went totally astray in the times before the Great Flood, with the exception of 3 men: Methuselah, Lamech and Noah and their family. After Noah's father Lamech and his grandfather Methuselah had died, shortly before the Great flood, only Noah and his three sons and their wives survived to live through the Great Flood, and they were the few whom God used to re-populate the earth in the days after the Great Flood.

Modern Times. What about the times in which we are living today? Jesus clearly also warned us 2000 years ago:

Luke 17.26-27 And **as it was in the days of Noe**, so shall it be also in the days of the Son of man. 27 They did eat, they drank, they married wives, they were given in marriage, until the day that Noah entered into the ark, and the flood came, and destroyed them all.

Luke 18.8 Nevertheless when the Son of man cometh, shall he find faith on the earth?

Mark 13.34-37 For the Son of man is as a man taking a far journey, who left his house, and gave authority to his servants, and to every man his work, and commanded the porter to watch. [35]Watch ye therefore: for ye know not when the master of the house cometh, at even, or at midnight, or at the cockcrowing, or in the morning: [36]Lest coming suddenly he find you sleeping. [37]And what I say unto you I say unto all, Watch

SALVATION
SALVATION - www.outofthebottomlesspit.co.uk

APPENDIX XV: LONGEVITY CHART ADAM TO JOSEPH

ADAM | 130|--------------------800---------------------- LIVED 930 Years (A.C. 930)

SETH |105|------------------807----------------------- LIVED 912 Years (1042)

ENOS | 90|-------------------815-----------------LIVED 905 Years (1140)

CAINAN |70|-----------------840--------------- LIVED 910 Years (1235)

MAHALALEEL|65|----------------830---------- LIVED 895 Years (1290)

JARED | 162----------   800--------- LIVED 962 Years (1422)

ENOCH | 65|------300-----LIVED 365 Years (987)

METHUSELAH | 187 |---782----(FLOOD) LIVED 969 Years (1656)

LAMECH | 182 |----------595-----------LIVED 895 Years (1651)

NOAH|---------502--|(FLOOD) ↓ --448- LIVED 895 Years (2006)

SHEM|

334

SHEM|

   |ARPHAXAD (FLOOD)↓35|-------------403---- LIVED 438 Years (2096)

       SALAH|30|----------403------ LIVED 433 Years (2126)

         EBER|34|----------430---- LIVED 464 Years (2187)

           PELEG|30|209 LIVED 239 Years (1996)

            REU |32|207 LIVED 239 Years (2026)

             SERUG |30|200 LIVED 230 Years (2049)

              NAHOR |29|119 LIVED 148 Years (1997)

               TERAH |70|135 LIVED 205 Years (2083)

                ABRAHAM |100|75 LIVED 175 Years (2123)

                 ISAAC |60|120 LIVED 180 Years (2228)

                  JACOB |91|56 LIVED 147 Years (2255)

                  |JOSEPH

APPENDIX XVI: ALL MY BOOKS IN ORDER OF PUBLICATION:

REACTIONS BY THE PUBLIC: ' INSIGHTS' BOOKS' - www.outoft-hebottomlesspit.co.uk

1) OUT OF THE BOTOMLESS PIT: http://www.outofthebot-tomlesspit.co.uk/411702511

2) ENOCH INSIGHTS: ENOCH 'INSIGHTS' - www.outofthebottomlesspit.co.uk

3) EZDRAS INSIGHTS: EZDRAS INSIGHTS - www.outofthebottomlesspit.co.uk

4) JASHER INSIGHTS BK I: JASHER INSIGHTS - www.outofthebottom-lesspit.co.uk

5) JASHER INSIGHTS BK II: JASHER INSIGHTS - www.outofthebot-tomlesspit.co.uk

6) JUBILEES INSIGHTS: JUBILEES INSIGHTS - www.outofthebottomless-pit.co.uk

7) EDEN INSIGHTS: 'EDEN INSIGHTS' - www.outofthebottom-lesspit.co.uk

APPENDIX XVII: OTHER USEFUL TOPIC LINKS ON MY WEBSITE:

GARDEN OF EDEN - HOLLOW EARTH? GARDEN OF EDEN - www.outofthebottomlesspit.co.uk

HOLLOW EARTH BLOG: HOLLOW EARTH - BLOG - www.outofthebot-tomlesspit.co.uk

HEAVEN IS REAL: HEAVEN - www.outofthebottomlesspit.co.uk

ANCIENT STRUCTURES FOUND: ANCIENT TIMES - www.outofthebottomlesspit.co.uk

THE GODS OF EGYPT? CH 7 FALLEN ANGELS - www.outofthebottomless-pit.co.uk

WHO REALLY BUILD THE PYRAMIDS? THE PYRA-MIDS - www.outofthebottomlesspit.co.uk

LIFE AFTER DEATH LIFE AFTER DEATH - www.outofthebot-tomlesspit.co.uk

CREATION: DREAMS & VISIONS - www.outofthebottomlesspit.co.uk

WARRIORS: WARRIORS OF THE WORD - www.outofthebottomless-pit.co.uk

SALVATION SALVATION - www.outofthebottomlesspit.co.uk

ABOUT THE AUTHOR: About the Author - www.outofthe-bottomlesspit.co.uk

RADIO SHOWS: Stream 245. NIGHTLIGHT (Jubilees Insights - with Steven Strutt) by NIGHTLIGHT | Listen online for free on SoundCloud

'INSIGHT BOOK' VIDEOS: 'INSIGHT BOOK VIDEOS - www.outofthebottomlesspit.co.uk